THE IRAQW OF TANZANIA

Westview Case Studies in Anthropology

Series Editor

EDWARD F. FISCHER
Vanderbilt University

Advisory Board

THEODORE C. BESTOR
Harvard University

ROBERT H. LAVENDA
Saint Cloud State University

Tecpán Guatemala: A Modern Maya Town in Global and Local Context
Edward F. Fischer (Vanderbilt University) and Carol Hendrickson (Marlboro College)

Daughters of Tunis: Women, Family, and Networks in a Muslim City
Paula Holmes-Eber (University of Washington)

Fulbe Voices: Marriage, Islam, and Medicine in Northern Cameroon
Helen A. Regis (Louisiana State University)

Magical Writing in Salasaca: Literacy and Power in Highland Ecuador
Peter Wogan (Willamette University)

The Lao: Gender, Power, and Livelihood
Carol Ireson-Doolittle (Willamette University) and Geraldine Moreno-Black (University of Oregon)

Namoluk Beyond the Reef: The Transformation of a Micronesian Community
Mac Marshall (University of Iowa)

From Mukogodo to Maasai: Ethnicity and Cultural Change in Kenya
Lee Cronk (Rutgers University)

Black Skins, French Voices: Caribbean Ethnicity and Activism in Urban France
David Beriss (University of New Orleans)

The Iraqw of Tanzania: Negotiating Rural Development
Katherine A. Snyder (Queens College, City University of New York)

Forthcoming

The Tanners of Taiwan: Life Strategies and National Culture
Scott Simon (University of Ottawa)

Urban China: Private Lives and Public Culture
William Jankowiak (University of Nevada, Las Vegas)

Muslim Youth: Tensions and Transitions in Tajikistan
Colette Harris (Virginia Tech University)

THE IRAQW OF TANZANIA

Negotiating Rural Development

KATHERINE A. SNYDER

Queens College
City University of New York

A Member of the Perseus Books Group

To the barise *of Kainam ward*

Copyright © 2005 by Westview Press, a Member of the Perseus Books Group

Published in the United States of America by Westview Press, A Member of the Perseus Books Group. Find us on the world wide web at www.westviewpress.com

Westview Press books are available at special discounts for bulk purchases in the United States by corporations, institutions, and other organizations. For more information, please contact the Special Markets Department at the Perseus Books Group, 11 Cambridge Center, Cambridge, MA 02142, or call (617) 252-5298 or (800) 255-1514, or email special.markets@perseusbooks.com.

A Cataloging-in-Publication data record for this book is available from the Library of Congress.
ISBN 0-8133-4245-7 (paperback).

The paper used in this publication meets the requirements of the American National Standard for Permanence of Paper for Printed Library Materials Z39.48–1984.

10   9   8   7   6   5   4   3   2   1

Contents

Series Editor Preface

The value of anthropology rests with its ability to bring local concerns and lived experience to bear on larger social issues. Nowhere is this more apparent than in anthropological contributions to development studies. Development has long been a concern of cultural anthropologists, who tend to work in the world's more impoverished regions and position themselves as advocates for the peoples they study. At first blush, development might be seen as an unambiguous good. But, in fact, there are very different views on what development is and what it should be—there is no one-size-fits-all economic formula to bring about local and personal visions of progress.

In this book, Katherine Snyder presents a nuanced view of development and cultural change among the Iraqw of Tanzania. She balances ethnographic detail with national and global issues, showing the ways the Iraqw coopt and redefine development projects toward their own ends as well as how their culture changes in the process.

Snyder's sensitivity comes from her fieldwork for over more than a decade in Irqwa Da'aw ("the Iraqw Land of the East"). The Iraqw are a patrilineal society organized around kinship and clan ties overlaid with the formal structures of the Tanzanian state. Agropastoralists who depend on communal labor within communities and amiable trade relations with neighboring pastoralists, they have a reputation as "a peaceful people." Maize and beans are the principal subsistence crops, and most households also keep some cattle and pigs. These two forms of livestock capture a division in Irqwa Da'aw over *maendeleo* ("progress" or "development"): cattle belong to a system of sharing within and between families that reinforces kinship and community relations; pigs, however, are part of a new market-driven economy, considered the private capital assets of individual households.

Snyder relates the tensions in Iraqw communities between elders and youths over what development should entail, over what the future should look like. Working with this theme, Snyder is also able to present the reader with a holistic ethnographic portrait of Iraqw life. From kinship and history to religion and witchcraft, she shows how each of these aspects of local culture and society is intimately linked to issues of development. Christianity, for example, is associated with modernist notions of development and progress. About half of the Iraqw identify as Christian (mostly Catholic), but Christianity coexists with a strong tradition of native religion and beliefs about witchcraft that serve as mechanisms of social control. In these ways, Snyder builds on the tradition of anthropologists such as Akhil Gupta and James Ferguson, who humanize our understanding of development by looking beyond economic formulas to the meaning and impact of development on individual lives.

The Iraqw are an extremely reserved people, making fieldwork difficult. But Snyder shows how such secrecy also serves as an effective weapon of the weak—just as sorcery and witchcraft offer a means of circumventing government control. Longstanding traditions such as circumcision, although modified today, remain an important feature of Iraqw personhood. Circumcision is an important life stage for Iraqw boys and girls, marking their passage from children into marriageable (and, it is hoped, responsible) adults. Female circumcision is a controversial practice from the Western perspective, but Snyder shows how it is eagerly awaited by Iraqw girls as a status symbol—and how hospital circumcisions have become a progressive alternative for boys.

Snyder relates changing Iraqw cultural patterns to their position in national and international political economies. The Iraqw were relatively favored under first German and then British colonial regimes. During Tanzania's experiment with isolationist *ujamaa* ("familyhood") socialism, which started in the late 1960s, traditional territorial divisions remained while new forms of state organization were imposed. By the mid-1980s, Tanzania could no longer support the *ujamaa* experiment, and the country was forced to adopt structural adjustment policies mandated by the International Monetary Fund. As a result, private ownership (of pigs, of land, of milk) is irreversibly changing social relations and conceptions of progress—sometimes for the better, sometimes for the worse.

The Iraqw of Tanzania makes an important contribution to the Westview Case Studies in Anthropology series and to the discipline as a whole. This series presents works that recognize the peoples we study as active agents enmeshed in global as well as local systems of politics, economics, and cultural flows. There is a focus on contemporary ways of life, forces of social change, and creative responses to novel situations as well as the more traditional concerns of classic ethnography. In presenting rich humanistic and social scientific data borne of the dialectic engagement of fieldwork, the books in this series move toward realizing the full pedagogical potential of anthropology: imparting to the reader an empathetic understanding of alternative ways of viewing and acting in the world as well as a solid basis for critical thought regarding the historically contingent nature of ethnic boundaries and cultural knowledge.

The Iraqw of Tanzania brings the anthropological gaze to bear on issues of development with implications that reach far beyond East Africa. Snyder interrogates received knowledge about "development" and reaches some surprising conclusions. All the while she manages a fine balance between humanizing ethnographic particulars and social analysis of broader, even global, trends. Snyder has written this book in an engaging and accessible style, advancing our understanding of cultural diversity while uncovering the often hidden webs of global relations that affect us all.

Edward F. Fischer
Nashville, Tennessee

Acknowledgments

Countless people have contributed to this book, and it would be impossible to name them all. My greatest debt is to the many Iraqw, particularly those residing in Irqwa Da'aw, who made this work possible. I want to thank the elders of Irqwa Da'aw in particular, most specifically the male elders' councils of Hareabi and Tsaayo, who invited me to their meetings, and the women's council of Tsaayo, who allowed me to attend their meetings and to participate in their protest march. In Kainam, I have an enormous debt of gratitude to Mzee Dagharo Dawite, Mzee Uo, Maiba Garsa, Akonaay Gabarish, Afa/ayangw Singda, John Humbaay Dagharo, Basili Awett, John Quffa, Maghway, Mzee, and Mama Benedicti, Mama Elgi, Qamshinda Qamera, the teachers and students of Kainam and Tsaayo primary schools, and many more for their friendship, guidance, and wisdom. The list is long and I apologize for any omissions. It would simply fill too many pages! My research assistant, John Qamlali, was tireless, patient, and a first-rate anthropologist in his own right. I would not have accomplished this research without his aid. At the University of Dar es Salaam, I owe thanks to Nestor Luanda for serving as my advisor and to Yusufu Lawi, who has been an enormous help to me over the years and who keeps me, I hope, from straying too far from the truth.

In Dar, Arusha, Karatu, and Mbulu, many have provided logistical support, hospitality, friendship, and advice over the years. Chief among them are Patrick and Martha Qorro, Vincent Cidosa at the U.S. Embassy, Dr. Wilbrod Slaa, Jeremiah Siay and family, Anthony and Mama Malley, Coleta Lagwen,

Amedeus Deodatus, Otto Humbaay, Edward Bee, and Daniel and Joan Paresso, who were my home away from home in Karatu.

In my early work on foot, Hans Duinmeijer, Giampaolo Mezzabotta, and Gabriella Rossetti took pity on me and loaned me their vehicles for periodic sojourns into the countryside. I am eternally grateful, as I saw parts of Mbulu, Babati, Hanang, and Karatu Districts I would never have seen otherwise. Giampaolo and his wife, Eva, and Corinne Whitaker and John Tucker provided home bases and generous hospitality in Arusha and Dar, respectively.

Throughout my years in Tanzania, I have enjoyed the friendship of Maia Green, Joe Lugalla, and Todd Sanders. Not only have we shared many a Safari beer, but they have been helpful critics and suppliers of crucial logistical information over the years. Thanks in particular to Todd for various readings of this manuscript and to Maia as well for last-minute help. Thanks also to Kana Dower, Mandana Limbert, and Murphy Halliburton for commenting on the introduction.

At Yale University, I am indebted to John Middleton, William Kelly, Harold Conklin, and Ann Biersteker. From my original dissertation committee, Angelique Haugerud has provided advice and encouragement for many years now. Tanzania scholars Donna Kerner, Deborah Rubin, and most recently William Arens have been supportive with their advice and insights. Fellow scholars of the Iraqw and neighboring Tatoga have been wonderfully generous in sharing their work with me, and I have benefited greatly from their ideas. They include Martin Mous, Ole Bjørn Rekdal, Astrid Blystad, Lars Hagborg, Nils Gunnar Songstad, Garry Thomas, and of course, Yusufu Lawi.

My research has received the generous support over the years from a Fulbright-Hays Doctoral Dissertation Fellowship, grants from International and Area Studies, Agrarian Studies, and the Anthropology Department at Yale University, a Social Sciences Postdoctoral Fellowship from the Rockefeller Foundation, and most recently, two PSC-CUNY grants from the Research Foundation of the City University of New York and a Fulbright-Hays Faculty Research Abroad grant. I am grateful to the Tanzania Commission for Sciences and Technology for granting me permission to conduct research in Tanzania, to the University of Dar es Salaam for support from the departments of history, sociology, and political science, and to the Tanzania National Archives and its tireless and helpful staff.

To my editors, Ted Fischer, Karl Yambert, and Steve Catalano, I give many thanks for the editorial advice and for making the publishing process an enjoyable one.

Finally, I'd like to thank Sasha Cooke for his willingness to keep disrupting his life and returning to Tanzania for extended periods of time. His companionship, support, and knowledge of car mechanics has made life in Tanzania that much more enjoyable. He has also been a careful reader of this book in its various incarnations.

CHAPTER ONE

"PROGRESS IS A LONG JOURNEY"

Negotiating Development in Rural Tanzania

Maendeleo ni safari ndefu.
(Progress is a long journey.)

In 2002, the rap song "I Am a Maasai, Bwana" soared to popularity in Tanzania, broadcast every hour on the radio and accompanied by video on television. The rapper, Mr. Ebbo, claims, "We are the only community to retain our culture in Africa." The video shows him in warrior dress, using a cell phone and drinking tea at a food stall in Dar es Salaam. As he walks the streets of the city, tourists gawk at him. These images are contrasted with scenes of Maasai in the countryside looking after cattle and other more "traditional" portraits. In July of the same year, I came across an opinion piece discussing the song in *The Guardian,* an English-language daily in Tanzania. In the article, Michael Eneza writes, "The song is set within the modern sector but its intention is to state the case for refusal to join this sector by many of the Maasai people." He criticizes the hit for "its false glorification of stagnation" and asserts that "we wish for development—which means abandoning these bits of culture that makes one African. . . . The song is aware of the contrast between modernity and tradition . . . and chooses tradition. . . . When one isn't modern it is because he is yet to make a choice" (*The Guardian,* July 27, 2002).

Eneza's contrast of "tradition" with "modernity," his equation of "tradition" with "stagnation," and his suggestion that "tradition" must be abandoned in

1

the pursuit of "development" are widely held views in the media, in development agencies, and even among many rural residents in Tanzania. It is believed that _maendeleo,_ Swahili for "progress" or "development," will lift people out of their traditions to a modern world formed on what Eneza calls "European" ways. Many anthropologists have rejected the dualism of "tradition" and "modernity," and indeed even mentioning these terms often raises eyebrows (see Weiss 2001). Yet, as ideological concepts these categories remain powerful and are very much at play in Tanzania and in much of what is classed as the "Third World."[1]

The academic dismissal of the categories of tradition and modernity parallel anthropologists' rejection of the concept of race as a valid category. Although biological anthropologists have argued successfully against the biological or genetic validity of the category, race is still a very potent ideological term in popular discourse and politics.[2] I will show how the ideas entangled in _maendeleo_ affect the lives of Iraqw people living in rural north-central Tanzania, thereby illustrating the ideological weight of these categories. I look not at a series of development projects, though I mention projects initiated in the Iraqw homeland, but instead at the cultural politics of _maendeleo_ on the ground in rural communities.

The imagined categories of "tradition" and "modernity" are ways of understanding various actors' views and experiences of the processes of globalization that began in the colonial era and continue at an accelerating pace today. Development entails bringing individuals and communities into a national and global political economic system. So, the story of development in rural Tanzania and elsewhere entails the chronicle of change and specifically how once "local" cultural forms and practices have been transformed or sustained by the ever-changing global political economy. While this is a story with resonance for communities around the globe, it is important to keep the "local" in mind because, as Feierman so aptly states, "local cultural forms (the rituals or narratives of a particular place) deserve to be given special weight, yet the framework of domination can never be understood within narrow boundaries"(1990:4).

This book shows how notions of tradition and modernity have resulted in a struggle over identity as well as the meaning of community. This struggle takes place at a national level, in the form of what aspects of "modern" life Tanzanians really want to adopt, as well as a local one. In the Iraqw homeland, these concepts are at the center of how community is defined and what rights and responsibilities people have in their communities. For many, the notion of a local community to which one is morally bound no longer has resonance. Rather, many Iraqw see themselves as part of more "modern" communities, the boundaries of which are not fixed and are definitely not local but rather regional, national, and global in nature. For those Iraqw, particularly male and female elders, who see their idea of moral community eroding in the face

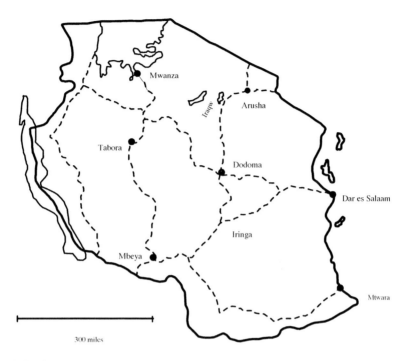

Map 1.1   Tanzania.

of development, this change is perceived as bringing a greater "selfishness" or individualism, which has its costs at the level of community.

I first arrived in Tanzania to carry out fieldwork in November 1989. After spending a little more than a month in Dar es Salaam, I set out for Arusha Region in northern Tanzania to begin fieldwork among the Iraqw, a Southern-Cushitic, agropastoral community in Mbulu District. On the way to what Iraqw describe as their homeland, known by Iraqw speakers as Irqwa Da'aw (or sometimes Kainam) and in Swahili as Mama Issara, I stayed briefly in the town of Karatu, about 78 kilometers north of Mbulu. Karatu, populated largely by Iraqw, is a dusty, expanding town on the main road from Arusha to the Serengeti National Park. One afternoon, as I drank tea in a local restaurant, a few people gathered at my table to ask what brought me to the area. I explained, as best I could, that I was pursuing a doctoral degree in anthropology and was on my way to Irqwa Da'aw to study the history of agrarian and cultural change. This explanation was greeted with incredulity by one young man who exclaimed, "You're going to live in Mama Issara? You should stay here in Karatu where people have developed. Those people in Mama Issara are from the past. You won't like living there. It's a remote and backward place." An older man countered, "No, you don't know what you are talking about. Mama Issara is where she should go if she wants to know the real Iraqw culture."

The remarks by these two men eventually came to take on greater significance as I settled in the Kainam ward of Irqwa Da'aw and carried out research for the next two years. Since my initial fieldwork, I have returned nearly every year for periods of several weeks to several months and more recently for a year in 2001–2002. Throughout this decade, _maendeleo_ has remained a central preoccupation for Tanzania and for many Iraqw. In Tanzania, _maendeleo,_ as Ferguson notes of "modernity" in Zambia, provides a "set of categories and premises that continue to shape people's experiences and interpretations of their lives" (1999:14). In a speech given to Parliament and broadcast on Radio Tanzania on February 2, 2002, President Mkapa said, "To boil water is _maendeleo,_" "to have a latrine is _maendeleo,_" and so on. Yet, _maendeleo_ is a bit of a moving goalpost, for both the government and Tanzanian citizens, as once one milestone is achieved, another appears on the horizon. As a farmer in Botswana noted, "Things modern . . . seem always to be in the next village" (Comaroff and Comaroff 1993:xii). At the national level, _maendeleo_ becomes a yardstick by which Tanzanians measure their country's status in the world economy, as well as a way of gauging their own achievements and those of their village and their neighbors' villages.

Development, and the modernity it is supposed to bring, are frequently contrasted with the past. This past is most often conceived as the precolonial past but more recently has also included reference to the era of socialism following independence. Peoples within Tanzania who may actively try to preserve cultural practices that they or others label "traditional" are often viewed as standing in opposition to progress and clinging to the past. This classification frequently takes on ethnic dimensions, yet even within ethnic groups, some sections, places, and subgroups are considered more "backward" and lacking in _maendeleo_ than others (cf. Walley 2003; Hodgson 2001).

An example of a common prejudice against peoples who attempt to preserve cultural practices appears in the remarks of Botswana's foreign minister in an interview he gave to BBC radio on February 1, 2002. When asked about the country's policies regarding the hunter-gatherer populations within its borders, he talked of the need to "modernize" these peoples and remove them from their "backward" way of life. Furthermore, he said that "communing with flora and fauna" is primitive and that Botswana is a nation of people who want to advance and develop, to drive Mercedes, have the best machines, and have the good things of life. The hunter-gatherer's lack of interest in these things was seen as an embarrassment and a disgrace. This opinion is not unique to Botswana and is clearly found in the discussion surrounding "I Am a Maasai, Bwana." However, views on tradition versus modernity are never simple or straightforward and indeed are frequently contradictory.

There is considerable debate within Tanzania and among the Iraqw about the negative aspects of Euro-American culture and the quest for modernity.

ACADEMIC DEBATES

James Ferguson (1994), Arturo Escobar (1991, 1995), and Marc Hobart (1993) have written widely cited accounts that are critical of development discourse and projects. They point out that the discourse of most development agencies reflects Enlightenment era ideas of a linear chronology of progress in which the West is held as further ahead in the march of civilization, and Africa, Asia, and Latin America are classified as "backward." Ferguson's analysis of discourse draws upon Foucault's examination of verbal or written expressions that are practices which have real effects (Ferguson 1994:18). Ferguson rightly argues that even debates on "'globalization,' 'democratization,' 'civil society,' and 'economic growth' rely on nakedly evolutionist narratives that reduce a complex and differentiated global political economy to a race for economic and political advance" (1999:16). Although I agree with the basic thrust of these critiques, they often overlook or fail to point out that, without some form of "development," as it is defined by local or national actors, many people's lives will suffer, as there is no community that has not been affected by the global political economy.[3] With incomes below $1 a day, it is extremely hard for many Tanzanians to afford education for their children or to pay for health services and vital medicines. Most Tanzanians are keenly interested in some form of development in hopes of improving their economic circumstances. Ralph Grillo notes that many critics are guilty of classifying the "targets" of development as simple "victims," which ignores the complexity and indeed multivocality of development in communities around the world (Grillo 1997). There is also a danger of perhaps overprivileging the success of development. Jonathan Crush states, "As most of us are aware, development rarely seems to 'work' or at least with the consequences intended or outcomes predicted" (Crush 1995:4). Ferguson's (1990) work in Lesotho illustrates this well. Yet, while development may rarely produce the intended results, the effects of development and of development discourse are apparent and often surface in what Escobar calls a "hybridization" of culture or what Louisa Schien (1999) has noted are the multiple modernities that arise from the bricolage of ideas and practices. Certainly the discourse of development has come to influence the views of a wide swath of people, from government officials to rural farmers. Emma Crewe and Elizabeth Harrison (1998) provide intriguing evidence on how the symbolic distinctions between developed and not developed have permeated life for many of the "targets" of development.

In looking at how _maendeleo_ is viewed and acted upon by Iraqw in the homeland, this book responds to anthropology's challenge to examine the relationship between the local and the global and to investigate the interplay between individual agency, structure and social change (cf. Bourdieu 1977; Ortner 1989; Moore 1986). It becomes apparent how individual Iraqw actions and decisions affect both their own lives and the wider community but also serve to transform cultural practices and beliefs. While perhaps providing an example of the "multiple modernities" in the world, I share Englund and Leach's (2000) reservations about the analyses of modernity that assume a unified vision of modernity without being sufficiently ethnographically grounded in the field experience.

In Ferguson's work on modernity in Zambia, he explores the cultural dualism between "localism" and "cosmopolitanism" by borrowing some tools from cultural studies to look at "cultural styles" (1999:95). He argues that using the approach of cultural styles gets away from evolutionist typologies that often accompany the tradition/modernity dualism. Instead, cultural styles of localism or cosmopolitanism are "contrasting styles within a single social setting" (1999:102), rather than two co-present societies that might represent historical sequences. Styles, he further argues, are both consciously and unconsciously deployed, and people tend to specialize in one style or another. Although Ferguson does not want to reduce "cosmopolitan" style to "Western" or "European," as these terms contain references to many African and international tastes, he admits that "cosmopolitan styles in urban Africa are dominated by Western and Western-derived cultural forms" (1999:108). This observation holds for rural Tanzania as well.

Whereas Ferguson looks at mine workers in primarily urban settings who draw on cosmopolitan or localist styles to establish certain alliances, I look at these styles within a rural setting. In Tanzania, and indeed throughout much of Africa, most of the population still lives in rural areas. In this rural environment, younger Iraqw, like Zambian mine workers, adopt a cosmopolitan style as a way of joining, or attempting to join, a wider national and often global world, one that is often as imaginary as it is real. While those adopting cosmopolitan styles are attempting to participate in the wider world, their ability to participate economically, culturally, and politically in this wider arena is clearly constrained. Iraqw, and indeed most Tanzanians, as Weiss's (2002) work in Arusha illustrates, are keenly aware of their marginal status in the global political economy. In carrying out fieldwork in Irqwa Da'aw, I learned that there is no single, coherent "local" or rural culture that stands in contrast to an urban one. Instead, there are many "local" variants as well as cosmopolitan ones within the homeland setting. Furthermore, there is no easy contrast between rural and urban, as each environment and style informs and is infused with the other.

An examination of cultural styles and the political-economic context in which they operate clearly reveals that the idea of cultural uniformity among Iraqw is not a realistic one. Certainly, there are practices and beliefs that most Iraqw will claim as recognizably Iraqw and to which they may subscribe, but there are many practices and beliefs linking Iraqw to other Tanzanians that have no basis in a precolonial tradition. For example, let's look at a day in the life of two men (one could also find these contrasts in women, but because women often do not have the same economic and social opportunities as men, differences may be slightly less marked in the homeland setting). Marmo is younger, educated through Form 4 in secondary school (the equivalent of twelfth grade), a Catholic, and a primary schoolteacher. Margwe is an older man of about sixty-five who speaks little Swahili; owns a few cows, goats, and sheep; and cultivates the land he inherited from his father with maize, beans, sweet potatoes, and pumpkins.

Marmo awakes; lights his charcoal stove; makes tea, which he pours into his thermos; and eats some chapati his wife has made before gathering his things. He takes his bicycle out of his small, sheet-metal-roofed brick house and starts off for school. His attire, mostly purchased at the used-clothing stalls in town, consists of leather shoes, a dress shirt, khaki pants, and a jacket, all pressed by his wife with a charcoal iron the night before. When his day at school is over, he passes by the local hoteli (restaurant) on his way home and drinks some soda with his friends while they watch the news on the television that an entrepreneur has brought to the village and hooked into international communication with a satellite disk.

Margwe wakes early, pulls his blanket close around him, and waits while his wife grinds maize into flour on the grinding stone and prepares porridge. He eats his porridge with milk, takes some milk outside, pours a small libation on the ground and then on the heap of manure piled outside to use in the fields, and prays to the Creator and thanks her and his ancestors for his blessings. He then sets out for the pastures with his livestock. He wears a blanket over his torn and ragged shorts and old sweatshirt his daughter bought him. He wears tire sandals bought years ago at the monthly livestock auction and traveling market in Mbulu. In the afternoon, he returns his herd to the homestead, eats some stiff porridge, and then heads out to the _kilabu_ (beer club) to drink sorghum beer with his friends.

These vignettes are brief, stereotypical portraits of two different cultural styles. They are not meant to represent entire groups but rather elements of different groups' styles. They are widely recognizable to homeland residents, and they express socioeconomic, as well as subcultural, differences within the homeland. The deeper implications and elements of these styles will become apparent throughout the chapters of this book. Attention to styles is helpful for interpreting much of Iraqw daily life, but consideration of wider political and economic factors must also be taken into account.

Although Tanzanians may aspire to some of the goals of modernity, they do not all subscribe to the idea that it necessarily brings "the infinite advance towards social and moral betterment" (Habermas 1990:343). This caution about "modernity" was even expressed by Tanzania's vice president Dr. Mohamed

Shein in a speech he gave to mark the end of Ramadan in December 2001. The *Daily News*, in the "comment" section of the December 19 issue, quotes Dr. Shein:

> There is a mistaken belief among some Tanzanians, and indeed people of the developing world, that everything Western—values, norms and the like—constitutes "modernity" and should be embraced without question. Imitating Western traditions and cultures in wholesale is often seen as a sign of "being civilised" or "moving with the times."
>
> But it is this blind adoption of Western traditions at the expense of positive local customs and values, which is putting our nation on a dangerous course to moral decay and heightened juvenile delinquency.

This hesitation or caution about embracing all that development or "Westernization" has to offer is present in both rural and urban contexts in Tanzania. It is evident in exchanges ranging from conversations about the value of beauty contests to debates about the adoption of genetically modified seeds.

Discourses on Tradition and Development in Tanzania

In Irqwa Da'aw, tradition is a fluid category of beliefs and practices that in usage is manipulated and reformed, as well as rejected, by various actors and interests. In both Swahili and Iraqw, there is no one word that sums up tradition. Most Swahili speakers refer to tradition by using a variety of words such as *mila*, *desturi*, *utamaduni*, and *mambo ya zamani*, which translate approximately as "habits," "customs," "civilization," and "things of the past." Iraqw, when discussing many cultural practices, often refer to *balgeera*, or "in earlier days" (Mous et al. 2002). Development, which often stands in contrast and opposition to tradition, brings with it *mambo ya kisasa*, or modern things (literally "matters of the present"). Much of the discourse on development in Tanzania and in the Iraqw homeland focuses on material concerns such as land use and acquiring Western goods. The goods that are considered markers of modernity include radio-cassette recorders, manufactured pots and pans, clothes purchased in stores, and bicycles. Many younger Iraqw aspire to build a "Swahili"-style brick and cement house with a sheet-metal roof as opposed to a "traditional" wattle and daub, round, thatched house.

Initiated by the colonial state, development, in both theory and practice, justified many of the state's policies (taxes, cattle culling, etc.) as the necessary cost of establishing modernity. As a result, "despite the internal complexity of colonial societies, they tended to be perceived and represented, from within, in highly dualist, oppositional terms; terms that solidified the singularity of, and distance between, ruler and ruled, white and black, modernity and tradition" (Comaroff and Comaroff 1997:25).

While the postcolonial state developed a different ideology of development, the effects were often the same. From the colonial era to the present, in the minds of most Tanzanians, development has been associated with the state and various government or donor-driven projects. The shift in the perceptions of midwives in a community in southern Tanzania provides an example of how closely linked development and the state are in people's imaginations. After undergoing training in a government hospital, "these midwives had been moved conceptually to another category, were thereafter associated with the government *(kiserikali)*, and were said to have adopted modern methods" (Tripp 1997:18).

I first began systematically to collect people's views on development in 1997 when I asked a class of Standard VI (sixth grade) students to write essays in Swahili about what they thought *maendeleo* was or how they would define it. Below are some of the students' statements (see Prazak 1999 for similar views among Kenyan adolescents):

1. *Maendeleo* is when a person goes from an inferior state to a better one.
2. *Maendeleo* is to go from a poor condition to a better one, for example from the way it was for our grandparents to the way it is now. . . . During our grandparents' time, they did not have clothes. This would be shameful [today]. . . . But we must remember that *maendeleo* has its costs. For example, those *wazungu* [European] scientists make bombs that can blow the world up. All of those things are the costs that come about because of *maendeleo*. We must remember that everything has its good and bad side. Everything has its time. Today *maendeleo* seems to be speeding up.
3. Our country can get *maendeleo* if we grow cash crops like coffee and bananas.
4. In our village, we have different kinds of *maendeleo* . . . farming, keeping cows for milk. The villagers have progressed because there are different schools that teach lessons. Children learn much about *maendeleo* from their teachers. The ward officer told the villagers to plant cash crops and they would get foreign money.
5. There are many today who are trying to develop but they are not able. Life today is very hard unlike the past. . . . Many young people run to the towns, but life there is not good.
6. *Maendeleo* is when someone is able to succeed on his own—when he can get all the things he needs on his own.
7. *Maendeleo* is when a person is able to meet his needs without relying on anyone else.

These thoughts expressed by the students clearly reflect what they have been taught in school and what they hear often at government meetings. A number of ideas emerge in their comments. First is the association of development with farming practices or types of crops or livestock that the government or donors have introduced or encouraged villagers to adopt. These changes in agricultural practices (which are discussed in a later chapter) have helped to link the residents of Irqwa Da'aw with the wider regional, national, and, in the case of pyrethrum and coffee, international markets. These connections are seen to be central to _maendeleo_, and indeed many Iraqw in Irqwa Da'aw and elsewhere have pointed out that the homeland's development has been limited by its isolation. Yet, obviously, being at least in part dependent on world markets for such crops as coffee and pyrethrum has its myriad dangers. The drawbacks to participation in supposedly "free" global markets have now become the subject of much debate in Tanzania and even in the United States, as a recent _New York Times_ editorial titled "Harvesting Poverty" indicates.

Maendeleo implies a linear progression, going from a poorer condition to an improved one. A temporal dimension is also indicated, as many refer to moving from the past (when in a poorer state) to the present (to achieve a modern life). Those whose development is not seen as significant are linked to the past, especially to the precolonial past. Yet, as indicated earlier, not everyone embraces the goal of achieving "modernity." Many Iraqw expressed reservations about _maendeleo_, particularly the new embrace of a more capitalistic economy. As one man said to me, "I am afraid we will end up like Kenya. There, they care about money more than people." Stereotypes of neighboring countries aside, this man's comments reflect strong sentiments in the Tanzanian consciousness, ones that emphasize "fairness, justice, and egalitarianism" (Tripp 1997:190). With economic liberalization has come a discourse on what many Tanzanians and certainly many Iraqw in the homeland see as increasing selfishness, or _ubinafsi_.

Elders' views of _maendeleo_ are more critical than those of youth. An excerpt from a pre-prayer speech given at a harvest festival in the village of Gidbuger outside of Mbulu town in 1991 illustrates their concerns: "These days people are angry. There is no understanding between a man and his parents, a man and his neighbors, and this has led to trouble among our entire family, among our Iraqw people."

I often heard elders recite this refrain of "no understanding," together with their view that today people are increasingly selfish, throughout my initial fieldwork and into the next decade. It was usually an accusation leveled at the youth, but today elders accuse even other elders of this fault. When asked what led to these problems, many were hard-pressed to come up with a specific cause, but others echoed the statement of one older man who said, "The reason Iraqw do not get along with each other as they did in the past is _maendeleo_. These days _maendeleo_ means that young people do not respect

Figure 1.1   A 102-year-old elder.

their elders and that everyone has become selfish and interested only in their own good." When asked to elaborate further, many older men and women claimed that, in particular, once children are educated (and exposed to national ideology and the agenda of the nation-state), they lose respect for their elders and the "ways of the past." As one old woman told me, "Once my children grasped a pen, they looked at me as though I was a fool."

ETHNICITY AND PLACE

Throughout Iraqw territory, and indeed throughout Tanzania and the so-called Third World, ideas about tradition and modernity are mapped out spatially, culturally, and politically. These positionings identify some people as further along the path toward modernity, while others appear caught in a distant past, unable to move forward. These ideas are pervasive and shape the plans of both the state and international development agencies, as these institutions often direct their projects toward those areas, communities, and individuals identified as "progressive."

Ideas about tradition and _maendeleo_ situate Iraqw identity within the nation as a whole. In Tanzania, communities that are seen to hold onto tradition are viewed as "tribal." As both Arens (1979) and Rekdal (1996:31) have observed, Iraqw tend to be grouped, along with pastoralist communities such as the Maasai and Datoga, as _watu wa kabila_ or "tribal people." Persistence of various cultural practices believed to have originated before the colonial era, such as clothing style, religion, use of language, and so on, are indicators of this presumed "tribal" proclivity. The common view of the Iraqw as "different" from other Tanzanians, in appearance, in language, and even in personality, is exemplified by the following description: "They are a proud people, noted for statuesque, immobile posture and sharply defined features. They tend to be withdrawn, growing their own food, tending their cattle, and selling only crops or beasts when essential to purchase their few needs" (Hatch 1972:17).

Hatch then further notes the Iraqw "lack of interest in modernization" (1972:17). These views of the Iraqw are common all over Tanzania, yet these stereotypes mask what is actually at stake in the process of "modernization," which is essentially self-determination and the ability to choose the course of change rather than have it imposed from above. The ways in which the colonial government valorized their own practices as right and "modern" while simultaneously classing those of the African population as "backward," "primitive," and "traditional" are not dissimilar to how the postcolonial Tanzanian state approaches various cultural practices and the peoples who maintain them.

Although some other Tanzanians may see Iraqw as stubbornly traditional, most Iraqw certainly do not view themselves this way. After all, many Iraqw point out, the prime minister is Iraqw. Nonetheless, Iraqw may use these ideas to classify other Iraqw within their own community or within certain regions of Iraqw territory. In so doing, Iraqw themselves contribute to what Giddens states about modernity: it "produces _difference, exclusion_ and _marginalisation_" (1991:6).

In 1995, Karatu, north of Mbulu District, became a separate district. Karatu residents stated that the major reason to seek independent district status was to pursue development. Many felt that Mbulu, which they asserted was "behind" Karatu and much more "tradition-minded," was holding the more "progressive" Karatu back. Karatu has a very different socioeconomic context, in part because it is situated on a major road linking Arusha to Mwanza on Lake

Victoria. This road is also the main tourist route for the northern national park circuit, and so this region sees a steady flow of foreigners who pass through and often stay in the town. In addition to the many businesses that have sprung up in response to this flow of people, Karatu also has many farmers who each cultivate hundreds of acres to produce wheat, barley, maize, and beans for both national and international markets. There are also many poor farmers and those without land in Karatu who work as laborers for farmers with large landholdings or those with businesses. As Karatu has become more integrated into national and global markets, the sense of ethnic unity with their relatives to the south has lost some of its salience.[4]

Many in Tanzania would agree with the view proffered by the bishop of the Catholic diocese in Mbulu that Mbulu is the "back of beyond" (personal communication, 2001). In February 2002, the government declared that a new region would be carved out of the Arusha region. Speculation quickly arose as to where the new headquarters would be located. Maasai in Ngorongoro began complaining that to be cast into a new region with primarily Iraqw could mean the loss of their landholdings to these agropastoralists. In Mbulu, people debated the pros and cons of the town's being selected for the regional center. Many believed that if the town were selected, it would no longer be the "back of beyond," and trade would grow, businesses would spring up, and roads would be improved and possibly expanded. Another faction within the town viewed the potentiality with distaste, stating that the town would no longer be mostly Iraqw and that *hoomo* (non-Iraqw) would take over. This debate illustrates again not only the ways in which *maendeleo* is a topic central to people's concerns but also how some people view *maendeleo* as a threat to cultural unity.

ETHNOGRAPHIC SETTING

North-central Tanzania is an area of great linguistic and cultural variety. Around the Iraqw live their pastoralist Datoga and Maasai neighbors, the agriculturalist Bantu-speaking communities of Ihanzu, Iramba, Mbugwe, and Irangi, and finally the small hunter-gatherer community of Hadza. Within this cultural mix, Iraqw certainly consider themselves unique, as well as perhaps more developed than their neighbors. Within this region, the Iraqw have been very successful in expanding their landholdings, and they now occupy an area roughly fifteen times that of their precolonial territory within the homeland. Iraqw used ritual practices (discussed later) to bring new land within their control and to turn these areas into Iraqw communities. Iraqw are unique within the region and throughout Tanzania for their Southern-Cushitic language and for their emphasis on space as an organizing principle. This emphasis has been discussed at length by Winter (1968) and Thornton (1980, 1982). Rather then dwell on spatial organization per se, I instead focus on what Iraqw communities do to emphasize a sense of community within territorial boundaries. It is this emphasis on community, and specifically locally based communities, that is often at odds with the national objectives featured under the banner of *maendeleo*. The tension between local and global and between "tradition" and "modernity" fuels much of the local dynamics within Iraqw communities in the homeland.

Within Mbulu District, within Tanzania, and indeed within a globalized context, the Iraqw homeland is certainly a marginalized area. The homeland is essentially hidden from view from the low-lying regions as it is surrounded by high mountain ridges. Iraqw originally fled to this mountain fastness to escape from hostile pastoralist neighbors. There is one main road that circles through Irqwa Da'aw, though it becomes largely impassable during the height of the rainy season. Farmers have very small landholdings, and agriculture is carried out by hand hoe. There are many people within the homeland who have never or rarely ventured out of it. One of the reasons for its economic marginalization, cited by many government officials and even those living within the homeland, is the physical and social isolation of the area. Many Iraqw stated that lack of exposure to other ethnic groups and to regional and national markets has led Iraqw in the homeland simply to "inherit the practices and beliefs of their grandfathers without change." This inheritance, many feel, is what has led to economic stagnation. This book examines some of these ideas and looks closely at what are supposedly inherited beliefs and practices. Although some Iraqw may argue that tradition has remained the same, I instead assume, as Sally Falk Moore has observed, that "the tradition of a modern ethnic group, and the tradition of its past, though they have a family resemblance, are not the same thing" (1986:11).

The homeland is significantly different from the neighboring areas to which Iraqw have migrated. The small size of landholdings per household, together with the topography and agro-ecology of the area, results in very different economic options for Iraqw residing there. Significant surpluses of food crops, and cultivation by plow or other forms of mechanization, are not possible in the homeland. Although Iraqw create myriad strategies for making a living and pursuing development, lack of transportation, poor roads, and numerous other infrastructural deficiencies constrain their efforts.

While those residing outside the homeland claim that outmoded traditions are one factor holding homeland residents back, I hold that much has changed within Irqwa Da'aw, and residents are hardly rooted in maintaining some sort of archaic tradition. The struggles for power and authority that accompany cultural transformations, together with the cultural richness of the homeland, are the focus of this book. My goal is to demonstrate to the reader that economic and political marginalization has little to do with "tradition."

SCOPE OF THE BOOK

This book draws on more than a decade of experience in Mbulu District and particularly in Irqwa Da'aw. I have resided for brief periods in Karatu District as well and have also traveled and conducted interviews in neighboring Babati and Hanang Districts. Over the years, I have investigated many topics: agricultural change, ritual, gender ideology, witchcraft and divination, education, democracy and civil society. My fieldwork has most definitely become a "peculiar form of current history" (Moore 1986:7). Each visit to the area reveals new changes and new twists and turns in people's lives. The children who were entering first grade in the primary school next door to my house in 1990 are now in their twenties, and some are studying in secondary school. In 2002 I hired one of those students as my research assistant, and he regaled me with stories about his classmates' astonishment that I, an _mzungu_ (European or white person), had lived in the school compound a decade ago. The chapters that follow provide a story of transformation. Not only have people's individual lives changed, but the cultural forms I observed in 1990 continue to be modified and contested today. Throughout, I insert specific cases to illustrate the ways in which people draw upon cultural ideas and practices and mold them to their circumstances. For the most part, references to other literature, both ethnographic and theoretical, can be found in the footnotes. There has not been a great deal written on the Iraqw, but various studies have looked at religion (Johnson 1966; Winter 1964; Snyder 1993, 1997), agriculture (Fukui 1969; Snyder 1996), marriage (Wada 1971, 1980), language (Mous 1988; Ehret 1974; Whiteley 1958), livestock markets (Winter 1962), personhood (Snyder 2002), gender ideology (Snyder 1999), migration (Fukui 1970b; Wada 1969b; Winter and Molyneaux 1963), and beer brewing (Fukui 1970a). Thornton's (1982) ethnography examines Iraqw spatial ideology, and more recent ethnographic contributions by Rekdal (1996, 1998, 1999), Hagborg (2001), Songstad (2002), and Simon (2002) highlight various aspects of Iraqw culture and society from the consumption of milk and beer to myth making, politics, health, and ritual. Lawi (2000) has focused on agrarian and cultural history in the homeland. My own work draws from this literature but seeks to address rather different questions.

Chapters 2 and 3 look at how Iraqw are situated within the wider region of north-central Tanzania and examine the organizational structure of Iraqw communities. Chapters 4 and 5 examine kinship, marriage, and circumcision. Chapter 6 shifts to a study of land use in the mountainous landscape of the homeland. Chapters 7 through 10 focus on religious beliefs and practices. Throughout these chapters, attention is paid to how things have changed over time in Iraqw communities as a result of their incorporation into first the colonial and then the postcolonial state. The ideology and practice of development have touched nearly every aspect of Iraqw culture and society.

Notes

1. The Comaroffs (1993, 1997), Gewertz and Errington (1991, 1996), and Pigg (1992) have illustrated the complex ways in which modernity and tradition become defined and acted upon in Southern Africa, Papua New Guinea, and Nepal respectively.

2. Ferguson observes that the cultural bifurcations described in the literature produced by the Rhodes Livingstone Institute in Southern Africa are still apparent among today's mine workers in Zambia: "[W]e might well reject the terms in which these authors described this duality (primitive/civilized [Wilson]; tribal/urban [Epstein]; low urban commitment/high urban commitment [Mitchell]), but the ethnographic fact of a certain duality remains to be explained" (1999:91). And as he states elsewhere: "Listening to informants discuss the contrast between 'the village' and 'the town,' or 'African' tradition versus 'European' modernity, I often had the unsettling sense I was listening to an out-of-date sociology textbook" (1999:84).

3. For one critique of Escobar from the perspective of anthropologists engaged in development, see Little and Painter (1995). For other useful reviews of the literature on anthropology and development, see Gardner and Lewis (1996) and Crewe and Harrison (1998).

4. Yet, as the work of both Raikes (1975a) and, more recently, Hagborg (2001) shows, there is enormous cultural similarity between these two areas.

CHAPTER TWO

CONSTRUCTING A HOMELAND

Place and Identity

Tanzania rarely gets noticed in the Western press, yet it is one of the few countries in Africa that has remained politically stable and peaceful since its independence in 1961. If the country does emerge in the Western imagination, it is because of its famous landmarks such as Mt. Kilimanjaro and the Serengeti Plains. In the global political economy, Tanzania is certainly a marginal participant, an identity it is keenly aware of. It has been ranked as one of the poorest countries of the world, yet this statistic does little to capture the rich vibrancy of Tanzania's many cultures. In Tanzania, Mbulu District is an area with a fascinating history. It is arguably one of the most diverse areas in the country if not in East Africa, containing the agropastoral Southern-Cushitic-speaking Iraqw, the hunter-gatherer Hadza, the Nilotic Datoga and Maasai pastoralists, and Bantu-speaking agriculturalists. This cultural and linguistic diversity makes the area intriguing, particularly for anthropologists. Yet, relatively little has been written about the Iraqw, certainly in comparison to the Maasai, about whom there is the joke that every Maasai village contains an anthropologist.

It is believed the Iraqw came into Tanzania from Ethiopia centuries ago. According to well-known oral history, the Iraqw arrived in Irqwa Da'aw[1] (by Iraqw speakers) or *Mama Issara* (by Swahili speakers), the place they call their homeland, from a place called Ma/angwatay to the southwest.[2] In Ma/angwatay, as the story goes, the Iraqw had many cattle and an abundance of milk and food. Yet, the young men grew bored in this prosperous land and went to the diviner Haimu to appeal to him to lead a war against the neighboring Datoga. Haimu disapproved of war and refused their request. To force him to agree to their demands, the young men kidnapped Haimu's son and refused to return him until a war had been arranged. So, Haimu journeyed to Datoga territory and made arrangements with warriors there to engage Iraqw youth in battle. He returned home with the Datoga warriors in tow and demanded the return of his son. He pointed the Iraqw youth in the direction of the warriors and refused to participate in the battle. He then withdrew from the area, along with others who were uninterested in this battle, and began his march to Irqwa Da'aw. Meanwhile, the Datoga overpowered the Iraqw fighters, and the survivors of the battle beat a hasty retreat to join Haimu and his followers. And this is how the Iraqw came to live in their mountainous and remote homeland of Irqwa Da'aw, passing through the Nou Forest to the south and settling in Murray. Fosbrooke (1955) estimated that approximately one hundred families made up the original settlers.

This story illuminates a central tension that exists in Iraqw society between the interests of the elders and those of the youth. Thornton has observed that "the distinction between the *barise* (elders) and the *masomba* (youth) is constituted as a political polarity" (1980:114–115). The youth are often perceived as clamoring for potentially dangerous change, whereas elders seek to maintain the status quo that has, in this story and in others, produced prosperity. Yet, as elders control the means to this prosperity, it is not surprising that youths chafe at their position. Today, tensions between youths and elders are redefined as the youth draw upon the resources and rhetoric of the state and the churches. They deploy the term *maendeleo* to seek independence from elders who want to hold them back and mire them in "tradition." For the youth then, it is not the maintenance of the status quo that leads to prosperity but rather the pursuit of change.

The story of the homeland's founding points to another feature of Iraqw culture and identity: peacefulness. In both historical accounts (Iliffe 1979) and in the wider Tanzanian imagination, Iraqw are characterized as a peaceful people. In the story of the homeland's founding, the elders promote this peace. Irqwa Da'aw appears as a place of safety and a refuge from hostile neighbors. In the narrative, there is no mention of the land being inhabited by anyone when the Iraqw arrived there; instead the Iraqw's role in transforming wild untamed land into socialized space is emphasized. In Irqwa Da'aw, the residents prospered, better protected from attack by the Maasai and Datoga who conducted raids for cattle. They also benefited greatly from the favorable climate and natural resource base. The homeland suffers less from many of the health problems, particularly malaria, that plague the surrounding lower zones. Once resident in Irqwa Da'aw, the inhabitants quite happily isolated themselves to some degree from the rest of the region. This isolation provided protection and indeed is a theme throughout Iraqw history and cultural practices. There

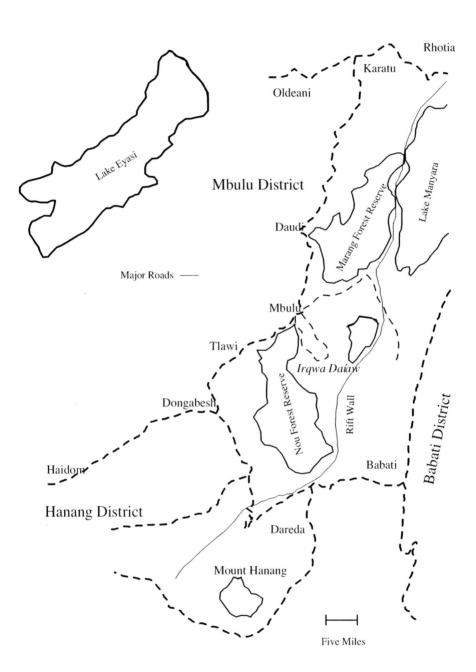

Map 2.1   Mbulu District.

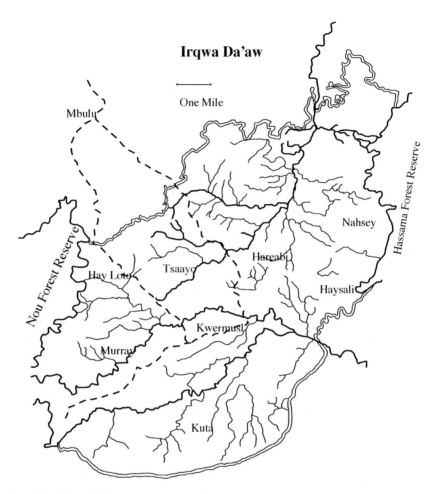

Map 2.2   Irqwa Da'aw.

are various rituals designed to protect and hide Iraqw households or even entire communities from hostile outside forces. In addition, Iraqw pollution beliefs, which are described in detail later, also focus on isolating and containing misfortune.

The landscape of Irqwa Da'aw is unique in the surrounding environment of north-central Tanzania. It is a highland area, of approximately 128 square miles, with elevations ranging from 6,000 to 8,000 feet, on the plateau overlooking the dry Maasai Steppe below the Rift Wall to the east. The land is composed of high ridges transected by well-watered valleys. Surrounding these ridges and enclosing Irqwa Da'aw is a line of mountains topped by forest reserves to the north, southwest, and east. Within this enclosure, the green hills and valleys seem endless. However, if you climb up any of the mountains forming the border of Irqwa Da'aw, the entire landscape can be viewed as a fairly small, contained bowl formed by the higher mountain ridges.

The climate in this mountain environment is cool and moist, and even during the dry season, the landscape remains green and the streams continue to flow. Every time I walked back from my weekly shopping trips to the town of Mbulu, I was struck, as I climbed the last steep hill into the homeland, by how the air seemed different, cooler and moister as I reached the top of the hill's crest and crossed the border into Irqwa Da'aw. Dew replaced dust, and moist fog often lingered in the valleys seen in the distance. This climate enables Iraqw living here to cultivate crops throughout the year. Outside of Irqwa Da'aw to the west, the land falls away to elevations of 5,000 feet and eventually the lower elevations of the shores of Lake Eyasi. A more abrupt descent is found on the eastern border that is the Rift Wall. From Irqwa Da'aw, the wall plummets straight down to the valley almost 2,000 feet below. These lower regions surrounding Irqwa Da'aw are much drier and sustain cultivation only in the rainy season. I have traveled into the homeland with Iraqw from the expansion areas who were visiting the area for the first time. All remarked on the marked difference between the homeland and the surrounding regions and expressed surprise at how green and mountainous the area is. Even in the nearby town of Mbulu, Iraqw living there describe the homeland as cold, isolated, and damp. The environmental features are just one of the elements used to define Irqwa Da'aw as different by both those residing within it and those outside.

Exactly when the Iraqw originally came to this region of Tanzania is difficult to establish. Cushitic-speaking ancestors of Iraqw preceded both the Nilotic and Bantu migrations into Tanzania. Ehret estimates that Southern-Cushitic settlement in Tanzania "antedates the first millennium B.C." (Ehret 1974:7). He approximates Cushitic occupation of the West Rift area (which encompasses what is now Mbulu District) at the first millennium A.D.

Several authors (Thornton 1980; Fosbrooke 1955; Thomas 1977) have suggested that Iraqw colonization of Irqwa Da'aw occurred from 300 to 400 years ago, but there is insufficient evidence to fix a specific time. Although the oral history describes all who arrived with Haimu as being Iraqw, today's elders say that only three of the clans (Tipe, Massay, and Irqa) are of pure Iraqw origin (a clan being a group that claims descent from a common ancestor). The rest of the clans found among Iraqw today were established by individual men from one of the various neighboring ethnic groups in the area who married Iraqw women.

The assembly of refugees following Haimu came to the land together with their livestock and began clearing it for cultivation. Initially, they divided the land into large family holdings that, over time, became clan holdings. The majority of neighborhoods in Irqwa Da'aw today bear clan names. Each holding occupies a portion of one of the many ridges that crosscut this mountainous bowl.

Figure 2.1   Two views of the homeland.

Although the mountain ridges surrounding the homeland are forested, it is unclear what vegetation was present in the area when the Iraqw arrived. However, in the 1930s British colonial officials described the area as virtually "treeless" (Tanzania National Archives, File A3/1), and older Iraqw women declare that they used primarily bracken ferns for their cooking fires. These ferns even today cover the land in great abundance in areas that are not cultivated or forested.

Due in large part to its geography, Irqwa Da'aw remained relatively isolated for centuries. Iraqw embraced and actively maintained this isolation. One of the chief functions of Iraqw community-wide rituals was to keep hostile individuals or groups from entering the territory. Several Iraqw elders explained that these rituals, and the actions of the paramount diviner at the time, successfully kept out slave traders. When faced with Europeans, however, their rituals failed to stave off the incursion. Although Iraqw tried to control who came into the homeland, they did have contact with neighboring communities, venturing out of the homeland during famines to trade for food and accepting immigrants into Iraqw society. For all Iraqw, Irqwa Da'aw is perceived as their homeland, but this identity means different things to different people. For those who established themselves or grew up in what are called the "expansion areas," the homeland is revered as the place of their forefathers and is considered to be historically and culturally important. But it is also viewed by these migrants as a "backward" place, somehow stuck in time and rooted in a primordial tradition. Obviously, Iraqw living in the homeland do not view it this way, and indeed they are acutely aware of the changes that have occurred and continue to occur in their home. Yet, they are also aware of the views of their kin in migration areas, who classify them as backward. Although they are quick to refute this characterization, it does affect their self-perception in various ways, which will become clearer in the chapters that follow. This perception of the homeland also shapes district council development policy.

Irqwa Da'aw in a Regional Context

Let our houses expand to point toward the north
Let us multiply until we reach the end of the country
—Lines from an Iraqw prayer

Those Iraqw who initially migrated out of the homeland were usually younger men in search of new opportunities, often anxious to make their own way and get out from under the control of their fathers. Thus, the tensions in Iraqw society between elders and youth, evident in the founding story of Irqwa Da'aw, manifest themselves in the history of Iraqw expansion as well. Within the homeland, Iraqw elders often say it was the headstrong and troublemakers who migrated north to form the communities of Karatu and Mbulumbulu. Today, Karatu District is a seat of opposition politics, and Iraqw in the homeland joke that those in Karatu have inherited the character of their troublemaking forefathers. Those who migrated to the west and south were not described in the same way but rather as sons who, faced with the population pressure in the homeland, sought their own land for a more prosperous life. In interviews with elders in these expansion areas, many confirmed that they left the homeland because they were attracted to the opportunity of greater landholdings. Most Iraqw in these settlements also suggest that they are more progressive and forward-looking than those who remained in the homeland. This is perhaps most pronounced in Karatu, as is evident in the conversation in the restaurant related in Chapter 1.[3] With these internal differences, to speak or write of "the Iraqw" is problematic. In addition, the Iraqw have cultural practices similar to many of their neighbors, a product no doubt of intermarriage but also of cultural borrowing from long-term residence and interaction. Yet, for Iraqw in all areas there is still a sense of common identity founded in part on identification with the homeland as the place from which all Iraqw came and on their shared language. The Iraqw language is pointed to by all Tanzanians as very different; the non-Iraqw regard it as very strange sounding and impossible to learn. Most Iraqw agree that few non-Iraqw are able to learn the language.

Beginning in the late 1800s, the Iraqw expanded steadily west, north, and south into areas previously occupied and controlled by other ethnic communities. The acquisition of land in the territory of neighboring groups has been a primary goal and one that they have managed to achieve. In the precolonial era, Iraqw engaged in small-scale trade with neighboring groups in axes, metal hoes, machetes, pottery, and, in times of famine or drought, foodstuffs. There was some migration into the homeland from members of other ethnic groups in the region, with migrants marrying Iraqw women and founding their own clans. Many male elders claim that prior to the colonial era, during which Iraqw were often given favored status first by the Germans and then by the British, Iraqw were particularly averse to leaving the homeland for fear of attack by Maasai or Datoga or the bewitchment of their Bantu-speaking neighbors. In addition, because of the climate in their mountain homeland, they have little resistance to the diseases that plague those living at lower elevations, particularly malaria, and they venture into lowland areas with some trepidation. Those who do travel outside of the homeland to lowland regions to work or study return to Irqwa Da'aw and regale their friends and families with stories of their bouts of malaria and other diseases.

Iraqw expansion was facilitated by both the British pacification of the raiding pastoralist communities of Maasai and Datoga and the rinderpest epidemics that preoccupied and decimated the wealth of their cattle-keeping neighbors. The British greatly favored the Iraqw because they were agriculturalists, but also because they perceived the Iraqw to be willing and easy subjects compared to the more confrontational pastoralist communities. Underlying their perceptions was a belief in Iraqw racial superiority that appears throughout the reports in the Mbulu District Book. As agriculture officer J. Hartley wrote in 1942: "The Wambulu (the British name for the Iraqw) seem a tractable people, and in comparison with most of the Bantu tribes of the territory, above average intelligence" (TNA, File 9/10).[4] Iraqw were very quick to figure out a strategy for appeasing colonial authorities. They listened dutifully and appeared to agree with colonial government dictates but inevitably found ways to avoid them or maneuver around them. This strategy is one many continue to employ in dealing with the postcolonial state as well. An illuminating quote by an Iraqw informant points out the differences separating the Iraqw and Datoga: "We, the Iraqw, know what to keep quiet about, and therefore we win. Our two tribes are as sheep and goats: the one is quietly watching the world before it is slowly moving; the other is passionately acting upon it for everyone to see and hear" (Rekdal and Blystad 1999:130).

With the sanction of the colonial government, Iraqw expanded rapidly into former Datoga and Maasai territory. By 1927, Iraqw had established their control over the former Datoga area of Dongabesh by moving into the area when Datoga had journeyed temporarily to other seasonal pastures. They also began to move southeast into Dareda, another Datoga area. Iraqw continue their steady encroachment into Datoga land today, and intermarriage is common. As in the colonial era, the state still favors the interests of agriculturalists over pastoralists and thus does little to ensure Datoga rights to land. In areas where Iraqw live together and intermarry with Datoga, there is considerable fluidity in ethnic and individual identity. Datoga adopt more sedentary practices and take up farming, while Iraqw put more emphasis on pastoralism. Language, dress, and other cultural practices are similarly mixed.

Iraqw feel a greater kinship with Datoga, as there are similarities in physical appearance and in dress style. The Datoga, like Iraqw, carry staves or spears and wear cape-like cloths, though the color and style of the drape (obvious to the Iraqw eye) is different. Facial scarification marks are also similar, the Iraqw having copied some of the Datoga styles. In areas where Iraqw and Datoga are both resident, many Iraqw continue to wear beads around both their necks and waists, the latter practice having been long abandoned in Irqwa Da'aw. At a harvest celebration I attended in Dongabesh, both Iraqw and Datoga elders recited ritual prayers, in Iraqw and Datoga languages respectively.

Datoga are frequent visitors to Irqwa Da'aw, where they trade metalwork and livestock for tobacco and maize. Iraqw, with the help of the British colonial government, were very successful in overturning the precolonial political order in which, greatly fearing the Datoga and Maasai, they kept to their mountain home. However, though Iraqw have managed to take over a large area of Datoga land and have intermarried in significant numbers, they nonetheless continue to express fear of the Datoga, citing instances of their ferocity and cruelty. These stereotypes of the Datoga stand in binary contrast to the gentleness and peacefulness that Iraqw claim are the hallmarks of their own cultural identity.

Other neighbors who have lost territory to the Iraqw are the Maasai. Again, as with Datoga, the British favored and encouraged Iraqw interests over Maasai and enabled Iraqw to push north into Maasai land. Maasai lost control over land from Karatu north to Mbulumbulu in the 1930s and 1940s. Their lands now border Iraqw territory to the west and north, and Maasai do occasionally still sweep into Iraqw land to raid for cattle.

As Arens observed in Mto wa Mbu, a rapidly growing town at the foot of the Rift Wall on the road entering Iraqw territory, Iraqw and Maasai are disdained as _watu wa kabila_ (tribesmen) and _wapagani_ (pagans) (1987:252). Although Iraqw do not share these sentiments of commonality with their pastoralist neighbors, they do admit to similarities in dress style and interest in livestock. They are adamant however in distinguishing themselves as "peaceful" people unlike these neighbors. Younger Iraqw men, who had left the homeland for school or military service in other parts of Tanzania, told me that Iraqw men in these multicultural environments tended to band together with Datoga and Maasai more than with other communities. One man explained, "When I was doing my military training in Tabora, I stayed mostly with other Iraqw, Maasai, and Datoga. We have all been circumcised unlike many other Tanzanians."

On a trip to Mbulu District in 1998, the driver of the vehicle I traveled in kept remarking on Iraqw dress, asking, "Why do they wear those primitive capes? That is not very modern. These people are very backward like those Maasai." I told him that he would understand why after spending one night in the cold highland environment in which these capes do much to keep people warm. What was particularly amusing about this exchange was that the driver was himself from the south of Tanzania, near the border with Mozambique, an area classed by the rest of Tanzanians as very "backward" and "primitive."

Traditional and Modern Places and Identities

Throughout the country, Tanzanians associate certain places and the people who inhabit them with either modernity (Kilimanjaro) or with traditional ways of life (Kiteto District, the southern border with Mozambique, among others). The Iraqw also define areas where Iraqw live and the residents who inhabit them in similar terms. Within the districts where Iraqw live, Karatu asserts itself as more modern, and areas such as the Iraqw homeland are viewed as "backward." In defining themselves as more modern, Karatu residents point to a variety of features of their lives: their integration into national and international markets; their cultivation of "modern" crops such as

Figure 2.2   Road heading north from the town of Mbulu.

wheat, barley, and new bean varieties; their use of combine harvesters and
other mechanical equipment; and the prevalence of Christian religions, particularly the Catholic and Lutheran churches. They also have regular contact
with foreigners (*wazungu*), as Karatu lies on the road from Arusha to the
Serengeti Plains. The road sees regular tourist traffic but also bus traffic taking passengers from Arusha to Mwanza in the west. Although Karatu is indeed more integrated into national and international markets, Irqwa Da'aw is
also tied to markets—some local, some international—through the sale of
fruit, charcoal, wood, and increasingly coffee and pyrethrum. Christian
churches are equally prevalent there with the population being roughly split
equally between Christians and non-Christians.

Within the homeland, a similar classification of some spaces as modern
and some as more traditional occurs. For example, Kuta, the community far-
thest from Mbulu and situated high on the Rift Wall overlooking Babati below, is perceived as more traditional, whereas communities nearer to Mbulu
are considered to be more modern. Furthermore, spaces within these communities, such as schools, churches, government offices, health dispensaries,
and the collections of small shops, are associated with modernity and with a
national identity. As Rekdal (1996) has found, these "modern" spaces are often exempted from the actions involved in certain traditional beliefs and
practices. Thus, tradition and modernity are ways of defining space and the
practices taking place within this space, as well as the people who take part in
these activities.

The Iraqw word *hoomo*(m)/*hooma*(f) illuminates some of the complexities
in the tradition/modernity dichotomy. This word is used to refer to a person

Figure 2.3   One of the main roads out of Mbulu down the Rift Wall.

from another ethnic group, or an outsider.[5] Yet, the term can be applied to any Iraqw who is seen to be acting in what might be said to be an un-Iraqw, and often "modern," way. I knew one ambitious young man who was given the nickname of *hoomo* after he returned from secondary school. He was the only member of his family who was a Christian (Catholic), and he was eager to set himself apart from tradition to lead a modern life. His often open rejection of traditional practices, together with his "quick," aggressively open nature ("he has no secrets," a friend of his explained to me) and his modern aspirations, were the basis of this nickname. Interestingly, this young man (as of 2002) now lives in Karatu District where he feels less constrained, he says, by the limitations of life in the Iraqw homeland and by the demands of kin. He has a cell phone and spends his evenings with his friends watching satellite television at a local bar. Meanwhile, his wife and children remain at home in Kainam, caring for his aging parents and farming their small plot of land. The behavior and aspirations of this young man are not unique in the Iraqw homeland. The nickname of *hoomo* is very telling. A word that was previously used simply to refer to people of non-Iraqw origin is now being used to refer to someone who asserts a "modern" and thus non-Iraqw, non-ethnic identity.

An important strategy of Iraqw in their dealings with one another and particularly with outsiders has been to maintain a high degree of secrecy about their affairs. Various ritual practices, which are described in later chapters, emphasize protection through establishing barriers or enclosures to pro-

Figure 2.4   Conditions of the main road to Mbulu during the rainy season.

tect individuals from view. Older Iraqw in particular stress that this has been a strategy for survival in dealing with first the colonial and then the postcolonial government. Rekdal and Blystad (1999) have also commented on the secretive and reserved quality of Iraqw and report that elders note that youth today are losing this reserve and see this loss as a cultural one as well. The noted reserve of the Iraqw does not make ethnographic research among them easy, and it takes some time to convince people of your good intentions. It took a year's residence in the homeland, for example, before I began to be invited by both male and female elders to their council meetings.

Secrecy is also one of the principal strategies used by the diviners to maintain their authority and position in Iraqw communities. This secrecy protects their power and knowledge and allows them the opportunity to carry on with their activities without interference. In 1993, on a visit to the Kuta area I learned of government discussions concerning the repair of an old road that runs through Irqwa Da'aw to the town of Babati, a trade center and now regional capital in the Rift Valley below the steep escarpment. Many of the elders and most of the diviners in the Kuta area were opposed to the proposal to make this road passable for vehicles. Fear of opposing the diviners led many residents to reject plans for the road.

In a meeting held to discuss the plans for road repair, diviners and other elders explained that they did not want *hoomo* to come into Irqwa Da'aw and destroy their "culture and traditions." In response, a government official, himself from Kuta, said, "We already have *hoomo* here. Look at the young people who have converted to the Church of God or the Pentecostalists. Are they not *hoomo*? They no longer follow the customs of the past. So, we already have *hoomo* among us." This debate reflects the ways in which, for many Iraqw, ethnic identity is tied both to residence and to cultural practices. In the past, before making any journeys outside of one's home community, and particularly before going into foreign territory, men would visit the diviners to get protective medicine for their trip. Diviners thus benefit from the us/them dichotomy that is inherent in ethnicity. Diviners have power over space and people's movements in it or out of it by the application of "medicine" to either bless or curse arrivals or departures. Although Iraqw have long welcomed foreigners into their midst (as is indicated by the fact that the majority of clan founders came from other groups), they are still wary of outsiders. The diviners potentially have much to lose by certain aspects of development. For example, if people convert to Christianity (conversion is seen by many Christian Iraqw and government officials as a hallmark of progress), or if health services become more easily available, the diviners may lose clients. Certainly, both the church and the government discourage people from visiting diviners, who are considered to be both "backward" and "pagan." In 2002, improvements to the road to Babati were again being discussed. This time the Catholic diocese was trying to find funding for the project, and many residents of the homeland thought the road would improve their economy greatly by making the transportation of goods to market much easier. I talked with some elders in Murray about this project, and most of them claimed to be in favor of it. Today, very few households are not in some way dependent on trade with local markets, and most see modern transportation as a desirable improvement in their lives.

From this overview, various contradictory and ambiguous views about Iraqw identity emerge. Other Tanzanians often characterize Iraqw as conservative and backward people, secretive and aloof. They are grouped with the Maasai and Datoga as being stubbornly traditional and evading the state in its efforts to modernize. Even among Iraqw, these views are not entirely absent. Young men and women often describe older men and women in such terms, as they increasingly associate themselves with a national and "modern" identity as either Tanzanians, or Catholics, or school graduates.

The Iraqw have incorporated many immigrants from the different ethnic groups in the diverse region and, along with them, elements of their cultural beliefs and practices, from weddings to witchcraft. Nonetheless, at certain moments, an assertion of an Iraqw identity, distinct from these neighbors, is made, particularly by elders. The elders in Kuta, in their opposition to the rebuilding of a road, drew upon these images of Iraqw identity and linked them with tradition in an attempt to control the influx of *hoomo* into their community. Obviously, the more outsiders there are in local communities, the less likely residents will be to follow the dictates of elders. Now *hoomo* is a term applied not only to those of another ethnic group but also to those who adopt a national identity and assert their modernity in the process. As Arens observed in Mto wa Mbu in the late 1960s, residents there prided themselves on their identity as *waswahili* (Swahili people), which in fact few of them were. But the term *waswahili* has become commonplace in postcolonial Tanzania to stand not for Swahili identity but rather a national identity, one formed on the Swahili language and house style, the wearing of Western clothes, participation in organized religion, and so on. By claiming to be *waswahili*, they were identifying themselves as members of a "category that is national and even international, and not a parochial one" (Arens 1987:252). In the homeland, the word *hoomo* was often used interchangeably with *mswahili* to denote a more modern, less local identity. For elders, this national identity strikes at the foundation of their power and moral authority in the community. Their authority rests on their knowledge of tradition, which is a very local, and very specifically ethnic, realm. For young people, a national identity enables them to circumvent parental control and seek opportunities for advancement through the churches or the state. This community-wide tension between elders and youth is most pronounced within households, a dynamic that is explored more fully in the next chapter. Schools promote a national identity over an ethnic one, and the embrace of an ethnic or local identity is viewed as an impediment to *maendeleo* and a possible threat to peace and national unity. Thus, young people in particular are exposed to pressures from both government and church to abandon "ethnic ways."

Notes

1. Irqwa Da'aw translates as "Iraqw land of the east."

2. See Fosbrooke (1955) and Thornton (1980) for full accounts of this oral history.

3. In her work among the Marakwet, Moore observes similar such divisions: "they themselves link the escarpment with the traditional way of life, and the families who have moved down on to the valley floor are those with a stated interest in change and development" (1986:122).

4. See Rekdal (1998) for an analysis of the ways in which Iraqw drew upon these colonial myths of Iraqw origins.

5. Rekdal and Blystad (1999) note that frequently Datoga are not included as *hoomo*.

CHAPTER THREE

"LIKE WATER AND HONEY"

The Making of Moral Communities

Let us get along like sleep and bedtime stories
Let us get along like the mouth and the hand while eating
Like water and honey
— LINES FROM A RITUAL PRAYER

Ideally, residents in Iraqw communities should get along together "like water and honey,"[1] blending together in a harmonious union. In precolonial Irqwa Da'aw, local communities, or *aya*, were independent of one another, and individuals had rights and responsibilities within, and to, that specific community. Ritual and religious beliefs developed these political units as moral communities in which there should be harmony. In bringing local communities throughout Tanzania under a central government, colonial and postcolonial governments changed the nature of communities. One of the main ways the state has engaged with local communities is through the agenda of development. To bring *maendeleo,* the state has reorganized social and political structures, "improved" indigenous agriculture and land-use practices, and encouraged the integration of local economies into national and international markets. Today, discussion about the proper course of development can be heard in households, at the local tea stall, or at the cluster of local shops in Kainam. Although many Iraqw never leave the homeland to live in towns or the expansion areas, or to further their education, all are amply acquainted with national ideology and discourse about *maendeleo.* At independence in

1961 and in the 1968 Arusha Declaration, _ujamaa_ (familyhood) socialism was the path taken to achieve the goal of a more modern, developed Tanzania. Under _ujamaa,_ the state's penetration into the everyday lives of Tanzanians increased dramatically (Rubin 1984). A state representative known as a ten-cell leader _(balozi)_ was put in place to represent roughly every ten households.

While penetration of the state was extensive, its effectiveness in achieving its goals of development was by no means complete. The limits to the effectiveness of the state has been analyzed by Hyden (1980) in his groundbreaking study, in which he suggested that the peasant population retreated and evaded the state by withdrawing into an "economy of affection." Hyden's assertions were later challenged by scholars who pointed out the myriad ways in which the peasantry was indeed incorporated into the state, including through the payment of taxes, the sale of cash crops, and the payment of school fees (Barkan 1984; Ergas 1980; Fleuret 1980; Kasfir 1986; Kerner 1988; Raikes 1978; Rubin 1984). In some areas of Tanzania, where the local population proved resistant to state interventions, the use of force proved highly effective in "capturing the peasantry." Although parts of the Iraqw homeland were affected by _ujamaa_-era policies of communal farming and villagization, many people avoided having to move their homes, as the landscape and density of population made it difficult to force house placement along organized lines. In the Iraqw homeland, and indeed throughout Mbulu District, Iraqw were often very successful at evading the state. Yet, taxes, community work duties, cooperative boards, and school fees were and remain features of state penetration into the daily lives of homeland residents. Throughout the country, Tanzanians suffered under the shortages of manufactured goods and foodstuffs that came about as a result of _ujamaa_ economic policies.

Rising oil prices, a decline in the trade of its major exports, droughts, and the 1978–1979 war with Uganda fueled an economic crisis in Tanzania that reached a critical point in the 1980s. The domestic crisis was matched by pressure from the World Bank and the donor community to sign an International Monetary Fund (IMF) agreement to implement a structural adjustment program. In 1986, Tanzania agreed to the plan and launched an Economic Recovery Programme, and controls on trade, both internally and externally, were relaxed. Over the course of the next decade, the state began withdrawing resources from social services such as education and health. The social costs of the state's withdrawal have been high. In an in-depth study of Tanzania's economic liberalization, Tripp reported dramatic effects: "Suppressed wages and large cuts in social services continued to adversely affect the livelihood of Tanzania's people. Cost sharing in education and health services put additional burdens on the poor. For example, enrollment rates in schools fell from 92 percent in 1977 to 40 percent in 1994" (1997:77).

In 1992 the Tanzanian government allowed the formation of opposition political parties in preparation for its first multiparty elections in 1995. These transformations have shaped the everyday life of all Tanzanians. The comment of one man in his sixties, himself a former agricultural officer, are indicative of many people's attitudes toward some of these changes: "During *ujamaa,* there was nothing to buy in the stores. We had to wait in line for sugar, and there was often none to be had. We had no soap and had to use leaves that we discovered produced suds. Today there are many things lining the shelves of the shops, but we have no money to buy them."

While many people complain about prices and the increasing financial demands of the government, people are able to sell their crops to private individuals today and are able to make more money than they were in the *ujamaa* era of strict trade regulation. Yet there are many more demands for their money today, and inflation has made their shillings increasingly less valuable in purchasing goods. In addition, with the government cessation of price controls for crops, farmers now often find themselves at the mercy of middlemen who work together to keep their purchasing prices low and take advantage of farmers during times of stress brought on by drought or other circumstances.

From the precolonial era to the present, the actual territorial boundaries within the Iraqw homeland have remained much the same. But the political structures that have been imposed have ushered in many new possibilities as well as restrictions that did not previously exist. Ironically, whereas local spatial organization was paramount to life in the precolonial era, now that boundaries have become more solidified under the Tanzanian state, territory has lost some of its significance to Iraqw in the homeland, and kinship is gaining some ground. In belonging to specific villages and neighborhoods, Iraqw have certain responsibilities to others who share that space, but residence also secures certain rights. Along with transformations in the structure of communities have come different ideas of what community means. Younger Iraqw increasingly question notions of a bounded moral community and instead embrace a sense of belonging to a wider community, one that links them to other Tanzanians and, in the case of religion, a global community.

Upon entering Irqwa Da'aw, it is difficult to discern what boundaries or levels of spatial organization may exist beyond that of the household. Homesteads are scattered on the crests of ridges, and there are no outward signs of villages or other corporate units. Nonetheless, boundaries exist at the level of household, neighborhood, and village and are known by all who live within them. Yet, borders are still subject to manipulation and are a source of various disputes. When the Germans and British imposed their administrative structures on the Iraqw homeland, they employed, roughly, the existing borders. In the process, the boundaries became more permanently fixed in space and time. The independent Tanzanian state also made few changes in the spatial composition of Iraqw communities in Irqwa Da'aw. Thus, today, the boundaries of neighborhood and village are recognized and used by both the council of elders to define a moral and ritual community and the Tanzanian state to mark out administrative and political units. These two purposes exist side by side, sometimes reinforcing, sometimes undermining each other. The state's use of space to create its own political units has, in some ways, reinforced the idea of a bounded community. But the state system emphasizes allegiance of all local communities to the nation-state and to a Tanzanian identity. The incorporation of local communities into the wider state political structure has diluted their individual characters and differences and undermined the authority of the local elders' council. Although there is still a sense of individual community identity, young people today feel as great a sense of shared identity with, and commitment to, fellow members of their church or classmates from school, both categories that crosscut village or neighborhood community boundaries.

THE HOUSEHOLD

As Winter (1968) has noted, the household is the primary unit of social organization. I would also argue that the household is important for conferring identity and status. It serves as the basic blueprint for all social relations in Iraqw society. Here I concur with Grinker (1994), whose focus on the house as the fundamental unit of social relations among the Lese in Zaire questions the common assumption that there is a divide between the domestic and political spheres. In Irqwa Da'aw, a person's reputation is formed in part by how he or she behaves within his or her household. If a man is known to be a good husband and father and to manage his household well, then he will be respected in the community, and the same is true for a woman as a wife and mother. A man who repeatedly beats his wife or children, fights with his son, drinks too much, or squanders his household's resources loses prestige in the local community, as does a woman who is seen to be careless about her work or child care. Children, as they grow up, also form an identity and reputation in the community by their behavior within their household. How well they treat and respect their parents affects how others perceive them in the community. As I discuss in Chapter 5, this reputation is important when marriage negotiations get under way. Finally, it is within the household that a model of gender relations is constructed and passed on to children. The social roles, between men and women and between elders and juniors, within the household extend to the public sphere, and the spheres are mutually interdependent. Today, these roles are being stretched and challenged under changes brought about through Christianity, postcolonial state policies, and exposure to new ideas and economic opportunities.

Typically, a household consists of a husband and wife and their children. Sons, once they marry, establish their own households on land allotted to them by their father, or they seek land in new areas. Usually the youngest son stays near home to care for his aging parents, building a separate house near theirs when he marries. Although polygyny is practiced, in most of the households I surveyed the husbands had only one wife. In the past, I was told that although second wives had their own houses and property, they lived near the first wife and cooperated in much of the labor. However, one elder claimed that "today there is much jealousy, and co-wives do not get along." To avoid conflict, husbands often build separate houses in different neighborhoods. Having more than one wife is frowned upon by the Christian churches and is described as an "unmodern" and "pagan" practice. Today, women head many of the households in Irqwa Da'aw, as their husbands have abandoned them or live elsewhere because of work. In a few cases, husbands are living with second wives in other neighborhoods.

The household is the principal economic unit. Each household has its own fields, livestock, and some private grazing land. Land is passed from a father to his sons or may be obtained by asking close relatives or members of one's clan. In addition, one can petition the village chairman (an elected official) for land, but this is often viewed as a less favorable option because one is likely to end up with the least attractive parcel available. Livestock is also inherited by sons or may be bought or borrowed.

Relations within the house are ordered on age and gender hierarchy. The father is head of the household, and his decisions and views are to be respected and not contested. He makes most of the decisions regarding resources. Depending on his personality, he may or may not choose to delegate authority to his wife and children. Mothers also deserve respect and obedience from their children, but they often have more affectionate relationships with their sons and daughters than do their husbands. Women are responsible for the cooking and cleaning, basic household chores, and child care. Men do not enter the cooking area and leave this domain to their wives. Women I spoke with were happy with this arrangement, as their control over food gave them, they felt, some power, authority, and respect in the household. They did joke that men, while claiming they could not cook, proved to be perfectly able when put to the task. Women tend to stay close to home, though today they are increasingly involved in small trading activities that take them to Mbulu, the district capital. Men, however, herd the livestock away from home and journey long distances to visit relatives or pursue jobs or trade. Attitudes concerning the proper domain of either sex are asserted in the expressions parents use to proclaim the birth of their child. When a daughter is born, they announce they have a child who will "fetch water" (hheekuuso'o), that is, she will remain near the household and be in its service. When a boy is born, parents announce the birth of a child "of the bush" (hhee sla/a), that is, one free to roam far from the house. All Iraqw, both male and female, should ideally, be "gentle" in personality, but women, in particular, should be gentle, shy, and obedient.

As further described in Chapter 6, which focuses on resources and their use, the household is the site for competition over resources. As sons grow

Figure 3.1   Traditional round house.

older, they may challenge their father's decisions and suggest that he pursue more "modern" activities, such as tree planting or coffee cultivation, with the hopes that they will eventually gain from these investments. Today, as it becomes increasingly more difficult to find land outside of the homeland, sons have to rely on their fathers for land and livestock, unlike those who left for Karatu or other expansion areas years ago. These constraints are leading many younger Iraqw to seek nonagricultural opportunities. Jobs in the government, in schools, or in health services all require education, which has become increasingly expensive in the wake of the structural adjustment policies instituted in the late 1980s. To afford education, younger people may seek out wage labor jobs or rely on their fathers or other relatives to provide them with financial support.

Relations within the household and indeed within the wider Iraqw community are guided in part by the Iraqw moral code of *irange*. Although Thornton (1980) glosses this term as meaning "sin," I think this translation is a bit misleading. Certainly, it involves moral violations, but they are specific to violations of codes of conduct between the generations and particularly within the household. For example, incest is *irange*, as is a child striking a parent. Young people also should not utter profanity in front of their parents or those of their parents' and grandparents' generation. In particular, this rule applies to cross-sex interaction.

When a man marries, he builds his own house. Building a house is an important sign of independence for men, and the type of house a man chooses to build is one way he can assert his identity and status in the community. In pre-

Figure 3.2   House compound in Irqwa Da'aw.

colonial Irqwa Da'aw, houses were of two kinds: a round house with no windows and a small entryway in which both people and livestock lived, and houses, known as *tembe*, that were dug into hillsides, giving them a subterranean quality.[2] The latter style is almost completely absent in the homeland today but was popular as a method for hiding from potential outside livestock raiders. After independence, the Tanzanian government began pushing the construction of what people refer to as Swahili-style houses, which are square or rectangular with windows and doors.[3] Lawi notes that "to the government and Party officials, owning a rectangular house with elaborate windows and roofed with corrugated iron sheets was a sign of modernity and higher status" (2000:361). In the homeland, the Swahili-style house now predominates, and round houses are becoming rarer. Most of the houses are made out of poles from black wattle trees, which are plastered with locally available mud and a white sandy soil, creating an almost whitewashed appearance. Thatch is utilized for the roofing material. The goal of many younger people, having internalized the government views on housing styles, is to construct a brick and cement house roofed with sheet metal. This modern housing style is considered by younger Iraqw to be of higher status and prestige, and it is recognized as a key symbol of _maendeleo_. In fact, in this highland climate, these sheet-metal-roofed houses are often colder in the cold season and hotter in the warm season than the houses made of traditional materials. A few of these modern houses dot the landscape, though more are appearing every day. This style of house remains beyond the reach of most Iraqw because of the prohibitively expensive materials.

From the precolonial era to the present, if a young man chafed under the authority of his father and was anxious to set off on his own, he could leave his natal household and establish his own in another community. In this way, Iraqw expanded and formed new communities outside the homeland. In these communities, allegiance to one's neighbors and other community residents was primary. Because Iraqw expansion has slowed, it is currently more difficult for sons to find land elsewhere. Many instead remain close to home or choose to pursue lives in the distant towns and cities. Because access to important economic resources depends in part on a son's relationship with his father, young men must navigate this relationship with care. The tensions inherent in this relationship fuel much of the struggles over _maendeleo_ in the community. Unlike the Maasai (Spencer 1988), the Iraqw do not have the institution of warriorhood to provide an outlet for rebellious young men but instead must rely on social and supernatural sanctions to contain the youth.

The Neighborhood and the Ridge Community

All households are nested within larger social and territorial groupings.[4] *Mangu aya* is a group of neighbors who have the closest daily interaction with one another. This term comes from the custom of parceling out meat to neighbors from the legs (*manga*) of a cow that has been slaughtered for consumption after a communal work party. Neighbors cooperate in herding, farmwork, house building, and other exchanges. The tenor of neighborly relations is apparent in the practice of sharing fire. If a woman needs embers to start her cooking fire, she may approach any of the households in the neighborhood. This fundamental activity, on which the consumption of food depends, is seen as an important symbol of mutual interdependence. The importance of neighbors to Iraqw is clear in the following saying: "The death of a family member who lives at a distance is better than the death of your neighbor" *(Gwaawaw' inslaawumo mar'afumo' sauwu' ng'ir' gwaa'i)*. This expression points to the social and economic interdependence among neighbors. It may also refer to the potential danger of pollution, which results from the death of someone in close physical proximity.

Households are situated on the crest ridges. A ridge of houses, or a large portion of it, is considered a community. It is called an *aya*. Each ridge community has its own name and specific boundaries. When they were first established, these ridge communities were usually occupied or controlled by one clan, and indeed today they often bear the name of a clan. However, as there has been much migration in and out of Irqwa Da'aw, the ridge communities are now generally composed of members of several different clans.

Ideally, relations with neighbors are close and harmonious, and many Iraqw attested to positive and cooperative relations with their neighbors. One young man explained that although he now lived and worked in another community, he still relies on his home neighborhood cohort to assist him with various projects. He trusts these young men with whom he grew up far more than many of his relatives in neighboring towns or his new friends in the community where he now lives. Yet, neighborhood relationships are also often fraught with tension, as competition over resources such as pastureland, agricultural land, trees, and water strains relations. Disputes over land—arising from conflicting interpretations of boundaries—and disputes over livestock are quite common. If disputes are not settled, it may lead neighbors to cut off communication with one another entirely and enter into a formalized and public declaration of enmity *(wakari)* in which households sever all ties. The underlying current of tension in these relationships is revealed by the fact that neighbors are often the first suspects in witchcraft cases. Relations in the neighborhood in this way mirror those within the household. Residents must cooperate and share some resources but are also in competition with each other over scarce resources.

In each ridge community there are some shared resources such as pasture, woodlots, and, of course, water sources. In the past, neighbors would cooperate with one another in farmwork, but these communal work groups *(slaqwe)* have decreased over time. They are still important, however, for the clearing and preparation of fields in the valley bottoms. Beyond this expectation of cooperative farming, members of the ridge communities have other specific responsibilities. Men are to cooperate in house building and in carrying sick people to the dispensary or hospital.

An event that took place in 1993 illustrates how these expectations are embedded in the ridge community. A young man who had joined other young men of his ridge community in carrying a sick woman to the hospital in Mbulu refused to continue, insisting that he had work to do at home and there were more than enough people to finish the job of delivering the patient to Mbulu. His cohort did not accept the excuse and the following day fined him for failure to carry out his duty. They demanded that he prepare beer for all members of the ridge community to consume together in order for the matter to be settled and to restore harmonious relations. If he refused, he would be shunned by all. The young man complied, and he prepared and served the beer that week.

Ostracism is a powerful method of social control. If someone has been formally ostracized *(bayni)*, he or she receives no visitors nor any assistance in farming, house building, or emergencies. Informally and unofficially, people shun those who are deemed to be selfish *(qahangw)*, greedy *(ilatleeri)*, or jealous.

The *Aya*

As their numbers increased, the Iraqw expanded northward out of the southern portion of Irqwa Da'aw to fill the entire highland area. In this expansion, Iraqw pioneers created new separate, autonomous, and bounded communities. In all, pioneers established eight of these communities *(aya)* within Irqwa Da'aw. In the precolonial era, each *aya* was politically autonomous. Relations with other *aya* were, and continue to be, marked by the same ambiguity that marks a household's relationships with its neighbors. While, on the one hand, neighbors (and *aya*) join together in cooperation, on the other, they compete for resources. Iraqw notions of pollution heighten this tension as impurity endangers all those in close proximity. Just as all households are united in a common moral community, all *aya* are united in a larger moral unity, which is held together, in part, through relationships to the clan of paramount diviners who handle ritual matters for the *aya* and the entire Iraqw community. Today, all *aya*—or villages, as they are termed by the state—are incorporated into wards, divisions, districts, and finally the region.

The *aya* is the largest precolonial territorial and political unit, ranging in size from 14 to 25 square kilometers and in population from 1,967 to 4,353 people (Tanzania Census 1988). The *aya* unites a collection of households and ridge neighborhoods into one community. It is difficult to arrive at a precise translation of *aya*, as it refers to both the land and the community of people who live on this land. The boundaries of each *aya* determine membership, and the rights and duties of membership influence access to specific resources. Each *aya* has its own earth spirits who affect the health and fertility of the land and people within the community's borders. Community-wide rituals mark the boundaries of the *aya* and cleanse its members and the land of the misfortune brought about by the violation of moral codes by individuals. Thus, the "*aya*, then, is a moral community. . . . The ultimate welfare of the spatial unit . . . depends on the assent—and the unity of purpose that such assent implies—of the people who live on the land" (Thornton 1980:66).

In the precolonial era, a council of elders made up of men from all the households in the community handled the affairs of the *aya*. At the head of this council was the *kahamusmo* (*kahamuse* [pl.]), or speaker for the community (referring to his role as intermediary between the community and the diviner). New settlers, upon entering the *aya*, would petition the founding *kahamusmo* for plots of land. When the *kahamusmo* had parceled out all the land, land reallocations became the responsibility of individual landholders. As his authority over land allocation ended, the *kahamusmo* acted, together with a council of elders, to handle conflicts over land, domestic quarrels, and other disputes. The most important responsibility of the *kahamusmo*, however, was the ritual protection of the community and its land.

Figure 3.3   The *kahamusmo* of Hareabi.

Elders' councils continue, and the *kahamusmo* is still an important figure in the local community, but council activities today focus primarily on ritual matters. The *kahamusmo* is an inherited position and is passed down through the clan of the original founder or pioneer of the *aya*, usually from the *kahamusmo* to his oldest son by his first wife. Iraqw view the *kahamusmo* as the "father" of the *aya* community and stress that he takes care of its members like a father cares for his children. Elders' councils meet and discuss the affairs of the community and plans for community rituals. Any elder who has married and has children may attend, though today many choose not to show up. Elders represent the interests of their households but also their neighborhoods. In the past, those who did not attend meetings would be fined (in livestock), but it is increasingly difficult to enforce such fines. Also, elders who have converted to Christianity avoid these "pagan" affairs. The proceedings at elders' council meetings can be lengthy, as according to the format, everyone who wishes to has a right to speak. Anyone wishing to voice an opinion stands up in the center of the group and delivers his views without interruption. Only when he has finished and sat down will another elder rise to state his agreement or disagreement with what has been said. These deliberations carry on for many hours, and only when the group has reached a consensus on a matter and achieved the state of being of "one heart" will the group disband and consider a decision final (Snyder 2001).

Members of an *aya* have certain responsibilities and are expected to obey the wishes of the elders' council or risk a fine. One of the most important duties for able-bodied men is to respond to a cry of alarm *(hayoda)*. A *hayoda* is given when the community is in threat of some danger such as an attack by wild animals (for people, livestock, and fields) or by enemies such as the Maasai. In addition, a man might give the cry of alarm if one of his cows is injured or stuck in a ravine or ditch, and he needs the help of many people. Today, the Maasai and Datoga no longer raid the Iraqw homeland for cattle, so there is little reason to give a *hayoda*. There have been isolated cases of theft in the homeland, and by all accounts all able-bodied men have turned out to chase the thief. If anyone fails to turn out for a *hayoda*, he will be brought before the elders and fined.

On one trip out of the homeland to visit the garlic farms in Bashay to the southwest, I came across a large meeting of elders and youth on the outskirts of the community center. They were meeting under some large trees near the main road. I asked permission to join the meeting and sat down to listen to the proceedings. It transpired that the elders had been deliberating for several days about a case relating to a recent *hayoda*. Apparently, the person who had given the cry of alarm had done so falsely (he had mistaken someone's guest for an enemy attacker). Yet, the false alarm was not the concern of the elders. Instead, they were discussing what to do about the few men who had not responded to the *hayoda*. They felt that a fine must be given, even if the alarm was a false one, because there must be no laxness about responding to community danger.

The young men who had failed to turn up proceeded to stand up and state their case. They were followed by various elders who rose to support or disagree with their position. One of the young men was from an ethnic group from southern Tanzania and was living in Bashay to market the garlic produced there. He tried to use his ignorance of Iraqw custom as a defense, but the elders explained that while they were sympathetic to his position, everyone in the community had to abide by the rules of *hayoda*. Their response suggests how migrants have been incorporated into Iraqw communities over time. Newcomers are welcome, but they must learn Iraqw ways and conform to them.

When the young man saw that ignorance was proving a poor defense, he switched tactics and claimed that he had been sick that night and had not heard the *hayoda*. The elders listened patiently but explained that they still could not excuse him from the fine, as it would be unfair to exempt him and not the others so accused. If they agreed to such a course of action, they explained, those who were forced to pay the fine would be resentful, and the bad feelings generated would cause harmful disharmony in the community. Therefore, all would be treated alike. When the fines were announced, the accused were clearly not surprised, for they retreated into the nearby bush and brought out the goats to pay their fine. Although they may not have agreed with the elders' decision, they risked ostracism if they refused to comply. The matter was concluded by the slaughter of a bull that was roasted and eaten by all those gathered, thus restoring harmony in the *aya*. The negotiations conducted in this meeting were similar to many occasions I observed in the homeland where elders relied on persuasion, appeals to harmony, and moral responsibility to pressure younger men or errant individuals to conform to "community" ideals of behavior. Clearly, this strategy can be an effective way for elders to assert their authority, but they must do so by evoking community responsibility and community benefits. These situations and community responsibilities exist outside of the state's authority and continue today despite the presence of alternative forms of political organization.

REDEFINING POLITICAL ORGANIZATION: THE COLONIAL ERA

The Germans established a headquarters in Mbulu in 1892 and quickly imposed an organizational structure onto Iraqw society to facilitate their rule. In Irqwa Da'aw, they utilized the *aya* as the basic political unit and installed subchiefs or *akidas* to oversee their affairs. Rarely were these *akidas* traditional leaders. This new system enabled younger, ambitious men to seek out positions of power that previously were absent from Iraqw society. According to oral accounts, Issara Marmo, a young man and member of the paramount clan of diviners, had heard about white rule in other parts of Tanzania, and he was interested in the power accorded to native chiefs. So, he left the homeland to seek out the Germans and bring them to Mbulu. As a reward, he was installed as chief and proved himself to be quite a brutal one. This story of Issara Marmo and his ambition for power parallels in some ways the story of the homeland's founding. In both cases, youth seek to take power into their own hands, and the result of their doing so is inevitably a loss.

When the British drove the Germans out of Mbulu District in 1916, they built upon the German system, appointing a chief, three deputies, subchiefs, and headmen who oversaw the daily administration in the communities. Selection of the chiefs was in the hands of the elders, and the chief then appointed those who worked under him. The authorities appointed by the colonial government performed duties that were "quite outside the traditional structure" (Winter 1968:18), including collecting taxes, conscripting labor, and intervening in land-use practices. The method of administration, with its chain of command and its transmission of orders, was opposite to the Iraqw system of decisionmaking and governance based on consensus. However, reports from both a government sociologist (Fosbrooke) and an anthropologist working in the area during the late colonial period (Winter) indicate that the Iraqw quickly accepted and adapted to this new system. This new political organization resulted in a decline in the elders' authority, as the Native Authority and the local chief and his administrators took over the running of local communities.

The colonial government erected structures that created a village center, such as schools, dispensaries, a few shops, a court, a bar, and government offices. These have expanded since independence. The location for these buildings is somewhat arbitrary, as nothing like a village center existed in precolonial Irqwa Da'aw.

Elders attempted to discourage the colonial government from establishing permanent structures in Irqwa Da'aw. When colonial officials sought a site for the first primary school, the elders designated a location that was considered to be the territory of spirits *(neetlaamee)* and the home of leopards, who, it was thought, would surely strike out against anyone attempting to appropriate the area. When I came to Kainam to live, I was given a home in this very same primary school by the local government officials. Only later did I realize the appropriateness of a white outsider being housed on these grounds. The elders used the same tactic on the first missionaries to Irqwa Da'aw, assigning them a spot that was prone to lightning strikes. Two churches on this site in Kainam have burned to the ground as a result of lightning strikes, and one crumbled during an earthquake.

POSTCOLONIAL STRUCTURES

The transition from colonial rule to independence was initially met with resistance by many Iraqw. These dissenters had been influenced by the paramount diviner Nade Bea, who saw independence, and the Tanganyika African National Union (TANU), in particular, as a greater threat to the indigenous order than the colonial government. Nade Bea eventually backed down in the face of growing Iraqw support for independence. However, in the first election, the TANU, under Julius Nyerere's direction, selected a non-Iraqw as a parliamentary representative of Mbulu, an act that annoyed most Iraqw. Iraqw elders made their annoyance clear, as a popular tale about Nyerere's post-election visit to Irqwa Da'aw attests. It is said that the diviners put special medicine to bar his entry near the bridge leading into Irqwa Da'aw. According to the story, Nyerere, himself said to be descended from diviners, recognized the medicine and immediately turned around and returned to Mbulu.

The Iraqw candidate, Herman Sarawat, was the son of a former chief (Elias Sarawat) during the British era. When he was rejected by TANU, he chose to run as an independent candidate and won. He was the only non-TANU member of Parliament. This story illustrates the role diviners sometimes play in behind-the-scenes political maneuverings and in promoting Iraqw ethnicity and what they hope will be an accompanying maintenance of Iraqw tradition.

In Irqwa Da'aw, the independent government of Tanzania, like the colonial government before it, drew upon traditional and colonial boundaries and units. The state utilized *aya* and neighborhood boundaries in creating villages (*kijiji* [sing.], [pl.]) and subvillages (*kitongoji* [sing.], *vitongoji* [pl.]). These units are incorporated into wards, which are part of divisions, which are part of districts, and finally regions. Mbulu District is, at present, part of Manyara Region. At the smallest level of organization, there are cells, which at independence were linked to TANU (which became Chama cha Mapinduzi (CCM), the Revolutionary Party, in 1977 after unification with Zanzibar's Afro-Shirazi Party). Cells consist of approximately ten households.

The political structure that the state imposed bears little relationship to traditional authority. Within each of these administrative units are administrators who trace their authority to the central government or the national political party (CCM)—or both. Within villages, the government has built schools, health dispensaries, and government offices. Thus, the penetration of the state is quite thorough. As Thomas has observed, this political system is "a highly effective means of communicating information particularly from the District headquarters to the 'grassroots'" (1977:17). However, the intended outcome of this structure—to enable those at the grassroots level to communicate their wishes and affect policy at the district, regional, and national level—was never realized. The flow of information and power moves primarily in one direction, from the core to the periphery, in spite of stated national ideology.

Over the years, I have attended many ward-level public government meetings. These meetings are designed to communicate government policies to villagers and reiterate policy and plans for development. Word spreads throughout the ward that a meeting is going to be held on a specific day. All adult men and women are expected to attend these meetings or risk a fine if absent. Usually, villagers turn out and wait patiently in the sun on the open field used for soccer games. Sometimes they wait as long as four hours before the district officials and dignitaries show up. When these officials do arrive in their four-wheel-drive vehicles, they go to the local offices to sign in and often receive sodas and food while the villagers wait in the hot sun. Government officials sit in chairs behind desks in specially constructed temporary daises, which are shaded with thatch. Typically, the topic of the meetings concerns *maendeleo*. Often, villagers are admonished for their stubbornness, for being slow to adopt "improved" or "more developed" land-use or livestock practices. These meetings are obvious replicas of the colonial _baraza_ in both format and tone. Often, villagers are treated as backward, child-like, or errant in their civic responsibilities.

The structure and tenor of these meetings are obviously different from the men's elders' councils described earlier. Instead of being forums for the communication of directives, these councils are highly participatory and only enforce decisions that the entire group has decided and agreed upon. Although these councils are more democratic in this sense, juniors are not invited to attend, nor are women, who meet in their own elder women's groups.

Although it often appears that the state stands separate and sometimes in opposition to civil society, it is also seen as a potentially valuable community to join. The state is a significant employer, and involvement in local government can enable individuals to gain power that would otherwise be unavailable to them (Tripp 1997). Many then use this power for their own economic gain. The state, as it is represented by local government, is to be evaded, embraced, manipulated, or complied with according to both the situation and the individual.

PARALLEL SYSTEMS COLLIDE

In 1994, the _aya_ elders' council of Tsaayo mobilized to contradict the local government's reallocation of landholdings. The way in which they handled the case is representative of Iraqw strategies of dealing with the state from the colonial era to the present. They rarely choose direct confrontation but instead handle matters quietly and often offstage. This year, the elder women's council staged a sit-down strike in February at the ward soccer field and meeting grounds. They demanded that the men's elders' council hear their complaints. Meanwhile, the local ward official at the time told me that, hearing the women approach and recognizing their songs of protest, he locked himself in his house and pretended he was not at home. He told me, "What was I going to do with these women? These are matters for the male elders." Government officials tended to treat these types of meetings and protests as traditional and thus not matters for the state to become involved in. In treating them as traditional, the government is thus marginalizing those who participate in them, stressing that they will hear people's views only in the "modern" context and format of government meetings in which they have the upper hand.

The women claimed that a widow had taken a cow to a paramount diviner to request that the rain be prevented from falling and had done so to protest the allocation of her land to others by the local government. Her husband had left some sizable landholdings, particularly in the valuable fertile valley bottom fields. She had left a significant portion fallow for some time, and the government had decided to allocate it to others who had made official requests for land. The men's elders' council heard the case and told the women to return home, assuring them that they would take action. Initially, the elders approached local government officials and asked them to attend one of the elders' council meetings to discuss the matter. But the officials said all such discussions would have to be held at the government offices and must follow the proper procedures for such cases. A government official explained to me that attending an elders' council meeting was impossible, as the government had procedures to follow and places to conduct business, and local officials could not be expected to go sit under a tree and have lengthy discussions with elders. The elders took this response as an indication of the officials' lack of interest in handling the case, so instead they went directly to the men who had been given some of the widow's land. They put pressure on these men to do what was considered right for the whole community, and quite quickly the widow's land was returned to her. She then agreed to send another cow to the diviner to have him bring the rains back. Soon thereafter, rain began to fall in the *aya*.

SUMMARY

The incorporation of *aya* communities into state structures resulted in new structures of authority that did much to undermine the position of male elders. Male elders in the precolonial era had moral authority in the community based on their knowledge of tradition and customary practice. As space rather than kinship was the principle for organization, much attention was given to moral codes of behavior that created a sense of responsibility to others within community boundaries. Earth spirits, described in a later chapter, occupied specific *aya*, and ritual emphasized *aya* residents' relationship to these resident spirits. The key to community prosperity was seen to be harmony and the observance of moral codes of behavior. Violations of harmony or moral codes could result in the earth spirits' attack on the entire community. Harmony is obviously a difficult state to achieve or even to define, but from the elders' point of view, it meant, in part, that juniors and women should agree with and follow their directives. Today, these notions of harmony are widely contested, as *aya* are no longer contained and bounded communities in the ways that they were prior to the colonial era. All members of an *aya* do not necessarily share the same opinion about the rights and obligations of membership in that *aya*. The meaning of community is different for men and women, elders and juniors, Christians and non-Christians, and individuals with different education levels. For older Iraqw, community still has very local associations and is held together by tradition, whereas the sense of community for younger Iraqw is often defined more broadly, as they are linked to wider groups through work, trade, education, and religion. These alternative communities may also be less restrictive on their individual ambitions than local neighborhood and *aya* moral communities. Although the elders' idea of a moral community, situated in a particular territory and governed by their council, may appear to be fading away, there are indications that it still carries some weight. The widow's land case and the *hayoda* in Bashay show quite clearly that the elders do still have persuasive authority in many instances. Their appeals to communal harmony, fairness, and responsibility are still heeded in cases that have high visibility. They are much less successful in smaller affairs, as I show in later chapters, such as when they attempt to force individuals to observe the rules of traditional rituals.

Communal harmony and responsibility are themes that appear not only in elders' ideology but in state ideology as well. On holidays *(siku kuu)*, there are usually special ward meetings and celebrations at which government officials give speeches. At the national solidarity holiday in 1993, one ward official chose to discuss the change from a single party to a multiparty political system. He urged the audience to maintain peace and harmony during these potentially divisive changes. He stressed that national unity had been one of Tanzania's most significant successes and that, unless people remained vigilant, Tanzania might have problems like Kenya, Rwanda, Zaire, and other neighboring countries that were not as blessed with political stability. To emphasize his point, he said, "Look at Somalia, because they could not agree among themselves, they are now being ruled by foreigners."[5] A second official elaborated on this theme and incorporated a reference to Iraqw history, saying, "The elders remember our battles with the Maasai. We were able to keep from being ruled by the Maasai because we had unity among ourselves. If we have no unity, we could be like Somalia." What is interesting about the speeches by the government officials is their obvious effort to put national rhetoric into local terms and draw on local examples and illustrations.

The emphasis on agreement and unity is both a local tradition and a national one, yet the implications of each are quite different. In the local version, agreement means first that all elders should be of "one heart" and genuinely come to a consensus on local matters. Then unity will be a natural outcome of this agreement. Obviously, even in this local interpretation, the implication is that the youth and women should accept what the elders have decided and comply with their wishes. In the national version of unity, local communities are being asked to put aside their ethnic and local allegiances and agendas and comply with national policy. The boundaries of "community" are expanded to include all ethnic groups. However, again, the agreement being promoted is one in which those with less power are asked to accept the directives of those in power. In this case, instead of elders, it is the state government. To date, the appeal to unity in Tanzania has been quite successful, aided by the development of Swahili as the national language and the example set by President Nyerere. Tanzanians all take pride in this achievement and are ever wary of going the way of their more troubled neighbors.

Notes

1. "Like water and honey," a line from a ritual prayer, is discussed at greater length in Chapter 10 of this book. When water and honey are mixed together, they form one substance, and so should the people who reside in the *aya*.

2. See Thornton (1980) for an analysis of the symbolic construction and organization of space within Iraqw houses, ridge communities, and *aya*.

3. For a detailed historical discussion of house types, see Lawi 2000.

4. The smallest level of social organization is the neighborhood, followed by a collection of neighborhoods that Winter refers to as villages and Thornton terms ridge communities. I am following Thornton's terminology here, as I think it more accurate and less confusing. The Tanzanian state refers to these groupings as *kitongoji* (*vitongoji* [pl.]) (subvillage or hamlet). The *aya* has been translated by some (Winter 1966; Thornton 1980) as "county." Although this is a good approximation to the meaning, I prefer to employ the Iraqw word throughout or to refer to it simply as "community."

5. The foreigners about whom the speaker was referring were American troops who occupied Somalia during this time.

CHAPTER FOUR

THE TIES OF
BLOOD AND BONES

Amsi was born in Mbulu to a family of eight children. Her father was a civil servant posted in the town of Mbulu. When Amsi was five years old, she was taken to live with her maternal grandparents in a village about thirty kilometers southwest of Mbulu. Her grandparents were getting old, and it was felt they needed a child around to help them out. She went to primary school there and helped out with household chores, from herding livestock to fetching water and cooking. She loved her grandparents, and they all got along well. She rarely saw her parents or her siblings. When she reached the age of secondary school, she went to live with her mother's brother and his family in a small town along the main road from Mbulu. There her life grew more difficult as she attempted to handle the incessant demands of her mother's brother's wife, who expected her to care for the children and do the cleaning and cooking for the household in exchange for sending her to secondary school. Rarely able to get any studying done till at least 10 P.M. when she was exhausted, and given the demands put on her in her mother's brother's household, Amsi did poorly on her Form 4 exams and did not continue with school. Now living in Mbulu, working for a local guest house, and getting paid about $4 a month (plus room and board), Amsi regularly visits her mother and siblings nearby and helps her family with the farming and other chores. She continues to rely on her mother's brother for help in finding other jobs and in possibly returning to her studies, but so far no opportunities have arisen.

Amsi's story illustrates the primacy of kin in a person's life. Previous accounts of Iraqw (Winter 1968; Thornton 1980) have emphasized the importance of space as the key to their social organization. The Iraqw emphasis on spatial orientation was viewed as rather exceptional in Africa, where kinship and descent had been assumed to play the chief role in social and political organization. In focusing on space, scholars often overlooked descent and kinship issues. In many ways, Iraqw are increasingly turning toward relationships formed through kinship and descent as a means to widen their resources in an uncertain, competitive, and expanding world. As *aya* communities have been incorporated into a wider world, previous emphasis on local space has lost some of its importance. In its place, kinship ties have taken on greater significance. These relationships provide a network of ties that can be called upon for assistance in food, aid in school fees or school admittance, or finding a job or housing in the towns and cities. Particularly in recent times of structural adjustment, when school fees, medicines, and medical services must be paid for, drawing on assistance from kin has become crucial. Kinship ties provide assistance that the state cannot. Kinship ties obviously crosscut those of locality and space and enable individuals to draw upon a wider set of resources. Moreover, kinship and descent are important aspects of individual identity and reputation. The many stories I was told of struggles with kin, as well as cooperation and interdependence among kin, resonated with much of the ethnography of Africa written since colonization.

The organization and meaning of descent and kinship is related to broader cultural ideas about gender and about moral values. The ties of mutual descent and kinship link individuals in different *aya*, and as they connect people in four districts—Mbulu, Karatu, Hanang, and Babati—they create, as Thomas has pointed out, a "strong feeling of ethnicity and ethnic unity" (1977:14).

THE BONES: CLAN *(TLAHHAY)*

Descent among the Iraqw is patrilineal. Clans are the largest descent groups, and today clans number over two hundred. There are only three clans that elder informants agreed are purely Iraqw: Hay Masay, Hay Tipe, and Hay Irqa (Fosbrooke states that "Hay" is "analogous to the Scottish Mac" [1955:29]).[1] Since the time that the original pioneers of Irqwa Da'aw established the homeland, immigrants from various neighboring ethnic groups came into Irqwa Da'aw, married Iraqw women, and stayed on to form their own clans. Among the Iraqw, there are clans tracing their origins to founders from Datoga, Irangi, Iramba, Ihanzu, Gorowa, Alagwa, Mbugwe, Hadza, and even Maasai. Each person knows the ethnic origin of his or her clan. Even if an individual can trace his clan back to, for example, an Ihanzu founder, this does not result in a feeling of shared kinship or culture with Ihanzu (or Datoga,

Gorowa, etc.). However, clan background does occasionally come up as a way of explaining the personality of an individual. For example, one woman said about her husband, "He has a short temper because his clan is a Datoga clan." Although those from other ethnic groups who founded clans are not described as being Iraqw, their descendants are considered Iraqw. Within Irqwa Da'aw, criteria seem to emphasize being born to at least one Iraqw parent and being raised as an Iraqw, in Iraqw territory, and speaking the Iraqw language. A few Iraqw men I knew in the ward of Kainam had married Chagga women. These wives (who spoke very little Iraqw) were accepted into local society but were never considered Iraqw simply by virtue of marriage or residence. Their children, however, who are being raised in Irqwa Da'aw and who speak Iraqw, are considered Iraqw. The creative quality of ethnic identity is clearly illustrated by the ways in which Iraqw identity is crafted from such diverse strands.

I noticed early on in my field work that when walking through Iraqw territory, strangers who meet on a path will, after exchanging greetings about the day and the health of their families and livestock, begin asking one another about their clan affiliation, followed by lineage identity and ultimately the identity of their father. In this way, they ascertain whether they have a connection to one another, either by descent or marriage (that is, one of the women from their clan married a member of the other's clan, and perhaps of his particular lineage). They also use this information to form an impression of the stranger's identity based on the reputation of his or her clan, lineage, or father. Since the grandfathers and often even fathers of Iraqw who live outside of Irqwa Da'aw all originally came from the homeland, all Iraqw share a common knowledge of clan identities and even lineages. Thus, a person from as far away as Karatu shares a common network with someone from Irqwa Da'aw or from any of the expansion areas. People form judgments about one another based in part on the reputation (or stereotype) of their clan, lineage, and uterine kin.

As is common throughout Africa, Iraqw place emphasis on strengthening and building up the clan through numerous progeny. Children are seen as "wealth" or assets of the household and of the clan. Much like the prayers and blessings that Kratz (1994) has recorded for the Okiek in Kenya, Iraqw ritual prayers emphasize fertility, as the following lines indicate: "Let us multiply until we reach the end of the country" and "Let births increase so that new work can be done, so that new bush can be cleared and a new *aya* begun." Fertility is valued for its contribution to the clan and lineage, but also for its contribution to the Iraqw community as a whole. Through population growth, new territories might be acquired, which would potentially add to the resource base and opportunities of all Iraqw.

Although there are sections of ridge communities where household heads are from one clan, more often ridges are composed of households from many different clans. Residence patterns are neolocal, with sons establishing their own households when they marry. Men may obtain land from their fathers or ask others, both neighbors and kin, for plots. Typically, farmers living in Irqwa Da'aw today acquired their land from their fathers. Among the households of which I was most familiar, fathers had given land to their adult sons who had chosen to remain in the area. Other sons, seeing that opportunities for land were limited, or feeling constrained under the authority of their fathers, left the area and sought land elsewhere, usually outside the homeland, or they pursued jobs in Mbulu or as far away as Dar es Salaam. This pattern of migration has expanded the web of relationships for all Iraqw across different ecological zones. The advantages of this expansion are numerous. Having kinship ties to households in different ecological zones enables exchanges of agricultural produce and provides new locations for livestock loans. Sheep and goats, in particular, are thought to prosper in the lower, drier areas to which Iraqw have migrated, so many prefer to place some small stock in these zones. Kinship ties are becoming increasingly important to the economy of households in Irqwa Da'aw, particularly during times of hardship.

Clans, in theory, have control over property, primarily land and livestock, and individuals can appeal to fellow clan members for assistance in these resources. However, in practice, this notion of clan ownership of land and livestock is mostly symbolic, and control over the resources stays at the level of the household head. For example, some clans are said to have territory in Irqwa Da'aw, but these lands have long been occupied by members of many different clans. Although theoretically clansmen have a right to ask for a plot in these areas, realistically there is no space available and nonclansmen cannot be moved off the land. Nonclansmen are considered to have a legitimate right to residence, having at one point (in their household's past) been given the land by a member of the clan who originally occupied the area. The property of each man is considered his own and is not held corporately by the clan. Yet, the wealth of individual clan members is seen, at least symbolically, to reflect the wealth of the clan. In practical terms, individuals may appeal to wealthy clan mates for assistance in the form of livestock or land. Livestock is sometimes given a clan brand so that if animals are lost or stolen, they can more easily make their way back to the rightful owner.

In the past, each clan held meetings to discuss problems such as land disputes (between individuals and to reaffirm the boundaries between their clan lands and those of neighboring clans) or a curse on one of its members. Today, only a few clans carry on with the tradition of clan-wide meetings, as they have become more difficult to organize with members scattered far and wide over as many as perhaps four districts. Particular issues do, on occasion, bring a clan or lineage together, such as the removal of a curse.

Each clan has its own history and identity, as well as its own secrets that are carefully guarded. For example, some clans have a reputation of being belligerent, others of being diviners, and so on. Elders do not like to discuss their clan's history or affairs in front of people from other clans.

LINEAGES

Iraqw lineages[2] (*guuru'* [sing.], *guuru'ee* [pl.]) are composed of four generations of male descendants. These lineages are given the name of the founder. The maximal lineages from which these segments branched off have little significance to Iraqw, and most Iraqw do not know the other lineages within their clan. Lineages and clans are exogamous; that is, members may not marry within these groups. Again, residence and lineage do not necessarily have any relation to one another, though it is not uncommon for male lineage mates to live near one another. The lineage has land and livestock that have been passed down from the founder. Usually, a father selects one son to oversee this lineage property upon his death. This land and livestock have been kept separate from the land and livestock apportioned to each of the man's sons. After four generations, the executor of the lineage will divide the remaining property and each of the descendants (in the fifth generation) will start his own lineage. Figure 4.1 shows how descent is reckoned among Iraqw.

Inheritance often leads to tension and conflict over resources. Being named an executor has its advantages and its burdens. Control over property is a considerable advantage, but in order to become executor, a man may have to sacrifice his and his household's independence and submit to the authority and views of his father.

Lineages may come together for meetings, especially during a crisis that threatens the perpetuation, or fertility, of the lineage. Lineage mates unite to perform ceremonies to cleanse the lineage of a curse or the pollution resulting from incest. If they neglect to perform these ceremonies, the lineage risks fading out completely because supernatural sanctions will cause a decline in fertility.

To strengthen the lineage, a man hopes for many sons. If a couple is unsuccessful in producing sons, they may keep having children in an attempt to beget a son, or the husband may marry another wife. I knew of a few Catholics who had two wives. They evaded church prohibitions on polygyny by maintaining separate residences and marrying one wife through a traditional ceremony rather than through the church. The importance of producing sons is deeply felt by most Iraqw men. They feel both a sense of competition with their brothers but also a larger social expectation that they will have sons to follow them. Women obviously feel this pressure as well, particularly from their husbands, and this can lead to tension between the couple if they continue to have daughters. One woman confided to me after giving birth to her second daughter: "My husband will hardly hold the baby or look at her he is so disappointed that she is not a boy. I will have to keep

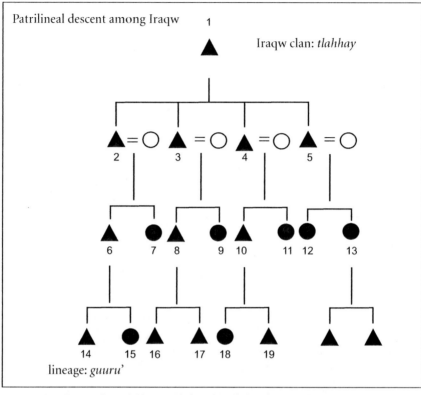

Figure 4.1   Iraqw clan *(tlahhay)* with founding father (1). Numbers 2, 6, 7, 14, 15 represent one lineage *(guuru'),* as do 3, 8, 9, 16, 17, and 4, 10, 11, 18, 19. Number 5 did not have sons so lineage stopped with 12 and 13.

having more children until I have a boy, though I think all this emphasis on boys is too much. What does it matter anymore? This is not <u>maendeleo</u>. Those ideas are the way of the past."

THE BLOOD: UTERINE KIN *(DAA'AWI)*

Conceptually, the Iraqw equate the clan with bones and the uterine kin with blood. The skeleton is the man's contribution to forming a child, as his semen is thought to produce bones and bone marrow.[3] The woman contributes blood and thus life to the child.[4] Blood is the substance that is shared among all uterine kin or *daa'awi*. The *daa'awi* links a mother and her children together with her mother and her brother and sisters, her sister's children, her grandmother, and so on. Women increase the *daa'awi*, whereas men perpetuate the clan. Thus, children belong to their father's *tlahhay* (clan) and to their mother's *daa'awi*.[5]

The *daa'awi* is important in a number of ways. It is a critical factor in assessing the marriageability of a couple. It is also through the *daa'awi* that witchcraft is inherited (whereas the knowledge of divination is passed through the clan). A person's *daa'awi* is more important in evaluating his or her character and suitability for performing *aya* rituals than is clan identity. For example, if a member of a person's *daa'awi* has committed a serious offense (such as committing suicide or murder), all members of his *daa'awi* are considered impure. The taint of this pollution is hard to remove. Even if a ceremony is performed to "cool" this dangerous pollution, members of this *daa'awi* will never be able to attend the *aya* rituals and may find it difficult to marry. Thus, the role of blood is perceived as more important in forming an individual's character and personality than the bones. Beidelman reports that for the Kaguru people of Tanzania, bones, providing form, also provide order and "measured judgement" (1980:145), but blood, being hot, requires moral control and direction. For the Iraqw, bones are perceived as cool and less affective than blood. Blood is not referred to in the same moral sense as the Kaguru example but instead is seen as a hot substance that provides strong emotional bonds.

Because of the strong affective ties among *daa'awi* members, it is often a more reliable source of assistance in times of need than the clan. This blood relationship is seen as nurturing and exerting a greater pull on its members than that of the clan or bones. The force of the *daa'awi* is believed to be felt physically. As one man explained to me, when a close member of your *daa'awi* falls ill (such as a child of your mother's sister), "you may also feel this illness as it affects your blood as well." The same is true when a wrong is committed against a close member of your *daa'awi*.

The *daa'awi*, like the *soog* among the Tallensi people of Ghana, is "essentially a personal bond, a bond of mutual interest and concern uniting individual to individual" (Fortes 1949:37). It binds particularly siblings and the children of one's mother's sister in ties of strong attachment. The mother/child bond is probably the strongest family relationship. The relationships with fathers are clearly more problematic, as they try to exert greater control over their children's, especially their sons', lives. The promise of future inheritance can lead to considerable tension between fathers and sons.

Like patrilineages, each *daa'awi* bears the name of its founder. As with clans and lineages, the ethnic origin of the founder is known. The *daa'awi* is also exogamous. Even the children of the mother's brother, who themselves are members of their mother's *daa'awi*, are unable to marry within the *daa'awi* of their father. After four generations however, a man may marry a member of his great-great grandfather's *daa'awi*.

For Iraqw, their most important kinship ties in daily life are with their immediate family (grandparents, parents, and siblings), with their *daa'awi*, and then with their lineage. Two individuals, the mother's brother *(mamay)* and the father's sister *(ayshiga)*, are of special importance to each individual and take a prominent role in an individual's life rituals such as birth, naming, circumcision, and marriage. The mother's brother is important in all aspects of a person's life, even outside of ritual occasions. He often provides assistance in the form of school fees, bride wealth, and other financial help and serves as an intermediator between his sister's children and the family of their fiancés at the time of marriage.

The way that descent and kinship shape people's lives can be seen in a conflict that occurred in the homeland between two people I knew well. The details of the case illustrate the significance of clan and uterine kin, as well as concerns about fertility, which pervade Iraqw beliefs and practices. Actors on both sides of the conflict related the events to me, though each had different opinions about the responsibilities of the other. The incident that gave rise to tension between the two families concerned the breaking of a man's leg.

Akonaay and Safari

One late afternoon around dusk, the paths leading into the homeland from the town of Mbulu were filled with people returning from the bimonthly livestock auctions *(minaada)*, which are the major social event in the area. As is common after a day of drinking the home-brewed beer sold at the event, many people were returning to their homes in various stages of intoxication. Akonaay, a young man in his late twenties, was among the crowd hiking up the mountain into Irqwa Da'aw. He was quite drunk from a long day of drinking and was trudging slowly up a steep incline when two cyclists came up behind him. Hearing them approach, Akonaay glanced back at the riders and recognized one of the men as a local government official. When the cyclists drew closer, Akonaay jumped in front of them to block their way. He began to insult Safari, the civil servant who was the first rider, accusing him of thinking himself important because he worked for the government and rode a bicycle. Akonaay then demanded that he be allowed to ride Safari's bike. Safari, trying to appease him, allowed Akonaay to get on his bike. As Akonaay was quite inebriated after a day of drinking, he promptly crashed the bike into the bushes. Safari, growing tired of this game, grabbed the bicycle and peddled off. But this incensed Akonaay even more, and he ran to intercept him by taking a shortcut through the bush. He leapt out in front of Safari and demanded a fight. Safari got off his bicycle and tried to push Akonaay out of the way, shoving him and causing him to fall to the ground. In the process and quite by accident, Safari tripped and stepped on Akonaay's shin while he was lying on the ground. The bone snapped under his weight. Alarmed, Safari then sped off on his bike to look for a local elder known for his ability to set bones. Safari paid for the bonesetter's fee and, according to Safari, gave Akonaay some cash for compensation. However, from the point of view of Akonaay's father and brothers, the case was not over, because Safari had not followed customary practice.

According to such practice, if a person breaks another's bone, they must go to the person's father and ask to be pardoned and present the father with a cow. If the father accepts, the case is considered closed and no animosity will exist between the two families. In my conversation with Tluway, Akonaay's brother, he agreed that Akonaay had behaved badly and provoked a fight but emphasized that still the issue of proper compensation remained, because Safari had not followed customary procedures and had not spoken with his father. A broken bone is thought to weaken the individual and his potential productivity. Compensation is aimed at reimbursing the family for the loss of that member's productivity. A person with a broken bone will never be considered "whole" again, and this can affect his chances of marrying.

Tluway, himself a primary schoolteacher, explained to me that this misfortune was seen as a threat both to their clan and to their *daa'awi*. Although he provided no defense for his brother's actions, he explained that he and his brothers were bound to support Akonaay out of both clan and *daa'awi* loyalty. Being of the same blood and coming from the same "stomach," they had almost a physical sensation of their brother's misfortune. Others have told me that even if you do not like someone in your *daa'awi*, you will be moved to help them because your very blood is affected by their misfortune.

Safari meanwhile assumed that in providing cash and paying for the bone to be set, he had provided enough compensation. He was annoyed by the time and effort the whole case took to resolve and wanted to bypass time-consuming tradition. Whereas Akonaay's family stuck to tradition to assert their claims, Safari wanted to pursue a more "modern" solution to this calamity by paying cash. As the case dragged on, Safari worried that the brothers might avenge Akonaay. He did not like living with this enmity hanging over his head, so eventually he provided compensation that the family agreed was sufficient.

The incident demonstrates how strongly ties of descent and uterine kinship bind people as well as how those who often profess to have put "custom" behind them call up traditional practices and beliefs to address specific situations. The central actors in this case had jobs that linked them to the state and wider national economy rather than relying on farming and livestock management. All were Christians. Yet, the more modern solutions to this conflict between two people did not sufficiently address the social context in which they were embedded. The emphasis in this case, and in many instances in which tradition was drawn upon, was on the restoration of harmonious relations between individuals and groups. While Safari thought that perhaps money was fair compensation to restore these relations, the others involved did not see cash as a solution. Cash, in these instances, has not successfully replaced the symbolic importance of livestock, which more adequately cements ties between individuals and groups. Cash can be used up rapidly by one individual and has little lasting power, whereas livestock multiplies and can benefit several people over time.[6]

Amsi's story, described at the beginning of the chapter, illustrates the importance of uterine kin, in particular the mother's brother, in people's lives. The mother's brother is often called upon to aid his sister's children. As Amsi's situation makes clear, however, this assistance does not come without a cost of its own. I knew several young people who were living with their mother's brother's families, and all had to work quite hard in repayment for the help these relatives were giving them. As Amsi experienced, this workload often led these youth to fail in school. When I asked why the mother's brother was chosen so often for help, most people explained that the ties of the daa'awi are simply harder to refuse. This type of assistance grows more common today, as families search for opportunities for their children to get an education or to learn a trade. Many families feel these opportunities are crucial for their children's survival, as agriculture and livestock-keeping provide little income, and land shortages are an increasing threat. Tapping into the national and global economy, starting with obtaining an education, is thought to lead to better opportunities for economic survival.

These stories show how uterine kin and clan are an important part of the Iraqw moral and practical universe. Ideas about kin contain ideas about gender as well. Clans, associated with men, involve inner competition and control over resources. They do not give rise to the same affective relationships as the daa'awi, which is bound up in ideas about mothers and relationships between mothers and their children. These ideas about gender and clans and uterine kin will become more obvious when I turn to a discussion about cosmology in Chapter 7. In the precolonial era, when all Iraqw inhabited the fairly small area of the homeland, kin were perhaps less important than neighbors, because kin in another homeland aya were basically laboring under the same ecological conditions and constraints. Yet, now that kin can be found in completely different ecological zones and in metropolitan areas, the importance of these ties has become more significant. In both the surveys I conducted, one in 1992, the other in 1995, all households surveyed reported that they frequently relied on kin from the expansion areas for help with food shortages. There is considerable moral obligation to help kin when they ask for assistance.

Today, a person's kin from Irqwa Da'aw may be scattered not only around the district but throughout the four districts into which the Iraqw have expanded. Many Iraqw live in the cities throughout Tanzania as well, particularly in Arusha and Dar es Salaam. Yet, many Iraqw who have moved to cities for salaried employment or work in the informal sector rarely send money home. If they come home for visits, they may bring cash and gifts, but it is unlikely that they will send regular assistance. Having kin in cities can be an advantage when looking for work, needing a place to stay, or seeking schooling opportunities. Those who have migrated to cities rarely return to reside in the homeland; once they have grown used to city life, they are not interested in returning to a rural way of life that lacks electricity and running water. Another disincentive to return is, as some told me, a fear of witchcraft. This suspicion is taken up in Chapter 8.

Notes

1. I differ here from Thornton, who states that the original Iraqw clans are Hhay Irqa and Hhay Tipu Bonday only (1980:204).

2. I am here relying on Middleton and Tait's definition of lineage as "a corporate group of unilineal kin . . . it is a single group that is assumed to be permanent, to which rights and duties may be attached as to a single unit. . . . It is generally named. . . . It includes both living and dead" (1958:3–4).

3. Semen is thought to resemble bone marrow.

4. Interestingly, the Kaguru in southeastern Tanzania have precisely the same notion (Beidelman 1980:145).

5. As among the Tallensi, "the fundamental distinction between uterine kinship and agnatic descent is that the former does not give rise to corporate units of social structure" (Fortes 1949:63).

6. For other intriguing examples of how cash does or does not "work" in specific cultural settings, see Shipton (1989) and Hutchinson (1996).

CHAPTER FIVE

THE MAKING OF
MEN AND WOMEN

CIRCUMCISION

One afternoon, I was sitting and chatting with one of my closest women friends in Mbulu. The conversation turned to female circumcision, and she began to tell me the story of her own operation: "I am telling you, that was some pain. When the day came, my mother and sisters grabbed me and held me down. I had one older sister sitting on each arm and each leg. I screamed so loud and gave the cry of alarm *(hayoda)* but no one came to my rescue. Then the circumciser cut me. Oh was that painful. I am telling you! Whew!" I then asked, "So, now that you have a daughter yourself and you suffered so much pain during your circumcision, will you circumcise your daughter?" She replied, "Oh yes. Of course I will. It is important for us. This is how we change from children to adults. Who would marry a child?"

Female circumcision is performed by a female specialist who uses a razor blade for the operation. For girls, the event is a private one, shrouded in secrecy. It is carried out in their own home with perhaps their sisters or a few neighbors' daughters who are a similar age and also need to have the ceremony performed. There are no festivities or public displays, and the male members of the house are banished during the proceedings. The girls lie on a grass mat during the operation and recuperate for up to a month, staying indoors and resting until they feel completely well. Iraqw female circumcision entails clitoridectomy and removal of the outer labia. The practices closely resemble those of the Datoga, who also perform the operation with little ceremony and in an air of secrecy.[1] The neighboring Maasai similarly have a private circumcision for girls and a public one for boys.

Tanzania has received pressure from international groups about the "inhuman practice" (as it is frequently called in the press) of what is now referred to in the English language papers as "female genital mutilation or FGM." Articles on FGM appear quite frequently in the Tanzanian press, mostly to expose a community in which it is still practiced. In neighboring Hanang District, where it is reported that FGM is "rampant," the district commissioner "has directed the Ward Executive Officer to punish all people engaged in female genital mutilation" (*Guardian*, March 12, 2002, p. 3). Although it is now illegal in Tanzania to circumcise girls, the practice continues, and there were even reports in the papers in 2002 that doctors in hospitals around the country have been involved in female circumcision. Although the government and nongovernmental agencies oppose the practice, this stance seems to have had relatively little impact on many Iraqw perceptions of the operation, and it is still very much practiced in the homeland. For many young women, circumcision remains an important ritual in their lives. Many Iraqw men would not consider marrying someone who had not been circumcised.

Through circumcision, children are transformed into marriageable youth. However, because these rites are usually held near or before puberty, youth are still not considered full adults after circumcision. Only marriage can transform individuals fully into adults. In the past, circumcision for boys, which involves the removal of the foreskin, was a public celebration held at the level of the ridge community. Although women did not participate in or witness the operation, they were present for the celebration that followed and sang songs of praise for the young men. Male circumcision rituals were events in which individuals were formally accorded greater community responsibilities and ties with kin were reinforced. Because of health concerns, families are now encouraged to take their sons to the hospital for circumcision. Girls, however, are circumcised privately, inside the home, and men and boys are strictly excluded. These differences mark the general distinctions between male (public) and female (domestic). Also, women's nakedness or any association with her sexuality carries with it an aura of shame. One man told me: "Today, as many of us are Christians, all nakedness is shameful. But in the time of our fathers, it was not shameful for men to be naked, and they often threw off their capes when farming. But for a woman, nakedness has always been shameful." Today, many households are circumcising their boys at the hospital, and community celebrations are becoming increasingly rare. Although circumcision practices are changing, the operation is still a very important hallmark of Iraqw identity.

Boys and many girls I spoke with are very eager to be circumcised. One woman in her early twenties told me: "I couldn't wait to be circumcised. Once my friends began to be circumcised, I begged my mother to make the arrangements for my own circumcision." Peer pressure plays an important part in boys' and girls' impatience. When they reach early adolescence, those who have been circumcised begin to tease their uncircumcised friends about their inferior status. Their interest in this operation obviously reflects their strong desire to be adults and to marry and start their own households.

One man in his early thirties told me the story of his circumcision, which was performed together with the other boys of his household and neighborhood:

My four brothers and I [he was about ten at the time] were awakened one morning before dawn and taken by our father to a big house in the neighborhood where we were told to climb up to the sleeping loft. When we climbed up, we saw many other boys there already. We stayed there until about 4 P.M. in the afternoon when we were given gruel to drink. Afterward, we were taken outside and told to stand in a circle. Meanwhile, the people who were gathered for the event began singing. All the while, we stayed in a circle, and two or three boys at a time were taken off to be circumcised. Then, they were taken into a special hut that was surrounded by people. Finally, I was taken out of the circle and forced down on my knees, and the specialist told me to watch myself. He drank some water from a gourd and then poured some out on my penis and pulled the foreskin forward. It stayed there without going back [this is one of the special skills of the circumciser; the water he drinks and pours onto everyone keeps the skin from receding and prevents excessive bleeding]. He then cut off the foreskin, and I was taken into the hut where we all stayed until dark. Once night fell, we were taken back to our house. Only those who lived very near were allowed to go back to their houses because the elders wanted to see all those who had been circumcised the next day in order to know whether the operation had gone successfully and that there were no problems with excessive bleeding. When the elders came to our house the next morning, we were all fine except my oldest brother who was still bleeding. So, we slaughtered a goat and ate the meat, without salt, together with porridge and milk. We remained inside for a month and a half. At first, we did not go outside at all in order to prevent being bewitched. Once we had healed, we began to go outside but not very far away.[2]

Several women told me that if a girl remains uncircumcised, she will suffer from a disease whose symptoms include terrible and constant genital itching. Others told me that it will be hard for an uncircumcised woman to give birth, as her uncut genitals will block the passage of the child. For both men and women, it is considered "unclean" (both literally and socially) to be uncircumcised. Attitudes toward female circumcision are changing among Iraqw, particularly outside of Irqwa Da'aw, and there is considerable government and church pressure against it.[3] One young woman from Mbulu in her midtwenties told me that when she was younger, an old woman who was the local circumciser kept coming to visit to confer with her grandmother, with whom she was then living. She guessed that they were planning her circumcision, and she vehemently protested and fled to her parents' house, where her mother supported her in her refusal to undergo the operation.

In a visit to Irqwa Da'aw in 1998, I attended a government ward meeting, which all adults of the area were required to attend. This meeting, held to celebrate the "day of the African child," involved district officials giving speeches on female circumcision and emphasizing that these "backward" practices must be abandoned for the sake of health and _maendeleo_. The Panafrican News Agency reported on August 12, 2000, that the Tanzanian government passed the Sexual Offenses Act in 1998, making it illegal to perform circumcision of girls younger than eighteen years of age. It also reported that the "government called the practice despicable." Although female circumcision is criticized for its backwardness, many Iraqw women I knew who lived in towns and lived far less traditional lives were still very interested in seeing circumcision continue. The woman quoted above who related the story of her own circumcision is herself a Catholic and works in Mbulu for the district council.

Parker (1995), who conducted research in the Sudan among people who practice female circumcision, makes a point very relevant to the Iraqw practice. She argues that the focus of female circumcision is on making girls into women and most importantly making them ready to become mothers. A woman's sexuality is important to her for its procreative aspects, not for her own individual enjoyment. For many societies who practice it, female circumcision is focused less on sexuality than on notions of femininity (Boddy 1989), fertility, and motherhood. It is these aspects of selfhood that are significant to the Iraqw rather than sexual pleasure and expression. Much of the international pressure to abandon this practice focuses on arguments about women being denied sexual pleasure. Thus, they do not confront the reality of this practice by confronting the community's association of circumcision with selfhood and fertility.

Like other circumcised groups, the Iraqw denigrate ethnic groups who do not circumcise males. For boys, circumcision involves a greater shift in responsibilities than for girls. As circumcised youths (_masomba_), they are expected to participate more fully in agricultural labor and to bear greater social responsibility. They are now eligible to participate in the _aya_-level rituals, though not until they marry and begin having children will they start to attend _aya_ elders' meetings. When boys' circumcisions were conducted at the level of the neighborhood, they acted to reinforce bonds between the members of a particular cohort (_qari_) of each neighborhood. These _qari_ are informal associations and are not marked like the age sets of the Maasai, but they promote strong ties, and members frequently turn to one another for assistance in work, or disputes, or financial crises.

Community-wide circumcision, like all rituals, is controlled by elders. As more young men are getting circumcised at the hospital, elders are less involved in their sons' transition. The same young man who related the story of his circumcision (above) told me that his younger brother came to him begging to be taken to the hospital to be circumcised, saying that their father was taking too long to have the operation performed. He agreed and took his brother to the hospital, returning him home later to recuperate. Their father was very angry at having had the decision taken out of his control but proceeded to look after his son until he had healed.

NEGOTIATING BONDS: MARRIAGE AND ITS TRANSFORMATIONS

Circumcision and marriage are the two most important rituals for transforming individuals into adults in Iraqw society. In the past, elders, both male and female (in the case of female circumcision), controlled these rituals. Marriage is a critical event in most Iraqw lives, marking the beginning of their full adult status and the change in their rights and obligations within the family and the community. Young men told me that they would receive little help from their fathers in terms of allocation of land or livestock until they got married. Although parents have the greatest authority over marriages, other kin as well as neighbors and even local elders get involved. Marriage in particular is a time when both kinship and descent, and relationships based on space, are brought together. Thus, these events can be fraught with tension in many ways. While harmony is emphasized in all Iraqw rituals, conflicts and contradictions are clearly brought out in wedding ceremonies.

Weddings in the homeland have become a very interesting combination of elements both traditional and modern. Clothing, food, dance, and song are features of specific cultural styles, both cosmopolitan and localist, to borrow Ferguson's terminology. During weddings, the display of cultural styles becomes very apparent. In the Iraqw homeland, I was often invited to wedding festivities, as I became the local wedding photographer. Weddings seemed to me to be the most public arena for the expression of the tensions that exist between young and old Iraqw and between Christians and non-Christians.

Marriage celebrations are one of the few occasions at which all members of the neighborhood gather together. Attendance and participation of local residents in the marriage celebrations promotes community unity. Weddings also promote solidarity among kin and are a forum in which the families of the bride and groom negotiate their future relationship to one another. Tensions and conflicts among kin and in-laws often surface during weddings.

At all times, a husband is expected to show great deference and respect for his parents-in-law. When I inquired about the relationship between in-laws, many Iraqw painted an ideal picture of unanimity. However, at the wedding ceremonies I attended, and in the conversations I had with people about their in-laws, tensions were clearly evident. One man, who was about forty and had seven children, explained his situation:

> Every year, my in-laws come to me asking for maize. Even my wife tells me to say we can't give it to them. But what can I do? They are my wife's parents. They come to me because they don't work hard in their own fields. My brothers-in-law, who are supposed to be providing for their parents, spend most of their time at the _kilabu_ (beer hall), and then they come to me for help. And my father-in-law is too gentle with them; he never demands that they get to work. They all go to the _kilabu_ together. If my brother-in-law comes again, I'll tell him I can't help him. But if it is my mother- or father-in-law, it will be very hard to refuse.

One young woman complained to me that her husband was being very lax in attending to his responsibilities to her family: "My mother has been sick for quite some time, but my husband has not made one single visit to her to ask after her health." The family of the bride, while able to make demands on their son-in-law, as they have provided him with a wife, must also show him respect. As the man quoted previously explained, "They respect me because I am taking care of their daughter, providing her with a home." When he traveled to other villages or towns, he often sought out his wife's relatives for a place to stay because of the debt that is created through marriage. One of the reasons he was so annoyed by his wife's brothers is that he felt they were not treating him with the proper respect, citing many instances of their verbally insulting him and taking his assistance for granted. An outstanding debt of bride wealth will make it even more difficult to refuse requests from in-laws. These debts are the rule rather than the exception, as most men take some time to pay off the bride wealth, and many even pass along this debt to their sons.

Another feature marking relations between a man and his wife's parents are name avoidances. A husband must not say the name of his wife's mother in front of her, or he will be fined. He should also not call his father-in-law by his name (but instead refer to him simply as "father"), but doing so inadvertently does not result in a fine. The same rules apply to a wife: If she says the name of her father-in-law, she will be fined. By emphasizing their identity as mothers and fathers, potentially dangerous incestuous relations are discouraged. This concern with inappropriate sexual relations appears throughout the wedding performance and in conduct after the marriage.[4]

Marriage expands the network of kinship relations that link households and their kin to one another. Clan and _daa'awi_ exogamy restrict individual's choices and promote a wider net of alliances. Couples rarely marry without consulting and seeking the consent of their parents. Even if they live as far away as Dar es Salaam, they will return or send an emissary to their respective places of birth to consult the elders of their lineage and *daa'awi* to determine whether they are related to their prospective mate. Most young people I knew did not know their genealogies very well and relied on their father and mother's brother for this information. In the past, if the prospective bride and groom were found to be related to one another in some way, their parents forbade them from marrying. The fear that they may not be able to have children, or that they may have very weak and frail offspring, dissuades most couples from pursuing marriage if they find they are related. All couples that I spoke with went through the procedure of determining whether they were related to one another. However, within the limitations imposed by kinship, young men and women tend to choose their own partners. One young woman told me that when she discovered she was distantly related to a young man who was courting her, they both agreed to end their courtship. Young couples tended to rely entirely on their mothers' brothers and fathers and other senior men to conduct the kinship reckoning. Most, even after calculations were performed, had no idea about how to conduct it themselves and said they would have to seek out help when the time came for their own children to marry.

Elders complain that young people today disobey many of the rules of betrothal and marriage. One elder, himself a respected marriage negotiator, claimed that most young people ignored the advice of their elders:

> Today, young people do not care. A father tells his son not to marry a girl because they are related, but the son goes ahead anyway and marries her. And now, you can see the problems that result. They discover they can't have children. Maybe the children are born, but they do not live long, or they are very weak.

After this man finished his explanation, I turned to his son who was sitting with him and asked him what he thought. He replied:

> I don't know. I don't think it matters that much these days. Few people of my age group understand these things. We don't know who we are related to. So, when my son is old enough to marry, who will be able to say whether or not he is related to someone? With so many men marrying women from other tribes these days, I don't think it will be a problem anyway.

Paradoxically, this son told me he would take over his father's position as marriage negotiator in the community in the future, a position whose authority is based on knowing the rules that forbid certain types of marriage and the procedures to ensure a good match.

Many young men resent the control that their fathers and the fathers of their fiancées have over their marriages. They find the lengthy negotiations frustrating and humiliating. One young man said, "It is as though you are somehow desperate, that you are some poor soul who is begging for the great gift of a wife." He added that he would prefer to avoid the traditional procedures of marriage: "I'd rather get married by the district commissioner. It takes too long to get married in the traditional way, and the girl's father likes to stretch matters out as long as possible, trying to get more bride wealth, or just being difficult."

This young man got married three years later, and contrary to his stated desire to simply get married by the district commissioner, he ended up following all of the customary betrothal procedures. The negotiations between his family and that of his intended bride lasted nearly two years.

It is when marrying that young men and women feel themselves particularly subject to their fathers' control, and many bristle at these restrictions on their autonomy. Yet, few men are able to disobey their fathers at this time because of their dependence on them for bride wealth and, in the future, inheritance. For young women, obedience to their parents is a sign of their good character, and this behavior is scrutinized by her future in-laws, with whom she may have to live closely.

It is considered a disgrace if a man or woman does not marry, and he or she will not be accorded the respect that married adults receive. If unmarried, a man or woman will continue to be called by his or her first name, as children are, or they will be addressed by elders as "boy" *(garma)* or "girl" *(desi)*. Women, once they are married, no longer are called by their given names. Instead, a woman is referred to by the title Deena or Ama.[5] Many Iraqw have adopted the "Swahili" practice of calling married women who have children the "mother of so and so," her first born child. Older married men and women who have children are called father and mother by all those junior in age to them.

In marriage rules and procedures, a number of important themes related to Iraqw concepts of fertility and pollution emerge. If a person fails to marry, it may be due to any of the following reasons: (1) the person is rumored to be a witch or to come from a *daa'awi* of witches; (2) the person is known to be very lazy (particularly important for girls); (3) the person has committed *irange*—a transgression against one's parents, or, worse, incest. In addition, if an individual comes from a *daa'awi* that is somehow tainted by suicide *(naysu)* or murder *(kundar/aatema'),* it will be difficult for this person to marry a fellow Iraqw. Often, his or her only recourse in such an instance is to marry someone from another ethnic group. Moral transgressions from *irange* or suicide or murder can bring pollution that threatens the fertility of the clan and lineage (in the case of *irange*) and the *daa'awi* (from suicide and murder). Christians may more easily overlook these traits, as many say pollution beliefs are "backward" and "pagan" and should be abandoned in today's world.

The taint of witchcraft, however, does launch a serious investigation even among Christians. Sometimes, parents delay approval of a couple's union by claiming there is a rumor of witchcraft that must be investigated. Although men may also be witches, usually rumors concern the bride or the bride's *daa'awi*. In the case of such a rumor (which is kept as secret as possible), a serious investigation into the allegations is conducted, a procedure that can take months. One man explained how his marriage negotiations were stalled by witchcraft rumors:

> My father was traveling back and forth to Lanta's parents' village. My brother had moved to this village several years ago and was doing odd jobs there in building and carpentry. There, my brother came to know Lanta's family. I have not been on good terms with my brother for many years now, and I think he wanted to make trouble for me. When my father was staying with him to begin the negotiations, my brother told him that all of Lanta's *daa'awi* were rumored to be witches. Well, this took a very long time to investigate. I knew it was not true, but the investigations had to be done anyway. They could not find enough evidence so the matter ended there. But it delayed matters for many months.

In the precolonial era, families arranged marriages, but today marriage is usually by mutual consent and interest. The families of the young woman and man conduct investigations into the characters of the potential spouses. Discovering a problem can end the betrothal. When investigations are finished, the two families enter negotiations about the marriage and bride wealth. Often, the groom's side will solicit the aid of a recognized and respected go-between, or *leehhtuusmoo*, to handle the matter for him. Customarily, the young man's father will give the go-between a goat for his services.

The work of a *leehhtuusmoo* does not stop with the wedding. If the couple has trouble getting along, if the husband beats his wife, or if there are other complaints and problems, he will be the first person the family turns to in solving the couple's difficulties. He will also be blamed if the marriage does not go well or if either the bride or the groom prove to have bad "characters" afterward. Thus, it is to his advantage to carry out his own investigation into the backgrounds of the intended couple and to intervene and recommend canceling a wedding if he thinks it might turn out badly. He may also intercede in the lives of the married couple if he sees that one of them is behaving badly (such as a man spending all the household money on beer, or a woman being "lazy" in her chores). He meets with the couple before and during the early stages of their lives together to counsel them on marriage. The *leehh-tuusmoo* is highly regarded in the community, and if he is particularly skilled, he may be called upon by people of even neighboring *aya* to perform this task. The respect accorded him is not simply for his skill in helping couples to marry but also for his service to the community by fostering positive relations between the in-laws. He is also appreciated for his role in mediating the couple's disputes and promoting harmony.

Neighbors can play an important role in marriage negotiations, as they are the people who have the greatest knowledge of the prospective bride or groom. They can impede a marriage by giving a bad report to the other side's family. For example, they may claim that the prospective groom is lazy or that he does not respect his parents or his neighbors. Or they may accuse the prospective bride of being a witch. Thus, how individuals comport themselves within the community is assessed at this critical juncture in their lives. Young people trying to find a husband or wife also value this information and look for mates who have good reputations and come from good families. One man explained to me: "You know Gwandu and the way he has of changing his mind all the time. People say he has no stability *(hana msimamo)* and is not trustworthy. So, you have to be careful about your reputation because when you want to marry these things come out."

COMPETING CULTURAL STYLES: WEDDINGS IN IRQWA DA'AW

Weddings in Irqwa Da'aw were stages for the performance of competing cultural styles. These cultural styles, built around notions of tradition and modernity, reflected struggles over power and authority within families and within the community as a whole. Most of the young people marrying today are Christians, and I was invited to their weddings either because I was their friend, a friend of the family, or the best bet for a wedding photographer. The weddings I witnessed combined Christian practices and traditional ones. In each wedding, a marriage ceremony was held in the church, and then celebrations were carried out at the homes of both the bride and the groom. Most of the weddings I attended were Catholic ones, and indeed the majority of Christians in Irqwa Da'aw are Catholic. The church service usually took place after the ceremony at the bride's house. Events at the bride's house loosely followed some of the practices elders had described as traditional, such as the recitation of bride wealth, the holding of a dance to celebrate the marriage, songs of teasing and insult sung about the groom's side, welcoming of the groom's party, throwing out of the ashes after the bride was taken out of the house, and the presentation of a sheep to the bride.

During the time I lived in Irqwa Da'aw, dances were held at both the bride and the groom's home. During the wedding season, one can hear dances going

Figure 5.1   Member of a primary school choir performing at a schoolteacher's wedding.

on nearly every night around the village. Iraqw dance in lines jumping up and down to a complicated rhythm and step, following the lead of the drummer, who is almost always a woman. The lines are differentiated by gender, but the steps are the same for all the dancers. Songs accompany the dances, and there are many songs specific to wedding occasions. At weddings, dances began in the early afternoon and stopped usually in the early evening, around 6 P.M., to adhere to the rules laid down by the Catholic Church that all dancing must stop before dark.

The Church, in its war on "backward tradition," targeted dancing in Mbulu District. In justifying this position, the Church claims that dancing encourages drunkenness, laziness, and promiscuity, which all lead to HIV/AIDS. In addition, it proclaims that dancing indoors is a health hazard, as people are exposed to one another's germs in a close environment. The priest threatened to refuse to marry couples if they did not see to it that the dancing at their respective family homes stopped at 6 P.M. Often, the priest came to the home to make sure that the dancing ended. In several instances, the rule was disobeyed, and the dancing either moved to another location or started up again when people believed the priest was not nearby. However, as the drumming and singing can be heard from fairly far away, this was not always effective. In the ward of Kainam, a few households were fined a cow by the Church for allowing dancing past 6 P.M.

Figure 5.2   Guests at a wedding.

Young Christian Iraqw often spoke of Iraqw dancing as "pagan" and "un-civilized" and were sometimes embarrassed by my viewing the dances. Others were embarrassed by various traditional rituals in weddings. At one wedding, a young man whose responsibility it was to lead the sheep to greet the incoming bride asked me not to take a picture of him while carrying out this task. However, whether they are bowing to pressure from parents or simply accepting these practices as part of the accepted ritual, younger Iraqw still incorporate them in weddings.

In the past, dances were held often by young people and were very popular. They were one of the few occasions attended by large gatherings of people. These dances were ways to meet new people and to prove oneself and were the primary forums for courtship and flirtation. For this reason, the

Figure 5.3   Older women watching wedding festivities.

Church has fought against these dances. Ironically, the result is that many young people now attend church services instead, as a way to meet and flirt with the opposite sex.

Although individual dancers' talents are respected and acknowledged, they do not have solos within the dance. At all times, individuals dance in a group, pressed together in tight formation. The songs that accompany dances relate tales of Iraqw heroes or other stories of their history. Few people today know these songs, and new songs are written to Iraqw dances to entertain government guests at ward government meetings.

The church ceremony commonly followed the celebrations at the bride's house. It was usually attended only by the Christian friends and family of the bride and groom, which meant that most of those present were young people. After the church service, the proceedings moved to the groom's family's house.

At the groom's house, a welcome party of older women met the bride and her entourage of kin and friends, singing to her in Iraqw and greeting her with the customary ewe and its lamb (this sheep is given to the bride and is meant to bestow fertility upon her). These women were dressed in blankets (*migorori; inqwari*), which are considered standard traditional garb.

Figure 5.4   Wedding dancing.

Figure 5.5   Going to greet the bride.

Figure 5.6   Greeting the bride with a sheep.

Often following on the heels of the older women, a group of young women sang church hymns in Swahili. They dressed in Western clothes covered by *kanga* or *kitenge*, the basic national dress for women throughout Tanzania. Rather than ushering the bride into a special chamber in the house from which she would be viewed by all the guests, as happened in the precolonial era, the bride and groom usually sat together behind a table, and food was served to them and songs sung. The youth choir sat inside as honored guests, together with schoolteachers or government officials or other respected and successful people who had been invited. They sat near the bride and groom, and the choir continued to sing hymns. Meanwhile, outside the house, other groups of young people sang Iraqw songs and danced. After the meal, the bride and groom moved outdoors and sat behind a table while people presented them with money or small gifts. The giving of presents usually marked the end of festivities, unless the dancers decided to continue past the 6 P.M. deadline.

Weddings are one of the few times that Iraqw come together in large groups; these occasions assemble people from the local community as well as relatives and friends who live outside the village. It was at these events that I witnessed the two competing cultural styles juxtaposed in the most obvious terms. The more "cosmopolitan" style, as Ferguson would describe it, was displayed among the younger generation. This competition between cosmopolitan and traditional styles was brought home to me on several occasions, when I witnessed the young choir members pressing up behind the old women as they welcomed the bride to the groom's house. These two groups of singers would often be singing at once—the older women singing songs in Iraqw and the choir singing hymns in Kiswahili. The result was quite confusing, as the choir would sing louder and louder in what seemed an attempt to drown out the voices of the older women.

Inside the house, the young people and special guests sat in an area specially prepared with store-bought decorations or strips of colored, twisted toilet paper twirled around the tables and chairs. Both real and plastic flowers were put in plastic containers around the room. Western clothes, either bought in stores or from used-clothes dealers, have become standard dress throughout Tanzania. But many Iraqw still wear *migorori* over these clothes, particularly young men and older men and women. However, there are categories of people within the homeland villages who very rarely wear *migorori*, particularly at public events. This category includes schoolteachers and all local government employees. Many younger people who are educated also choose not to wear them. At weddings, this "cosmopolitan" group always gathered inside the house and sat at tables, drank sodas or sometimes bottled beer, and ate specially prepared food, in particular *pilau*, a spicy rice and meat dish, which is a standard Tanzanian meal for a special occasion. They ate from individual plates and used knives and spoons. If available, they listened to church

Figure 5.7   Elders and youths at a wedding.

hymns on a cassette player. Meanwhile, outside, the older men and women, dressed in _migorori,_ sat on the ground, watching the dances and drinking traditional sorghum beer, which they passed around in a gourd. They wore tire sandals or were barefoot, and ate cornmeal porridge and a side sauce of greens and beans, or perhaps meat, with their hands from communal bowls.

The bride usually wore a long white wedding gown and veil instead of a traditional beaded leather wedding skirt. The atmosphere of the celebration differed according to the participants. The dancers and elders were usually quite festive and joyful. The bride and groom, however, wore fixed expressions of extreme seriousness, and most of the time the bride had her head lowered or hidden and sometimes cried throughout the event. This melancholy demeanor reflects her sadness at leaving her childhood home, her parents, siblings, and friends. Much was made of the bride and groom's clothes by the younger participants. It was considered quite noteworthy if a bride wore a store-bought wedding gown, particularly one that you might see in a big city such as Arusha or Dar es Salaam. The equivalent for men was a suit bought in a store.

The cost of these festivities today is quite high, as the guests of highest status (village officials, schoolteachers, the choir) are all given, by local standards, fairly expensive food in the form of rice and meat and bottled soda and beer. The other guests are usually fed maize porridge and beans, and beer is brewed for everyone who attends. This expense is leading some young people to dispense with traditional proceedings as well as those of the Catholic Church (which demands payment for the wedding mass) and instead get their marriage certified by the district commissioner in a civil service. However, having a big and well-attended wedding is important to most couples, and there is an element of competition among their siblings (over their weddings) and their neighbors. Preparations for weddings require months of organizing, and families make sure they invite important local people, such as government officials and schoolteachers. Weddings are ways for young couples to display their _maendeleo_ through having a Christian ceremony and by wearing Western clothes, singing church hymns, and preparing Swahili-style food for the younger visitors and special guests.

Wedding cakes have become a very popular cosmopolitan element in wedding ceremonies. At the wedding of two close friends of mine, a great deal of effort and money had been spent to get a wedding cake and to transport it up to Irqwa Da'aw. The cake was brought out in front of the couple, and they cut it together. They then fed each other and called on all the important family members (mothers, fathers, the fathers' sisters, the mothers' brothers, etc.) and special guests to be fed by the couple. The bride's mother drew back with considerable embarrassment when she was called to the front to be fed. She said, "This is too much. For my daughter's husband to feed me by hand is the same as _irange_ (violations of taboo between the generations). I won't do it." But soon after saying this, so much pressure was put on her by her daughters and other young people that she relented, looking very uncomfortable. So, although the Western practice of cake eating has been incorporated in many weddings, the Western symbolization of the conjugal union becomes expanded by the Iraqw to symbolize family interdependence. The underlying sexual symbolism of feeding cake to one another was clearly not lost, however, on the bride's mother, who was terribly uncomfortable with this association.

RECURRING THEMES AND INHERENT CONFLICTS

The network of rights and obligations in which an individual finds him or herself provides great opportunities and also considerable constraints. Inherent in this network are structural contradictions, and individuals learn to negotiate the conflicting claims and allegiances that result from these contradictions. Anyone growing up in the homeland is enmeshed in both community ties, in the form of neighborhood and _aya_, as well as kinship. Each group has overlapping and sometimes conflicting sets of responsibilities. At weddings, all these interests come together. Neighbors and other members of the community can support or sabotage an individual's wedding plans by giving him or her a good or bad character recommendation. At weddings, members of the local community attend and are expected to be treated with respect. They also contribute in various ways to the festivities by helping with food and arrangements.

Fertility is a theme throughout Iraqw weddings and marriage practices, particularly the fertility of the wife. This fertility comes under the control of the husband and lineage upon marriage and is channeled into a socially acceptable form—that is, legitimate marriage. Yet, it must be noted that the interests of the lineage are offset or balanced by the *daa'awi,* for children become members of their mother's *daa'awi,* and thus ties with the wife's home are still strong. Therefore, a woman's fertility is linked with the fertility of the lineage, but also of the *daa'awi* and finally of the entire *aya* community, as will become clearer in the following chapters.

At weddings, elder women are key participants. They greet the new bride and welcome her into her new home. In effect, through these actions they are also asserting their authority over her, as senior women over a junior. A new wife must be deferential and obedient to her new mother-in-law. If her husband lives close to home or is the last son (whose responsibility it is to care for his parents), the new wife will be continually under her mother-in-law's authority. The degree to which the two women get along with one another naturally varies a great deal. I knew many households where mothers and daughters-in-law had very good relationships. However, there were also many stories of conflict. If there is tension, the blame falls first on the wife and then on her husband, who will lose respect in the community for his inability to control his wife. The lengthy investigation conducted before the marriage is carried out is an effort to avoid a potentially difficult mate. If a man or woman does not show respect to his or her parents, then it is likely that he or she will not respect his or her in-laws.

Weddings are an occasion where a household's ties to the community, to the lineage, to the *daa'awi,* and to affines are acknowledged and strengthened. However, they are also a venue for the expression of antagonism and resentment. At one wedding I attended, members of the bride's party stormed away from the celebrations, claiming they were not being shown respect. They also complained that they had not been paid for the beer that they had brewed. This sparked off lengthy deliberations between the two sides. The conflict was finally resolved, and the bride's family was appeased. In fact, it is quite common for the bride's side to provoke some kind of confrontation in which they draw attention to the respect they feel they deserve.

Most young couples, while chafing at elders' control, still recognize the need for their parents' and other relatives' support. Most also view weddings as a time to please their families and as an opportunity to make statements about their own identity and status in their local community through having a Christian ceremony or wearing "modern" clothes and following "modern" procedures such as the cake cutting or presentation of small gifts. Wedding celebrations reveal wider tensions in Iraqw society between elders and juniors, men and women, and, in a more pronounced way, between Christians and non-Christians. These tensions and conflicts are transforming Iraqw marriage practices and wedding celebrations and illustrate the limits of elders' authority.

Through patrilineal inheritance practices, marriage arrangements, and even circumcision rites, parents exert control over the lives of their children. In these areas, elders assert themselves as experts who have the knowledge and wisdom to make decisions for their children. Resistance to elders takes many forms, but always at risk is inheritance and social disapproval. The local economy still provides relatively few opportunities for younger Iraqw to accumulate wealth (in land or livestock) on their own. Respect for elders, both male and female, is an important ingredient of character in Iraqw communities, and to fail to demonstrate this respect threatens one's reputation in the community and can jeopardize one's ability to obtain land, livestock, and a wife. Although many balk at the authority of their parents, young people are still quick to state that respect should be shown to elders. Weddings represent a step away from the control of parents, as once a couple establishes their own household and begins having children, they are considered to be fully adult and in charge of their own affairs. The songs sung at weddings acknowledge this transformation of status. To the groom, the women sing:

Oo hiiyoo heeee	*From the past,*
Toorero lakabero'	*From the time of our fathers*
Kainam harsiipa	*Here in Kainam*
Kooren aa urarey	*Today has entered a full-grown man*
Laa yaa/bo gaa baa/	*He will not be sent on errands again*

And to the bride, they sing:

Ma/oo hiyahaa ma/oo	*She has grown and will leave*
Ma/oor dasu'	*behind the work of fetching*
Ma/oo hiyahaa ma/oo	*Water and the water vessels*
Quurutlay kwarara/	*will have no work again for her*
Ma/oo hiyahaa ma/oo	*Their work for her has ended*

As will be seen in the chapters to follow, moral codes governing the conduct of individuals emphasize generational differences, boundaries, and proper comportment. To break these codes of morality may bring harm to the transgressor but also to the entire community. At stake is the fertility of households, their livestock, the land, and the entire community. Modernity as it is perceived and defined by Iraqw offers new challenges to these moral codes.

Notes

1. As with the Iraqw, Klima states, and Blystad (1992) confirms, that any "boy or girl who did not submit to these operations would not be able to marry another Barabaig in later years" (1970:56).

2. While the boys are healing they are vulnerable to attack by witches because they have little strength. Witches frequently prey upon people who are in weakened states, such as after circumcision or childbirth.

3. While female circumcision is illegal, it is not strictly.or easily enforced.

4. Although Radcliffe-Brown and Forde (1950) emphasize that name avoidances do not always have sexual significance, Iraqw themselves say that specific practices are designed to discourage the desire for incest between a father and daughter-in-law. As the name avoidances are the same for a mother and son-in-law, and incest between a mother and her son are considered serious breeches in the moral code, I can only assume that these name avoidances relate to these fears. Certainly, I would agree with Radcliffe-Brown and Forde that name avoidances also establish a social distance. Suzette Heald (1990) found that these avoidances centered on sexual prohibitions.

5. To differentiate married women from one another, the name of a woman's husband is attached to Deena—such as Deena Bura, or Ama Bura. In the past, deena was the term applied to all young women when they emerged from the female initiation rites known as *marmo*, after which they were considered marriageable.

CHAPTER SIX

THESE DAYS
THERE IS NO MILK

Changing Agrarian Ecology in Irqwa Da'aw

Competing styles of tradition and modernity can be seen in land-use and subsistence strategies as well as weddings. At independence, the Tanzanian state made agriculture a focus for development throughout the country.[1] In Irqwa Da'aw, decisions about what to plant, how to plant it, and how to manage a household's natural resources are framed by concerns both traditional and modern. Land and the natural resources it supports are the principal means for achieving *maendeleo* in the Iraqw homeland and indeed throughout Tanzania. This chapter focuses on the material conditions of Iraqw life: the farming and livestock management practices on which they depend, organization of labor, land tenure, ecological conditions, and cash-producing activities. Historically, Iraqw have been innovative and flexible in their land use and responses to modern introductions. Discussion of agrarian ecology is important for a number of reasons. First, and most obviously, farming and livestock keeping are the principal economic activities of homeland residents, both young and old. Second, the material conditions that they experience in the homeland shape their sense of themselves in the wider north-central region and in Tanzania as a whole. Finally, much of local, regional, and national discourse on development, whether that of farmers, government officials, or expatriate development officers, centers on agriculture and animal husbandry.

Regional Overview

The Iraqw practice a mixed economy of agriculture and livestock keeping. The balance of livestock with agriculture, the level of agricultural technology, and the participation in the national economy all vary by area, ecological zone, and household.[2] Although my research concentrated primarily on Irqwa Da'aw, a brief review of its neighboring areas is necessary, as Irqwa Da'aw is connected to these regions through trade in foodstuffs, livestock, and tree products, and this trade is important to Irqwa Da'aw's local economy.

The drier southwestern areas have both greater livestock numbers and larger household agricultural holdings. Due to the seasonal nature of rainfall and the soils outside of Irqwa Da'aw, the agricultural season outside the homeland is largely limited to the rainy season, and farmers usually harvest only one maize crop per year. As the field sizes are larger, and the slope of the land is not too steep, most farmers outside of Irqwa Da'aw employ ox-plows for cultivation. Unless there is a drought, households in these expansion areas are usually able to meet their needs in maize and produce a surplus to sell on the market.

In Karatu District to the north there are a number of wealthy farmers who cultivate upward of 500 acres of wheat, barley, maize, and beans for the national market, and in the case of beans, for the international market.[3] Much of the wheat and barley is sold to Tanzania Breweries. Many wealthy farmers in Karatu rent land on a sharecropping basis from farmers who are unable to cultivate all their holdings. Although Karatu has a number of wealthy farmers cultivating large acreages, the majority of farms range in size from ten to fifteen acres. Most farmers with smaller holdings do not cultivate wheat at all but concentrate on hybrid maize and beans, of which they often produce a surplus for sale on the market.

Farmers in the expansion areas, as well as government officials and international aid personnel, view the Iraqw homeland as "backward," in part because of their traditional land-use practices, particularly the use of the hand hoe instead of mechanized cultivation. In terms of wealth, however, many residents in the expansion areas are no better off than homeland residents. Yet, the reason for their migration to these areas in the past was to pursue better opportunities for accumulating land and livestock. The stated differences between themselves and homeland residents have come to form a kind of mythology, one that has at its core the traditional/modern divide. Frequently, Iraqw residents in the expansion areas perceive the natural resource management strategies of Irqwa Da'aw as traditional simply because they take place within the space of the Iraqw homeland. However, in examining homeland land-use practices, it is clear that homeland residents have always been keen and quick to adopt new strategies that make economic, and ecological, sense. Population density and the environment present constraints on what is feasible, not the tradition-bound sentiments of the residents.

Irqwa Da'aw remains unique among Iraqw communities for its ecological conditions and the nature of its agropastoral production system. Rainfall averages about 1000 millimeters (about 39 inches) per year, and the growing season is virtually year-round. Farmers in the homeland grow a greater variety of crops than in the expansion areas, though their holdings are smaller. This diversification is crucial to meeting their food needs but also provides them with crops to exchange with farmers outside of Irqwa Da'aw and to sell in the markets in the town of Mbulu. This crop diversity also provides them with a more varied diet.

Maize, which is the principal food crop, is harvested at different times in different ecological zones. When maize stores begin to run out in Irqwa Da'aw, farmers in the west and south are harvesting their maize and vice versa. These different harvest schedules enable farmers to call upon relatives in other ecological zones and ask for assistance in food supplies during respective harvest seasons. Today, the flow of these types of assistance goes primarily in the direction of the Iraqw homeland. However, when a drought plagues Mbulu District, the Iraqw homeland is usually in better shape because of its naturally moister environment and because of the variety of food crops grown there throughout the year. During a particularly bad year, I saw people traveling into the homeland from all over the district to ask relatives for aid in grain and in other food crops such as sweet potatoes or beans. In 2000, during a prolonged drought, while the rest of the region had turned into a dust bowl in July, Irqwa Da'aw was still green, and the livestock was doing fairly well.

Although the number of livestock per household in Irqwa Da'aw has decreased since the precolonial era, livestock is still an important part of the Iraqw economy and cultural identity. Iraqw have a complex cattle-loaning system, which establishes ties between households both within and outside of the homeland. It enables households without any cattle to start a herd and those who are wealthier to guard against all their stock being affected by disease. The cultural importance of cattle adds to the Iraqw sense of shared identity, to some degree, with Datoga and Maasai. Lawi (2000) suggests that the divide between humans and animals is often not a distinct one. This is particularly so with cattle, who are named and who fall under many of the same pollution beliefs and practices that humans do. Milk is an important symbol of fertility, and therefore the present-day decline in milk production is of great concern, particularly to older Iraqw, as it is equated with a decline in the fertility of the land, livestock, and the health of the people. In numerous interviews and discussions with male elders regarding livestock and agriculture today, many repeated a common complaint that "these days there is no milk." Milk, as Rekdal (1996) has discussed, has always been an important substance linking households together, emphasizing good will, cooperation, and reciprocity. To offer milk to a guest is to honor him or her and to bestow good intentions and wishes for fertility and health. Thus, when male elders complain that there is no milk these days, they are alluding to the loss of not only a food but also a way of life that they identity as "Iraqw."

Irqwa Da'aw in Independent Tanzania

The Iraqw have been very receptive to adopting agricultural innovations if benefits can be clearly demonstrated. During the colonial era, they began cultivating potatoes, various bean varieties, and wheat. They also began to keep pigs and to experiment with coffee and pyrethrum (a flower that is used to make pesticide) as cash crops. More recently, changes in land-use practices correspond with new economic opportunities and markets. New strategies are a way to pursue modern goals of individualized resources and a cash income. At independence, the state placed considerable emphasis on agricultural development for economic growth. As Nyerere stated, "the land is the only basis for Tanzania's development; we have no other" (1968:122). The policies regarding rural development have varied widely in postcolonial Tanzania from the emphasis on communal agriculture during the _ujamaa_ era to more recent liberalization efforts emphasizing cash crop production for international markets. However, the emphasis on a "modern" approach and doing away with "backward, traditional" practices has been a common theme, as Coulson has documented:

> [A]ll the institutional policies . . . co-operatives, extension, community development, and settlement—were justified by an appeal to modernization theory. The view that peasants are primitive, backward, stupid—and generally inferior human beings—dominates the rural chapters of the 1961 World Bank report and the Tanganyikan First Five Year Plan (1982:161).

Because of its importance to national development, agriculture _(kilimo)_ has been a part of primary and secondary school education curriculum since independence. In her analysis of the agricultural science syllabus, Stambach (1996) demonstrates how models of progress are applied to farming systems and the people who inhabit them in Tanzania: "Implicit in the economic scheme are categories of social differences that rank peasants above pastoralists, cooperative farmers above subsistence farmers, and certain social groups in Tanzania above others" (1996:550).

Stambach's work further shows that embedded in the syllabus is a deep-seated prejudice to tradition and that tradition is equated with culture: "The language of the syllabus suggests that 'traditional farming' carries a social stigma" (1996:551) and that furthermore "farming is seen as a menial task that ought to be left to unschooled peers" (1996:552).

This ideology, with its regional prejudices and bias against tradition, has influenced the way young Iraqw in the homeland, in particular, view their conditions. It has shaped decisions about land use and life plans. Contributing to young Iraqw's sense of despair at the marginalization inherent in this ideology is the concurrent decline in agricultural production that has been a feature of life in the homeland since independence.

DECLINE IN PRODUCTION

In the homeland, Iraqw farmers in the precolonial and colonial era regularly harvested surpluses of foodstuffs. The district books of the 1920s and 1930s document that Iraqw farmers provided grain to the Mbugwe to the east and to drought-stricken farmers in the west as well. Today, most farmers in the homeland rarely produce enough maize to meet their own needs.[4] They make up the shortages by buying grain in the markets, bartering with other Iraqw, or seeking assistance (_kuhemea_) from relatives in expansion areas. Farmers attribute this production squeeze to a decline in soil fertility, the small size of landholdings, insufficient organic fertilizer, and the poor and erratic rains that have plagued much of Tanzania in recent years.[5] Recently, El Niño has become a frequent topic of discussion and a catch-all term for climatic problems.

Although out-migration has relieved some of the pressure on the land, migration is increasingly difficult as the expansion areas are under growing land pressure. Today, population density in the homeland is approximately 186 people per square kilometer. Frequently, land previously left for pasturage is put under cultivation. Indeed, government officials have pushed Iraqw to open these areas to agriculture, emphasizing the importance of farming over pastoralism. Unlike areas to which the Iraqw have migrated, homeland farmers do not rely on their maize crop alone for subsistence. While most Iraqw will claim they have not eaten unless they have had _fa'a_ (cornmeal porridge known as _ugali_ in Kiswahili), when maize is hard to come by they eat sweet potatoes, European potatoes, and wheat. Sorghum and millet, while mostly used for beer, are also used occasionally to make porridge.

Labor patterns have changed in the Iraqw homeland since independence. Today, cooperative work groups supply less of the overall labor to household fields than in the past. Also, the loss of children between the ages of nine and seventeen, and even up to twenty, to primary and secondary schooling has reduced their contribution to household labor. Women are increasingly bearing more of the responsibility for farmwork, as men pursue wage labor, livestock herding, or spend time at the local beer clubs. The heavy workload of women and their increasing contribution to the household income is recognized and sometimes discussed in government meetings. One woman described her day to me from start to finish. Her account was similar to those of many women I spoke with.

Table 6.1   Household data

Average farm size	Average household	Mean no. of cattle	Mean no. of goats
1.4 ha	7.5 people	5.4	5
Mean no. of sheep	Mean no. of pigs	Households with cattle	Households with cattle on loan
3.6	1.8	82 percent	56.9 percent
Households with goats	Households with sheep	Households with pigs	
52 percent	48 percent	72.6 percent	

N =150

I usually get up at 5 A.M. so I can begin grinding the maize into flour for the mid-day meal of porridge. I also get to work on cooking gruel for the family's morning meal. Once I have finished with the meal, I sweep out the manure from the livestock enclosure so that it will dry in the sun. Then, I go to the fields where I work until mid-day. I return to cook the mid-day meal and grind maize again for the evening meal. I go back to the fields in the afternoon, and after a couple of hours of work, head home to collect the axe and go find firewood. When it begins to get dark, I prepare the evening meal and grind maize again for the morning's gruel. In between these activities, I must find time to care for the children, sweep the house, clean the cooking vessels, prepare bathwater, and attend to other chores.

Younger women rarely grind their maize by hand using grinding stones. Instead, they take their maize to a local grinding mill to have it ground, freeing them from some of the time demands of hand grinding. In addition to these daily chores, women perform most of the small-scale income-generating activities such as mat and basket weaving, beer brewing, and selling bananas and other fruits, potatoes, tomatoes, firewood, and charcoal. They transport these goods on their backs to the town of Mbulu. Men generally work as hired laborers on farms in Mbulu, or sell shop goods, or are employed in salaried positions as schoolteachers or rural medical assistants. Although the first priority of households is to meet their food needs, they still must raise cash for taxes and the purchase of clothes, school materials, and medical needs.

There are two rainy seasons in the homeland. The early rains begin in late October or early November and continue through January. From January to

March, rainfall drops off, and the sun is at its strongest. Then from March to early June the rains are heavy and constant, falling in sheets in the morning and clearing briefly in the afternoon. Even during the dry season, from July through September, a thick, moist, cold fog covers Irqwa Da'aw during the mornings and the early afternoon, which enables the cultivation of wheat. The climate in the homeland allows for two cropping seasons, and thus there is always work to be done in the fields. As the elevation is quite high, the weather is cool, and the crops take longer to mature than at the lower elevations outside of the homeland. Iraqw in the homeland, unlike those who have migrated out to drier areas, work year-round on their plots and have no season of rest. Farmers' decisions about pursuing other economic activities, such as wage labor in the towns or cultivating fields outside of Irqwa Da'aw, are constrained by the demands of agriculture in the homeland.

Iraqw elders, both male and female, complain that there are fewer cattle today than when they were young. They point to disease and the increasing lack of pasturage as factors in this decline. In most communities, the communal pasture known as *hindawi*, the use of which was regulated by the male elders, no longer exists because it has been put under cultivation. With the decline in cattle has come a decrease in milk production as well. Livestock remains an important indicator of wealth, particularly for older Iraqw. Diviners and the elders' council leaders are among those with the largest herds in the homeland. The Iraqw have a strong emotional attachment to their cattle. They keep the horns of their most beloved cows and hang them on the rafters of their houses after they have been ceremonially slaughtered. One man explained this reverence for cattle thus: "A cow is like the mother of the household; she gives milk to her calves and your own children. She is respected like all mothers are."

Livestock, through loans and communal neighborhood herding practices, creates and reinforces bonds of interdependence among households. Respect for a man with a large herd is apparent in elders' council meetings and in other community functions. In the two communities I was most familiar with, the men who had the largest herds of cattle were also the most involved in community affairs, often serving as mediators in disputes. But many younger Iraqw see keeping "traditional" cattle as less important than other income-generating strategies. One man in his late twenties explained it this way: "I would rather earn a wage at a job than have cattle. They are too much work. The world has changed, and there are better things to do to make money than have livestock. Those old men care more about their cattle than they do in paying school fees for their children. That is not *maendeleo*."

Younger Iraqw men's reluctance to pursue livestock management as a wealth strategy may also have to do with the stigma applied to those who do. In the school syllabus mentioned previously, and in government discourse, those who pursue pastoralist strategies, such as the neighboring Maasai or

Datoga, are typified as backward and primitive and holding the country back from _maendeleo_. Indeed, many young Iraqw pointed to elders' obsession with their cattle as a factor in what they perceived as the lack of development in the homeland.

Despite a national ideology that stresses the importance of agriculture for national development, many young Iraqw men and women aspire to a life away from farming. In the homeland, only hand-hoe cultivation is practiced, as the slopes are too steep for ox-plow or tractor. This form of cultivation is one aspect of life in Irqwa Da'aw that Iraqw in migration areas point to as a sign of the "backwardness" of the homeland. Young Iraqw are aware of this stigma and are frustrated by the limits to production that the resource base and technology place on them. Yet, opportunities for off-farm employment are few. To make money, many young men keep pigs that they sell for slaughter in the town of Moshi in Kilimanjaro Region. Others transport goods for local shop owners, try their own hand at opening a shop _(duka)_, or work in the beer clubs. Aside from pig husbandry, these activities bring in very little money. A minority of young people continue their education through secondary school, or beyond, and seek jobs as schoolteachers, office workers, health professionals, or civil servants. Many who have remained with farming have become discouraged by declining yields, poor rains, and persistent pest infestations that force them to replant several times. Most are unwilling to invest any more of their labor or financial resources in agriculture. One man explained:

> Today, many young men have lost hope in agriculture. Every year they work harder on their fields and seem to harvest less. That is why you see so many young men going to the beer halls in the morning and staying there all day. They see relatives in Karatu or even Daudi harvesting fifteen acres of maize and using plows. Here, they have given up.

"Modern" Production Strategies

Since independence, a variety of economic strategies have taken hold in Irqwa Da'aw. Investing in livestock remains an important strategy, but as pasture space shrinks, it is becoming increasingly difficult to maintain large herds. Many homeland residents resort to cattle loans with relatives or friends living in the expansion areas that still have space for herding. Others are turning to pig husbandry, as pigs can be fed household wastes and fattened for sale quite rapidly. The income from pig husbandry is quite substantial by local standards, with prices as high as $50 or more per pig. The drawback to raising pigs is the labor-intensive nature of the work. Most of this work falls on women, but the profits from sales tend to be pocketed by the men. In addition, pigs, because they are produced primarily for the market, are in a different resource category than other livestock. Unlike goats, sheep, or cattle, pigs are not loaned or borrowed or given in times of need. They are valued for their cash potential and are treated quite differently from other livestock. They are not herded with neighbors' herds, and the ownership of pigs is very individualized, with the one who has purchased it, or raised and fed it, being in control of its sale. Although some pork is consumed in the homeland, many Iraqw are still reluctant to eat the meat. Goats, sheep, and cattle all have a place in the symbolic, as well as the material, lives of Iraqw—in rituals, in weddings, and in establishing bonds between households. Pigs contribute to the material well-being of the household but have no symbolic associations attached to them.

Another popular land-use practice today is tree planting. Trees have a number of benefits to farmers. Most important, the trees planted in the homeland since the 1930s have become so numerous as to enable residents to be self-sufficient in fuelwood. Iraqw women in particular cite this as a great benefit, recalling with dismay the days they had to rely on bracken ferns or long trips to the forest reserves. In addition to fuel, trees produce much-needed timber for local house construction. After household needs are met, trees provide poles and timber for sale on the market. Farmers also listed fruit production, charcoal making, and boundary markers as important benefits from trees. Women are mainly responsible for selling fruit and charcoal, and these activities provide them with an important income. Again, tree planting is viewed as a very "modern" land-use strategy, and it has received a great deal of national attention. I have heard on Radio Tanzania more than one speech made by members of Parliament about the importance of planting trees for _maendeleo_.

The strategic importance of trees is another factor in their popularity. Planting trees gives farmers greater security over their land tenure. The government must compensate farmers for any crops on fields they are using if they decide to allocate the land to another person or designate it for another use. In the past, the government has waited until fields are under fallow before claiming land. In this way, minimal compensation is necessary. However, if trees are on the land, the government must compensate the farmer for the estimated value that those trees will have when they are at a harvestable age. Because of the potentially significant cost of this compensation, the government tends to shy away from taking land with trees on it. Farmers thus use this strategy as a hedge against the government taking their land.

Today, many of the black wattle woodlots planted as individual household reserves in the 1930s and 1940s are now considered communal property. These species flourished in the homeland and spread in an almost uncontrollable way over the landscape. Their abundance, and their use as fuel and building material, led to the shift from being private resources to being considered communal resources in many cases. However, other exotic tree species planted for the purpose of future sales of timber and poles are classed as private resources. Many Iraqw suggested that as private resources, trees are similar to bank accounts or stock on the shelves of stores. Building materials for housing and fuelwood for food preparation are seen as resources synonymous with life itself. Whereas aid in fuelwood and building materials for local house construction is given fairly freely, no one would ask a neighbor or relative to cut down a timber tree intended for sale, so they could use its products. As one man explained: "Trees are your property and your business. You don't see storekeepers giving their goods away. It is the same with us and our timber trees." Investing in trees enables farmers to avoid some of the potential demands of relatives and neighbors. They store their wealth in trees instead of in surplus food crops. Local moral codes hold that requests for food assistance cannot be refused, as doing so would be wishing someone harm or death. But denying a person the use of your trees is not denying them sustenance and thus can be done without criticism.

Tree planting on boundaries also allows farmers to cement their claims to land vis-à-vis their neighbors. Planting a tree on a boundary is a way of making it very clear where the boundaries between farms are. Because tree planting is a land-use strategy that reinforces individual or household claims to land, it can lead to conflicts within the community. Various disputes took place during my residence that involved trees. Most of these cases revolved around boundaries. In one case, two neighbors fought about the claims to ownership of trees growing on the border between their two farms. On one side was a lemon tree and on the other was a pear. The woman who had planted the lemon claimed that her land (she was the head of the household) also included the pear tree, whereas the other disputant claimed that the lemon was planted on her (also a female head of household) side. In the end, the local government heard the case and decided that the boundary ran in between the two trees but that the rights of access and use to the two trees would swap; that is, each landholder would have access to the tree on the opposite side of their boundary. The person granted access to the pear tree was given an opportunity for greater income in this case, because pears fetch a higher price on the market than lemons.

Tree planting can provoke conflict between sons and fathers. Usually, it is younger men who are most interested in planting trees. Tree planting is seen as a "modern" strategy and an investment for the future, one that can help pay for children's school fees, house-building costs, and so on. On the other hand, because trees can take many years before producing financial benefits, older men are less interested in them. Often, young men will plant trees on their father's land with the assumption that they will have control over these trees and will inherit this land in the future. This action can provoke resentment from both their fathers, who feel they are being pushed out, and also from their brothers, who may view this action as an attempt to make claims on all of their father's land. In one case with which I was familiar, a middle son planted seedlings of pines and *grevillea* on his father's land. His older brothers, who had moved out of the area and found land elsewhere, expressed no objection to this move. His two younger brothers, however, were upset by his actions and complained to their father and prodded him to pull up the seedlings. When he did so, the middle brother who had planted the seedlings was furious but had little recourse and decided not to pursue compensation.

Women have a different interest in trees. In the 1960s, a development project promoted the planting of fruit trees in the area. The trees did well, and it is now women who benefit from them. They harvest the fruit and take it to Mbulu to sell, providing them with an income, however small. They also value the trees for producing food for their children. For the most part, fruit is thought of as food for children, and many adults in the homeland do not eat it. Women view fruit as a valuable nutritional contribution to their households as well as a source of cash income that is largely under their control. In the households I visited where women were the household heads due to the death of their husbands or his residence outside the homeland, women had actively planted and tended fruit trees and were interested in increasing their numbers. Men, when asked what kind of trees they preferred, never pointed to fruit trees but rather to species useful for timber and building materials. Thus, concerning trees, men and women have different perceptions and interests.

Tree planting fits in with a more "modern" approach to land use that promotes individual rights to land and its resources. "Modern" trees, such as Australian fast-growing exotics like *grevillea*, are viewed as more individualized resources than livestock or food crops. They are not resources that are shared or loaned or redistributed. It remains to be seen what the full impact of trees will be on the local economy, as planting of timber species is a fairly recent strategy. The physical landscape of the homeland is already being transformed by this resource management practice, and it no longer is a "treeless" expanse as was reported by colonial officers in the 1930s.

Another tree product generating interest recently is coffee. Coffee was introduced by the British in the 1930s but never really took off in the Iraqw homeland. In part, there is little land to allot solely for cash crop production. Also, during the *ujamaa* era, farmers would take their coffee harvest to the coffee cooperatives but would never receive any financial compensation. This clearly did not engender a positive attitude to investing in coffee. But in recent years, as economic liberalization policies have encouraged privatization and outside investment, coffee buyers from Europe have occasionally come as far as Mbulu to buy coffee directly from growers. This turn of events led many farmers to plant coffee seedlings in the hope of reaping rewards. Still, coffee requires far more of a financial investment than timber trees, due to the high costs of herbicides and fertilizers. Furthermore, prices of coffee on the world market fluctuate significantly, and in recent years coffee farmers in Africa have had a very hard time making a living from this crop. In 2002, the

Figure 6.1   Examining a coffee tree.

district commissioner, in his speech to residents of the ward of Murray, told villagers that it is government policy that farmers plant one-quarter of an acre in coffee so that the community would bring in cash for development.

Another recent introduction to the homeland has been "modern" cows *(n'gombe wa kisasa)*. In general, European breeds of livestock, or even livestock such as chickens that are kept in enclosures and not allowed to run free, are called modern *(kisasa)* all over Tanzania. The modern thus refers both to the origin of the breed and also to the methods of management. My research assistant remarked one day, "I don't understand why those cows are more 'modern' than our own indigenous breeds. After all, they are both 'modern.' They are both existing here and now." In Tanzania, each district usually has one country that oversees development efforts. In Mbulu District, the Mbulu District Rural Development Programme (MRDP) is being funded by the government of the Netherlands. MRDP has encouraged soil conservation, agroforestry, and implementation of a heifer project to support women's control of cows beginning in 1990. The project laid down strict rules. First, only women could apply for these heifer loans. Then, they had to fulfill various conditions before they were approved for the project such as building a shed "fit" for zero-grazing, acquiring the proper equipment for dipping and spraying the animal to keep it tick-free, and keeping the animal separate from "local" breeds. Similar to the Iraqw cattle loan of *komi*, when the heifer

Figure 6.2   Mbulu bimonthly livestock auction.

eventually gave birth to another heifer calf, the women were allowed to keep
the cow but agreed to give the new heifer to the project. Among the Iraqw,
livestock ownership, in particular cattle, is the domain of men. The MRDP
obviously planned this program to circumvent male ownership and control
over a potentially valuable income-earning resource (from the sale of milk to
the town of Mbulu). However, in most of the instances with which I was familiar, men had their wives (or mothers or even sisters) put their names on
the project list simply as a means for getting the cows. Once the cow was obtained there was little doubt as to who would be the actual owner. It was men
who made all the preparations and who took over control of the heifer once
it arrived. While women may do most of the labor of stall feeding the animal,
it was not recognized locally as her animal, though it might have been considered such by MRDP. Furthermore, many Iraqw object to stall feeding as
both too labor intensive and as cruel to the animal, and instead some have
chosen to herd their "modern" cows with "traditional" ones in communal
pastures. One man said to me, "What kind of way is that to treat an animal,
keeping it confined to such a small area all the time? It will not be happy with
such a life." It is too early to tell what the ultimate outcome of the project will
be, but it is one that has gained popularity with younger Iraqw, particularly
those who are attempting to carve out more "modern" lives for themselves.

Development and Modernity

What these examples illustrate quite nicely are the ways in which Iraqw manipulate "development" for their own aims where they are able. Iraqw have always been quick to adopt changes that provide obvious benefits, yet who gets these benefits is always determined by those who are quickest to recognize the possible gains. Although the heifer project is intended to benefit women, it will most likely benefit men. Depending on the men involved, their entire household will also benefit from the program. Although the heifer project might alleviate the shortages of milk that elders cite as an issue today, their concerns of declining milk yields reflect wider concerns with community change and growing individualization of resources. Milk was, in the past, a substance establishing bonds of closeness among people. With the heifer project, milk is to become a commodity for sale on the market. Again, it is too early to predict the consequences of this project, but its orientation toward individual control over a resource is part of a wider trend in resource management. It is doubtful whether these "modern" cows will be incorporated into the Iraqw system of cattle loans that strengthens bonds across households and often across ecological zones. It is more likely that, like the pigs and fast-growing exotic tree species, these animals will become part of the set of resources linked with cash and therefore not available as part of a wider system of resources used to aid relatives and friends and thus to establish bonds of interdependence and obligation. Instead, these resources will enable those who choose to invest in them to further withdraw from social and communal obligations and engage directly with the market. Yet, this dependence is very risky, as fluctuations in prices leave farmers vulnerable.

Promoting private ownership has been a common feature of development programs throughout East Africa from the colonial era to the present. Another common effect of development programs is that when new cash crops or new income-generating activities are introduced, men tend to take control of these activities. However, as we have seen with fruit trees and fuelwood production, women also benefit if the economic gains are not substantial enough to interest men. What this allows in the Iraqw homeland is a small degree of independence for women. For instance, women can control the proceeds from fruit and charcoal sales for the most part (though women complain that men will ask them for this money). In Irqwa Da'aw, women use this cash to buy school materials for their children, soap, cooking oil, kerosene, and other household necessities. Women complain that men use profits from their activities for themselves, either to drink beer with their friends or to spend on their own projects, which may be of no direct benefit to the household.

What is clear from Iraqw encounters with development initiatives is that they are not powerless and deprived of agency. They are quite clever at circumventing the designs of development projects when they can. Furthermore, in examining the changes from the colonial era to the present, it is evident that the ideology of modernity has been important in shaping local decisions from land use to spending patterns. Part of the appeal of planting exotic tree species, raising pigs for sale on the market, raising "modern" cows for milk production, and growing coffee is that these activities and commodities are perceived as modern and leading to development and progress. Younger Iraqw, in particular, are interested in these strategies and use them as a claim for their own modernity. Many draw upon state ideology in noting that the elders' interest in their livestock herds and their reticence to take up cash cropping are examples of their "backwardness." Younger Iraqw are also more concerned with earning cash not only to pay for household necessities and school fees but also to buy material goods on the market that are associated with modernity. Most senior male elders I knew used any cash they obtained for medicine for their cattle, blankets for the cold, or trips to the beer clubs to drink with their friends.

Planting exotic tree species, having a "modern" cow, breeding pigs for sale, or planting hybrid maize seeds go hand in hand with other markers of a modern identity such as being a Catholic, finishing school, living in a brick house with a sheet-metal roof, wearing new store-bought clothing as opposed to used clothing sold in markets (or the more traditional capes and blankets), wearing shoes instead of tire sandals, and having furniture and factory-produced cooking pots rather than handmade clay pots. They are all part of the package of modernity in rural Tanzania. This package is one pursued mostly by younger Iraqw, whereas elders remain more interested in traditional markers of status such as large cattle holdings. These seemingly small features of modernity are ways in which younger Iraqw assert their own identity as different from their parents' generation and use this identity to make claims to power and authority. Modernity also enables many who pursue it to keep more of their economic resources to themselves. It is unlikely that anyone will request a loan of a pig, or to cut down your timber tree, or to borrow a "modern" cow. In the precolonial era, it was difficult to refuse requests for food or livestock loans, and household resources given out to others reinforced interdependencies and relationships. "Modern" resources fall under a separate and new category. This aspect of modernity, one that allows for individual advancement and accumulation, is one that is both highly sought after and also highly contested, as will be seen in following chapters.[6]

Finally, I would like to end this chapter with the story of one young man in his twenties who desperately wanted to pursue his schooling by furthering his studies through Form 6 and then, if he continued to do well, through university.

This story illustrates the struggles faced by young people but also how their aspirations place them in conflict with their parents. Frequently, these conflicts revolve around differing ideas about land use.

Struggling to Get Ahead

From Irqwa Da'aw and from a large family who depended entirely on the land for their livelihood, Nada had been trying for years to raise the money for his school fees. He worked various odd jobs, mostly for the local parish, and borrowed money from relatives. Still, he was unable to get enough money together for the fairly steep fees at the local seminary that offered Form 5 and 6 courses. He tried in vain for years to convince his father to allow him to take a small plot of land and plant tobacco or pyrethrum as a cash crop. He believed the sale of these crops would enable him to pay his school fees. He explained to me: "My father asks me why I can't just plant maize and beans like we have always done and settle down to life here in the village and farm and tend the cows like he has done and like his father did. I try to explain to him that times have changed and that nowadays it is no longer possible to rely on farming alone. Besides, I want an education. I want to do something more with my life than farm. And we barely make ends meet anyway. But he sees no point in these 'modern' ideas."

Nada's situation is not unique in Irqwa Da'aw. Although many young men do not pursue an education and do turn to farming, others flee and either struggle to get jobs or to further their schooling, or end up doing odd jobs for very little pay in the towns. These youth with few economic prospects are increasing daily in towns throughout Tanzania. In tandem with this trend is the increasing frequency of petty crime.

Notes

1. See Lawi (2000) for an extensive review of "modernizing" practices introduced by both the colonial and postcolonial governments.

2. See, for example, the work of Wada (1969a, 1969b, 1971, 1975, 1978, 1980, 1984) in the Katesh area.

3. Most of these wealthy farmers own their own tractors, combine harvesters, and other machinery and employ many agricultural laborers. Raikes (1975a, 1975b) has documented in detail the development of capitalist farming in this area.

4. In my survey, farmers reported producing only 62 percent of their annual needs. Farmers in areas such as Kuta may have access to greater holdings than those in

my own survey, which focused on the ward of Kainam, in particular the villages of Hareabi and Tsaayo.

5. See Bernstein (1982) for a discussion of the factors leading to decline in production.

6. Shipton's (1989) analysis of bitter money among the Luo of western Kenya provides another example of the ways in which communities grapple with the introduction of a money economy and the ways in which changes in the economy transform the meanings of resources.

CHAPTER SEVEN

COSMOLOGY AND MORALITY

One evening, as I was beginning the chores of preparing dinner and heating water for a bath, I glanced across the meadow in front of my house and saw a young woman I recognized from Sunday services at the Catholic Church performing a ceremony at the river. She removed her _kanga_[1] and put them back on upside down and appeared to be uttering something, although I could not hear what. She stayed about fifteen minutes and then walked quickly away. I had no idea what had been going on, but asked my neighbors the next day if they had seen her. They explained that the woman had been saying a curse _(lo'o)_ at the river, hoping to deliver justice to those who she felt had wrongly accused her of witchcraft. If the curse worked and brought harm to her accusers, she would prove her innocence and clear her name.

Religious beliefs and practices, rooted in the precolonial era, make up much of what Iraqw, both old and young, classify as traditional. When asked about precolonial religion, which younger Christian Iraqw refer to as pagan _(Upagani)_, many will tell you "_wakati yake imeshapita_" or "its time has passed." Those who adhere to "pagan" beliefs and practices are often viewed as lacking in _maendeleo_. Yet, these beliefs also inform Iraqw identity. The moral ideas embedded in religious beliefs provide substance for local debates about development. In precolonial Irqwa Da'aw, the relationships among _aya_ members were shaped by cosmology and moral codes of behavior that defined relations between the human population and the supernatural.

Today, the situation is more complex, as the Christian churches gain more adherents and put forth their own notions of community and morality.

There is a nearly even split between Christians and non-Christians in the homeland communities I surveyed. This divide also corresponds with age, with older Iraqw more often being non-Christian. Although younger Iraqw have all grown up hearing and learning about certain precolonial beliefs and practices, many claim to reject them and assert strongly their identity as Christians. For many youths, belonging to a Christian church is an important aspect of modernity, and one that connects them to a wider world and cultural community. As I grew more deeply involved in the community, I came to see, however, that Christians, even those who claimed disbelief in cursing, diviners, and witchcraft, would turn to these traditional beliefs and practices to handle a variety of situations.

Because young people are reluctant to embrace many of the cultural practices still observed by elders, many elders are concerned that they will not know what to do in the future to address some of their, or the community's, problems. One older man told me: "Young men today do not want to sit with their fathers and learn these things. We worry that when they have difficulties in the future they will not have the knowledge to solve them. They will not know how to perform the proper rituals." Although younger Christians may discard the beliefs and practices that focus on the welfare of the wider community, many, like the young woman described above, are less likely to reject those that help solve their more personal, individual, problems. Some scholars, as well as Iraqw elders, see this turn toward more individualistic concerns as a product of globalization.

Struggles over beliefs are struggles over power. In the moral ideology of Iraqw elders, individual moral transgressions anger the earth spirits that share a specific, bounded space with community members. Their anger can affect the entire community. It is the council of elders, in cooperation with paramount diviners, who act to appease these spirits to protect and cure the land and community. This role legitimates their claim to authority.[2] Those who do not relish being constrained by local male elders turn to _maendeleo_ in the form of the Christian churches or the state, claiming allegiance to a different belief system or a different sort of community, one in which Iraqw elders are clearly less of an influence. However, their ability to evade this traditional system has its limits. Particularly during times of stress, such as during a drought, or when a family suffers a death or other misfortune, many younger Iraqw will draw upon practices associated with traditions that, in the view of most of the local churches, are "matters of the devil" (_mambo ya shetani_).

LOOAA AND NEETLAAMEE

In Iraqw cosmology there are two main spiritual forces. _Looaa_ is the female Creator Being who is benevolent and maternal. She is conceived of as the sun and is remote from the day-to-day lives of Iraqw. She has the characteristics of an ideal mother. She is kind and gentle and only wishes health and fertility for her children. She gives fertility to people and livestock and sends the rains to fall upon the land. She is prayed to during times of need or distress and is thanked for good fortune, such as a bountiful harvest. No sacrifices are made to *Looaa*, for she is said not to demand appeasement.

Neetlaamee (*neetlaangw*, sing.) are earth spirits who are perceived to be male. They dwell in the rivers, streams, and springs, in rocky caves on mountains, and in certain forest groves. They resemble human beings in both appearance and personality and can be meddlesome and troubling to the human population. They are of much more concern on a daily basis to Iraqw because these spirits can cause great harm to the community. The earth spirits, like the human population, inhabit specific territory, so each *aya* has its own spirits.

In the precolonial era, it was the responsibility of the elders to maintain a harmonious relationship with the spirits through ritual practices. *Neetlaamee*, in particular, must be appeased through ritual sacrifices for any offenses of the human population. If not, they may prevent the rains or bring disease, death, leopard attacks, and so on. The earth spirits reinforce the idea of a bounded, moral community. All the inhabitants of a specific territory are responsible to others sharing that space, because if moral codes are violated, all within the community boundaries may be harmed by the resident earth spirits.

In addition to reinforcing a sense of community based on spatial boundaries, the beliefs in the Creator Being and the earth spirits also reflect ideas about gender. As Lawi states, "these two supernatural beings were mirror images of the social roles of mothers and fathers in the Iraqw society, as it existed at the turn of the century" (2000:135). The earth spirits "matched the typical nature and role of fathers just as closely" (2000:138). The ideal for Iraqw women is that they should be mothers and should put the interests of their families and the welfare of the household above their own personal concerns. They should be benevolent and generous and also a bit removed from the day-to-day political workings of the community. Iraqw men, like the earth spirits, are more directly involved in the affairs of the community, and it is through them that various struggles for authority and power are played out. Children often have a more fraught relationship with their fathers than with their mothers. Although many older Iraqw carry on a relationship with and knowledge of *Looaa* and *neetlaamee*, younger Christians often know little about these spiritual beings.

GIUSEE

Other less important spiritual beings are the ghosts or *giusee*. Iraqw male elders explain that both the dead and the living have a soul *(hinsla)*.[3] However, upon death, the soul leaves the heart, which it inhabits during life, and moves to another part of the body. In the afterlife, the person has the same body that he or she had in the living world and lives much as she or he did before dying, living below the living world and growing crops and herding livestock as before. Although attention to ghosts has decreased among the Iraqw, their presence is felt on occasion, and efforts are made to appease them from time to time. Most Iraqw, young and old, profess to believe that if you mistreat your mother in her old age, she will bear a grudge that will come to plague you when she dies.

In the past, it was customary to honor the dead through sacrifices of cattle or through the brewing of special beer. Iraqw sacrifice cattle to ghosts, as opposed to other livestock, because they are most highly valued and desired by both the living and ghosts. Ghosts, like the earth spirits, are easily angered and vengeful if not treated with proper respect. The only dead of significance to living individuals are those they knew, such as parents or grandparents. If a person did not know his grandparents or great-grandparents, he will not be a target for these ghosts. The Iraqw are not concerned with distant ancestors. Also, a man or woman who dies before marriage or before having children will not be a threat to anyone. He or she will become a ghost but will have no one to disturb from the afterworld. These beliefs demonstrate the importance of the relationships between elders and juniors within households, which continue after the death of the parent. In effect, the authority of both elder men and women continues beyond their deaths, and their children must continue to show them respect and deference. Although many younger Christian Iraqw do not follow the rituals honoring ghosts, they do fear reprisals from their parents after their deaths. In Hareabi, one man was rumored to be treating his ailing mother poorly, neglecting her or providing her with only minimal care. Sitting with a group of Iraqw in their twenties and thirties who were all Catholics, I listened as they discussed the situation. One man said, "When his mother dies, then he will have justice delivered upon him." All those present nodded in agreement.

When a man or woman is near death, he or she usually makes a request to be buried in a specific place. Often men choose to be buried in the *aya* where they were born so that they can reunite with their parents or other family members. The afterworld, like the living world, has territories and boundaries. Children rarely refuse to bury their parents in the place of their choice, as they fear, should they refuse, that their parents will strike out against them from the grave. In 1993, an old man born in the homeland *aya* of Tsaayo died in Karatu, where he had moved many years earlier. He requested before he died that his body be returned to Tsaayo. This journey was of considerable expense to his family, but they followed his wishes, and a funeral was held for him in Tsaayo.

If a person falls ill or suffers a misfortune, a diviner will usually attribute it to witchcraft, the earth spirits, or the ghosts. If the source of the trouble is ghosts, the diviner usually instructs the afflicted person to slaughter a bull and to put the hide of the animal on top of the place where the deceased was buried. If hyenas take away the hide during the night, it is seen as a sign that the ghost has accepted the offering and agrees to stop his or her mischief. As a daily ritual of respect for the dead, a man, at dawn, would stop at the threshold of the door before crossing it and pour out a small libation of milk. He would then proceed to do the same on top of the nearby dung heap. The use of milk acknowledges the ghost's membership in the family. By pouring the milk on top of the dung heap, a further connection to the family's livestock, their fertility, and the fertility of the household is being made. Very few Iraqw continue this practice today. Such "pagan" practices and beliefs are discouraged by the Christian churches, and most younger Iraqw do not perform them.

To establish harmonious relations with a recently deceased relative, the dead person's family may honor the deceased by holding a special beer party and by slaughtering a bull soon after the burial.[4] If this offering has been successful (that is, the ghost has remained peaceful), further ceremonies are unlikely to be held.

I attended one ceremony to honor the recently deceased father of a schoolteacher in his late thirties who lived in a neighboring village. The schoolteacher himself was Catholic but was advised by local elders to conduct the ritual. He did not know all the procedures he was expected to follow but relied on the elders to tell him what to do. He invited all the people from the neighborhood but extended a special invitation to the male elders of the neighborhood and male relatives from other areas. The family prepared beer from recently harvested sorghum and slaughtered a bull.[5] The ceremony was held in the house of one of the deceased's sons, in the compound of his father. This particular house was selected (from a compound of three houses) as it was built in the traditional round style. The participants thought it more suitable for the ritual than the Swahili-style neighboring houses, as it allowed the elders to arrange themselves in the customary circle near the doorway. The host bade me to sit at the end of the line of male elders along the wall to the left of the doorway, taking a place near the area that was occupied by the elder women. About twenty-five older men and a few youths were in attendance. Only four women were sitting inside. Most of the women remained outside and attended to the chores of the beer preparation.

The atmosphere inside the house was jovial and relaxed while people waited for others to show up and for the beer to be brought in. When everyone was assembled and seated, two large pottery vessels of beer were brought in and placed on the floor in the center of the front section of the house. Two large gourds, which had been cut in half, were then filled with beer and passed around to the elders. Each man took a few sips and then passed it to his neighbor. This drinking went on for about twenty minutes or two rounds of beer. When the men reached the dregs of the brew, they passed this portion to the women to drink. When I asked why women got the dregs, both men and women explained that women preferred the dregs because they were sweeter. However, this practice also acknowledges the men's higher status.

Once everyone had drunk, a youth was sent out to fetch some grass. He soon returned and handed the grass to the sponsor of the event. The host stood near the door, dipped the grass into one of the gourds of beer, and blessed those gathered by shaking the wet grass over them. Then he began to give a *firoo*, a ceremonial speech or prologue that commonly precedes the recitation of *sluufay*, the ritual prayer:

> *We will pray and be thankful and pay our respects to him whom we buried from this household. We do not know if the people of this house have undergone this affliction and suffered this loss because of a natural death from* Looaa *or not. Nevertheless, it is natural for people and all living things that were born to die later on. No one will remain on this earth forever. Everyone will die and go to where our father now is. Now, all of us have entered this house in goodness. However, in other places inside there are witches who cast their evil gaze on others. But,* Looaa *is here among us. Today, in our country people are sick, the hide (the country) is ill, so now, let us pray.*

Then, he began to recite a prayer to *Looaa* in which she was thanked for her protection and benefaction and also appealed to for future protection. Once he had finished, he handed the grass to a youth who placed it in the slats of the sleeping platform over our heads, signaling the end to the ritual. More beer was brought in and served, and people continued to drink informally well into the afternoon, when they consumed the meat from the sacrifice.

The supernatural beings in Iraqw cosmology mediate and judge the moral behavior of the human population. *Looaa* is concerned with justice and the maintenance of a specific social order. The male earth spirits help to define and regulate community among the Iraqw and create a sense of shared responsibility among people who share a specific, bounded space. And finally, the ghosts uphold the gerontocratic order. Christian Iraqw claim not to believe in earth spirits, *Looaa*, and ghosts. In contrast to the belief in an underworld of ghosts and earth spirits, they profess a belief in Christian notions of heaven and hell. Although they outwardly claim not to put any stock in the beliefs of their non-Christian forefathers, most of them are nonetheless uneasy at the idea of angry ghosts.

MORALITY AND ITS INFRACTIONS

Debate about social and political changes occurring in the homeland is often framed in moral terms. Iraqw moral codes emphasize a concern with com-

munity and household harmony. If not addressed, moral violations ultimately threaten fertility, both at the level of the community and of the household. For example, physical harm done to an individual is a violation of
community harmony but is also a threat to the well-being, fertility, and prosperity of that individual and their household. In such cases, a complicated ar-
ray of interests and concerns are brought to the surface. Relationships based
on kinship and descent and those based on shared space overlap and may reinforce or conflict with one another, as was seen in the incident between
Akonaay and Safari (see Chapter 4). The following account illustrates some
of these ideas more clearly.

Accidental Killing

In 1992, a tragic accident took place on the outskirts of Mbulu near a
maize-grinding mill. A young seminarian was getting a driving lesson
from a priest. As he neared the crowd of people waiting near the mill, he
panicked, and instead of braking, stepped on the accelerator and ran over
a young man who was resting at the side of the path. The young man died
from his injuries, leaving a wife and children. The seminarian was an or-
phan and had no means by which to pay compensation to the family, so
the priest took over this responsibility. The settlement of the case took
over a year, and in 1993 a ceremony was held to put the matter to rest. A
respected elder was called in to mediate the proceedings. At the ceremony,
the priest and other members of the church gathered in support of the
seminarian. On the other side, the deceased's parents, other relatives, and
neighbors were present. The two sides had come to the agreement that
compensation for the young man's family should be four cows, two
calves, two sheep, and a goat. At the ceremony, a sheep was led into the
middle of the gathering, and the elder told the seminarian to put his hand
on the sheep and ask *Looaa* for forgiveness and swear he would never
commit such an act again. On orders from the priest and other church officials, the seminarian refused to say one of the words told to him by the
elder. I was unable to discover the word, but was told that if the word was
uttered, the Catholics in the group would not eat with the others present.
The word was omitted with the agreement of the non-Christians. Then,
the mother of the deceased came forward and put her hand on the sheep
and said that now the matter was settled and that her family bore no ill
will against the seminarian. She also asked her son's ghost to remain quiet,
explaining that the matter had been resolved. She led the sheep away, and
another was brought in and killed, the meat of which was eaten by all
those gathered.

This case is interesting on a number of levels. As Christians, the seminarian and the church officials involved would usually stand in opposition to traditional and "pagan" beliefs and practices. Yet, they must have recognized that neither the Church nor the state had a better way of handling this tragedy. Although courts and other modern institutions are turned to with increasing frequency, they are still unable to provide adequate solutions to many of the issues that arise in rural societies, particularly ones that lead to possible ruptures of social relations. It is particularly interesting to note the degree to which the elders, in pursuing "pagan" practices, are willing to compromise with Christians to achieve the wider goal of harmony.

In cases such as these, regarding the breaking of bones, shedding of blood, or the killing (accidental or intentional) of a man or woman, certain forms of compensation are customary. The wrongs can be made right, and thus dangerous tensions and enmity avoided and harmony restored, by the payment of specific fines of livestock. Fines compensate not only the individual wronged but family members as well. Even if compensation is given and the matter considered finished, members of either clan should never intermarry. Compensation is meant to respect both the economic and emotional damage done to the family that has suffered a loss.

Accidental Death Caused by an Animal

In one unusual case, a young boy was gored while tending the "modern" bull of Boay, a schoolteacher in the homeland. These "modern" cows are not as docile as the indigenous breeds and can be quite a handful to care for. This bull terrorized most of the young boys that the teacher had hired to look after him. The youth who was gored had been on the job only a week when the calamity occurred. Boay was on his way to the town of Mbulu when word reached him of the accident. He promptly turned around his bicycle and peddled home to find the boy badly wounded. He then rushed to the local parish to request the use of its vehicle. He accompanied the boy to Mbulu, where he hired another vehicle to take him to Haidom hospital, one of the best health facilities in northern Tanzania, some three hours to the southwest. Unfortunately, the boy died on the journey, so Boay returned the boy's body to his parents. Boay was extremely upset by this disaster. He went to the elders in the village to get advice on what to do. The elders met and agreed on the transfer of small stock, agreeing that a cow was unnecessary as the death had not been caused directly by Boay, but instead by his bull. Boay presented the family with the animals, and they all sat and shared beer that Boay had brewed. Boay continued to send gifts of maize and other foodstuffs to the family.

Nearly a year later, Boay sent over a sack of maize, and the parents came to him and said, "You have done enough now. You cannot keep sending us food for the rest of your life." Yet Boay will always feel some responsibility toward this family, and in 2000 he was trying to raise secondary school fees for one of the other children in the family.

In all instances of enmity, fighting, or disputes, the act of eating and drinking together is given special attention, as a sign that the matter has been resolved and that all parties bear no resentment, and their hearts have "cooled." If a person feels that appropriate justice for a wrong committed has not been delivered, two courses of action are possible. A situation of formalized enmity might develop between the two, or the wronged party might put a curse *(lo'o)* on the offender.

WAKARI—FORMALIZED ENMITY

Wakari is a formalized state of enmity that occurs when two people, or two families, have a serious and irreconcilable disagreement arising from conflicts involving land, debts (in livestock) incurred but not repaid, accusations of witchcraft, or other disputes. In Irqwa Da'aw, disputes over land and livestock were the most frequent causes of *wakari*. To enter into the state of *wakari*, the protagonists cut off relations completely with one another. This enmity includes all household members and the descendants of the protagonists. Once the parties have entered into *wakari*, all those affected refuse to speak to or greet one another or to interact in any way. If this condition is not rectified, the children and grandchildren of the original participants will carry on this enmity. *Wakari* often, but not always, involves the saying of a ritual curse. I was told that *wakari* without a curse is worse than if it is accompanied by a curse, because a curse can be addressed and rectified by the elders. The ambiguity that ensues without a curse makes *wakari* harder to resolve.

In one *aya*, I knew a few families who were in a state of *wakari*. The tensions in one case originated over a failure to pay off a debt of livestock between neighbors. The other case concerned a dispute over land. This latter case involved brothers who were also neighbors. This family had a reputation for being unusually belligerent, so the enmity was not entirely surprising to the community. The hostility corresponded with structural tensions that are a feature of fraternal relations in which brothers compete with each other over the land and livestock resources of their father. This family was somewhat unusual, because all the brothers had chosen to stay in the area. Often brothers, possibly to escape such tensions, move to other areas. Two of the brothers entered into the formal state of *wakari* after one was said to have hired a thug to beat up his sibling at one of the bimonthly livestock auctions. This incident marked the culmination of hostility between the two brothers over disagreements concerning both land and livestock rights.

Interestingly, *wakari* is not singled out as "pagan" or "primitive" by churches or the state. This might simply be an oversight, or it may be due to the fact that *wakari* does not directly relate to what are often classified as "backward" beliefs. In any case, *wakari* continues, though it is not a common feature of local communities. Its continuation rests in part on the inability of the state or other "modern" institutions to fully iron out disputes and "cool" the hearts of those who feel themselves wronged or taken advantage of.

LO'O—THE CURSE

Iraqw resort to curses when they believe they have been wronged and have no other recourse.[6] Many elders I interviewed claimed that both *wakari* and cursing were more prevalent before the colonial administration's establishment of native courts. In the precolonial era, aggrieved individuals often felt that the elders' council was ineffective in enforcing settlements of grievances. The curse, which relied on assistance from *Looaa*, provided another avenue. On the other hand, other elders told me that cursing, in particular, is escalating, even among young people, because many of the actions that provoke curses are on the increase. Curses are used predominantly in cases where the proof deemed necessary for government court settlements is lacking, such as debts from the past or slander (for example, accusations of witchcraft). Several elder men suggested that women more frequently resort to curses than men. For women, seeking justice through the court system is intimidating (many do not speak Swahili, or do not feel comfortable speaking it) and time consuming. In addition, in cases where women feel themselves verbally or psychologically mistreated, the courts are not particularly effective at providing redress.

To utter a curse is to call upon *Looaa* to deliver justice upon an offender. Cursing is often conducted at rivers or streams or springs to enlist the aid of the earth spirits, together with *Looaa*, in striking down an offender. In these instances, *Looaa* and the earth spirits cooperate for the good of the community. The earth spirits are said to dislike wrongdoers in the same way that humans do. Curses can be said by individuals or, in rarer instances, by the elders as a group. If a person has been justifiably cursed (that is, he is guilty of the offense of which he is accused), the curse will work, and *Looaa* will punish him. Usually, what results are losses to the family of the accused, such as the death of his livestock or the death of his children, particularly male offspring. The objective is a slow eradication of his household and a weakening of his lineage and clan. To curse a woman brings about the same result. When her children are attacked, her husband's lineage is threatened, and her role as the perpetuator of that lineage is undermined.

For lesser wrongs, a person may curse only the individual he feels wronged him and spare the family members of the accused. The curser may openly inform the offender of the curse, thus giving the wrongdoer an opportunity to rectify the situation.

A person may take his complaint before the elders to seek sanction for a curse. He and the person he has accused both appear before the elders. If they agree that a curse is in order, the accused, his accuser, and the elders will meet again three days after the meeting to conduct the curse. The waiting period gives the antagonists a chance to resolve their differences without resorting to a curse. The elders will instruct the accuser on the proper words and etiquette for the curse.[7]

In the following case, the participants went before the elders to solve their dispute over an unpaid debt through a curse. Because the case involved witchcraft and diviners, the elders were a better choice than the state court system. The story, as it was told to me, is as follows:

Basso and Tarmo

One day, the mother of Basso fell ill. She was the sole surviving parent of Basso, as his father had died several years previously. Basso was the oldest son of his mother. The day that his mother fell ill, Basso went immediately to a diviner named Tarmo to ask him to divine the cause of his mother's illness to determine whether it was brought about by witchcraft, the earth spirits, or the ghosts. The diviner located the cause of the problem as the deceased first wife of Basso's father. In payment, Basso gave Tarmo a gourd of honey and promised him a sheep in exchange for a prescription for the ritual "medicine" to treat his mother. However, Tarmo demanded the sheep before he gave out the medicine, and Basso refused to pay him before the work was carried out.

When Tarmo realized that Basso would not pay him, he paid a visit to Qamara, the son of Basso's brother. Tarmo told Qamara that when he conducted his divination, he and Basso discovered that it was Qamara himself who was trying to kill Basso's mother through witchcraft.

Qamara was outraged and called a meeting of the elders and accused Basso of slander in suggesting that he was a witch. Basso responded that he had done nothing of the kind. He explained that he had gone to Tarmo, and Tarmo had told him that it was Qamara, the first wife of his father, who was causing the trouble, not Qamara, the son of his brother (some names are used for both males and females), and that Tarmo was clearly trying to cause trouble. The elders deliberated this case for five days. In the end, they decided that Basso and Tarmo should each say a curse and let *Looaa* decide the case.

So, Basso and Tarmo, together with a few elders expert in the procedure, went to an abandoned termite mound and took off their blankets and put them on again upside down and inside out. Then, Basso was told to say the following words, repeating them twice: "Oh *Looaa,* hear what I am saying. Take me before this year's harvest if truly I said that Qamara, the grandson of Baran (Basso's father), was a witch."

Then, Tarmo followed, saying, "Oh *Looaa,* if it is not true that I divined that Qamara, the grandson of Baran and not Qamara the first wife of Baran, was responsible for Basso's mother's illness, then let me not see the harvest of the coming year. If it is true that Basso did not pronounce the name of Qamara, grandson of Baran, as the source of his mother's illness, let me not eat the harvest of the coming year."

They then went about their lives, living in the same community but having entered into a state of *wakari.* Then, before the harvest of the new season, Tarmo died. Basso lived and eventually moved on to another village where he now lives with his family.

For Iraqw, the power of a curse is taken very seriously. They believe that when people fail to see justice brought about through their own efforts, the curse will eventually work for them. Young people, particularly Christians, are ambivalent about curses, which they have been told by the church are "primitive" and "pagan." Most young people will initially respond that they do not believe in curses but when pressed further almost all say they have indeed heard of curses among those they know. Cursing may not be employed when the option of going to court and obtaining a solution is available. Yet, in cases where debts have been handed down for several generations, or when a court case appears too expensive, many people still resort to a curse.

When I visited in 1993, *lo'o* was a frequent topic of conversation because of recent political developments. In an effort to make itself more competitive in the upcoming multiparty elections in 1995, the national political party—CCM—began to throw out corrupt and inefficient officials. In the ward of Kainam, the ward secretary and several others, who were not at all liked, were removed and replaced by more popular leaders, who were reputed to be clean of corruption. A common view in Kainam in 1993 was, "You see, *lo'o* finally got them." Because some of these former officials had greatly misused their authority (demanding bribes, stealing livestock, harassing women, and so on), it was said that many people had said *lo'o* and it had finally taken effect. One Iraqw man in his forties complained about these beliefs:

Iraqw would rather rely on *lo'o* to seek justice than to speak out directly against someone. *Lo'o* takes too long to work, and meanwhile we continue to get robbed and oppressed. Iraqw fear that if they speak out against someone openly, and that person (and thus indirectly his family) is punished, then he or she may say *lo'o,* and the person who spoke up will suffer. Iraqw think it's better to say *lo'o* and let *Looaa* decide whether her intervention is justified.

Another man told me that he used *lo'o* to resolve a case in which he had been accused of stealing. He claimed that he had been wrongly accused and asked a few elders to assist him in saying *lo'o.* With the elders present, he called his accusers (who he believed had set him up) to a meeting, explained that he was prepared to say a curse, and invited them to do likewise. Hearing this, his accusers immediately backed down and withdrew their accusation. I asked him why he had not chosen to go to court instead. He replied: "Going to court would take too long, and they could win the case if they bribed the judge. When a case can be won with a bribe, you can't count on the court for justice."

Slander is another matter more easily handled through a curse. Lying is strongly disapproved of because it sets off tensions that destroy the ideal of harmony and may erupt in violence. Elders said that in the precolonial era, liars (*lamussmoo* [sing.], *lamussee* [pl.]) were exiled or killed. In one case I was familiar with, a woman resorted to a curse in response to being accused of being a witch. Both the accused and her accusers were Catholics. Although the accusers dismissed the woman when she put a curse on them in retaliation, they did begin to use a different water source to distance themselves from the one that the woman had stood by when saying her curse.

Another case of cursing was brought to my attention while I was walking in the homeland with a friend who stopped on the path to talk with his father's sister. They talked for quite a long time, and then he joined me and explained that his family was caught up in a case of a curse that took place many years ago. Apparently, another sister of his father's had put a curse on his father's brother for an insult he had given her long ago. Apparently her brother had told her she was worthless because she had borne no children, and so, before she died, she uttered a curse on the man. Now his children had failed to have children, and they had discovered the curse. My friend's father's sister was on the way to a clan meeting to discuss the curse and how to remove it.

Cursing can also address very serious wrongs like murder. I was told of one instance in which an old man who had been a forest guard in the colonial era had killed a woman who was cutting wood in the forest. He had made a confession of his act while on his deathbed. Since his death, eight of his children had died, leaving two remaining. The consensus in the community was that the family of the dead woman had placed a curse on him, and procedures for removing a curse should be undergone. Another serious offense often handled by cursing is rape. One friend told me of a relative of his who was cursed by a woman who said he had raped her when she was young. Her curse resulted in his not having male children. After he and his wife had their third daughter, they sought the woman out to remove the curse. Obviously, rape is an offense difficult to discuss, and even more difficult for women to pursue in courts, so cursing provides some avenue for redress.

People will also take action to try and prevent a curse from being said. One elder told me his grandchild had hit a woman with a bicycle by accident. He was carrying a crate of soda on the back of the bike, so the impact was even greater than it normally would be. The woman was hospitalized for a week and then went home. Not long thereafter, she died, and many thought it was witchcraft that had caused her death. But the family of the young man who had knocked her down was very concerned that the deceased woman's family would put a curse on them. So, they negotiated compensation to the family, in the form of livestock, to prevent a curse from being said.

Curses are not irrevocable. If the person who has been cursed begins to suffer under the curse (through such misfortune as the death of his children), he may plead for mercy and forgiveness from the person who has cursed him. He first sends an elder as an emissary to plead his case. If someone has said a curse in secret, considerable investigation must be done to discover the source of the curse, as the following case attests.

Addressing the Wrongs of the Past

Akonaay Marmo had lost all eight of his male children. He traveled all over Mbulu and Babati Districts to search out the source of what a diviner had said was a curse. After months, it was established that certain of his relatives had cursed him, and he gathered together the parties involved. His lineage held a meeting to correct the situation. As he had lived in Matla (a neighborhood of Tsaayo) long ago together with the relatives who were responsible for the curse, he and they convened there. I was fortunate to be able to attend the proceedings.

The origin of the trouble began with Akonaay's grandfather, Matle' Kwaslema. Matle' Kwaslema had two sons: Ni/ima and Marmo. Following custom, Marmo, being the younger son, stayed with his parents to take care of them in their old age. Marmo had two wives. He and his wives lived in his parents' compound together with his two younger, unmarried sisters. One day, one of Marmo's sisters discovered that a piece of her skirt was missing. This caused some alarm in the household, as a theft of a personal item such as this quickly gives rise to the suspicion of witchcraft. Matle' went to a diviner and returned home, accusing one of Marmo's wives of witchcraft. He quickly banished both the wives from the compound and cursed them at the same time. Matle' lived to a very old age and saw no result of this curse in his lifetime. It finally began to take root in the life of Akonaay Marmo, the son of one of Marmo's wives.

Akonaay Marmo, Marmo's eldest son, had a bad temperament as a child, torturing and beating his brothers and sisters mercilessly. In revenge, his siblings cursed him (a rather unusual act by children and generally not approved of, as children are always getting into fights and disagreements with one other). In addition, Marmo's other wife cursed Akonaay's mother for slandering her as a witch. (After being expelled from the compound of Matle', the wives turned on one another and eventually it erupted into a curse.) As Akonaay was the only son who had married and had children, the full weight of the curse, from his grandfather to his siblings to the other wife of his father, all bore down upon him, causing him to lose all eight of his male children.

At the lineage meeting, Akonaay stood up to explain the trouble he had experienced and the lengths he had gone to appease his relatives and to rid himself of the curse. He begged their forgiveness and asked for their blessing. Shauri, the senior male lineage representative, encouraged all those present to forgive Akonaay and agree to release him from the curse. It was agreed that Akonaay's siblings would receive a goat for retracting their curses. After a consensus was reached, the participants left the meeting ground and proceeded to the grave of Akonaay's grandmother to begin removing the curse. Each relative of those who had originally uttered the curse said the following words:

> This curse, which was used by Bura against Ni/ima Da/ati, began the difficulty that we are here today to put right. Today, we will remove this curse. Let this curse end, let it stop its work of bringing death and misfortune to Akonaay. Because of this curse, Akonaay has lost all of his sons. Today, we say to this curse, "Stop this work of bringing death to Akonaay." Today, we will eat together and use new vessels [gourds used for serving food]. The branches and roots of the fig tree. We will eat together from new vessels, we will eat together with all the sons of Ni/ima Da/ati and Bura Gobre'. We will eat together and the curse will be at peace and stop bringing death. This curse of our mother Bura, stop at once your work. Do not bring death ever again.

After they had finished, all the participants and observers gathered to eat together. Akonaay negotiated with those who had been promised livestock about when he could deliver them. In addition, it was agreed that he would provide a drum of beer next year at the same time for all the participants to drink together. This would be the final gesture to wipe the slate clean and remove the curse once and for all.

This case brings to light many of the complexities of relationships in rural Tanzania. Tensions and conflicts between kin, between the sexes, and between the generations all emerge. Cursing shows how far people can stray from the ideal of harmony and how in doing so, they are believed to place their lives in jeopardy.

Cursing the Land

In 1998, I returned to the homeland and was told the story of a curse that a young man had put on his land. Apparently, the young man had left land fallow for a few years, as he was often away and out of the homeland altogether, sometimes working in the town of Mbulu and rumored to be cultivating land in the expansion areas to the west. The neighbors, whose land bordered his, went to the local village government and asked that the land be allocated to them, as they had need of more acreage. The local elders agreed to this reallocation. However, when the man returned to find others encroaching on his land, he went first to the village government to protest. He argued that the land was his to do with what he liked. He asked those who had been given allocations to get off the land, but they refused. The neighborhood elders attempted to intervene and reason with the man, but instead he grew more furious. His relatives in nearby areas backed up his claims and further incited him to action. In the end, the man resorted to cursing the land. The elders in the neighborhood claimed they had never seen a curse quite like this one and thought he must have obtained instructions for it from a Datoga expert. He performed a ritual for three days wearing only a goat skin and going to each boundary of his property muttering special curses. On the final day, he planted a spear on the border of his land and left the area, taking up residence in a village to the west of Mbulu. Since then, no one has encroached on the area, and elders doubt whether anyone would dare. Although the elders I spoke with agree that his curse was not just, they are still wary of treading on cursed land and in any case feel that if such enmity had developed, the land was better off avoided.

Iraqw believe strongly in the power of intention. Even though younger people and Christians may publicly proclaim disdain for such beliefs, if they feel that others harbor anger and resentment toward them, it is difficult for them to ignore it. As one Iraqw friend explained to me: "Whether or not you claim to believe in *lo'o*, if you know you have been cursed yourself, you will become uneasy, always thinking about whether or not it will work, about the bad deeds you may have done which have led someone to say a curse. As soon as you begin to think in this way, the curse will enter your life and begin its work." Even if curses are not said, older Iraqw believe that *Looaa* will see that justice is eventually done. So, when Iraqw feel that they have been abused by another, or taken advantage of, or wronged in any way, they reassure themselves with the belief that the wrongdoer will one day get his own back.

SUMMARY

Iraqw cosmology provides a blueprint for age, gender, and social relations within *aya* communities. Supernatural sanctions punish violations of moral codes that stress an individual's responsibility to the family and to the community. The goal of these moral codes is harmony within the community. The harmony promoted is one based on respect for age and gender differences and hierarchies. Cursing and feuds acknowledge that harmony is not always possible but ultimately should be restored. The cases described here show how complicated and strained relationships in rural communities can be. Conflicts, disagreements, and tensions emerge daily and threaten harmony.

A recurring feature in what are classed as traditional beliefs is the emphasis on elders' authority and their role in maintaining harmony. In theory, elders should be involved in approving curses and in recognizing and mediating cases of *wakari*. Yet, as we see from the numerous examples in this chapter, younger Iraqw often proceed on their own with such matters, bypassing the elders in their haste for retribution. Also, men and women use these beliefs and practices differently. For women, curses are ways in which they can seek justice for transgressions not easily taken to the government courts. For men, cursing concerns threats to the descendants and to their property. Curses are ways in which both men and women can circumvent the government and the more invasive aspects of modernity that threaten their access to resources.

Notes

1. *Kanga* are pieces of cloth with sayings and pictures on them that are worn around the waist and around the shoulders.

2. As Arens and Karp state, "in many African social systems . . . the exercise of political influence derives from access to and work upon the natural and supernatural spheres, both as the sources of power to control others and as the legitimization for actions" (1989:xvii).

3. Soul has also been translated by many as *fuqraangw* (Thornton 1980; Mous 1988). But all of my informants said *fuqraangw* is a person's intelligence, whereas *hinsla* means soul, or breath, which is equated with soul.

4. The ghosts who are of greatest importance are male, as mothers and grandmothers are not thought to demand respect to the degree that fathers and grandfathers do.

5. Rekdal (1996) describes the importance of sorghum beer for community unity in an Iraqw community to the south of the homeland.

6. See Hagborg (2001) for discussion of *wakari* and curses in Karatu. He argues that curses can be caused by court cases and their failure to adequately address the feelings of the litigants.

7. It is said that a curse will not work if the wrongdoer is not guilty of the offense for which he or she is cursed. Iraqw beliefs about the curse are similar to what Spencer describes among the neighboring Maasai:

> The belief in the power of the blessing and the curse is associated with legitimate authority, underpinning social order in Matapato. The belief in sorcery, on the other hand, expresses forces of chaos and evil that undermine this social order, and it is quite distinct from the curse. A curse is compared with arrow poison placed on the skin, which has no effect unless there is a cut; in other words, unless a wrong has been done (1988:219).

CHAPTER EIGHT

MEDIATING *MAENDELEO*

Divination, Witchcraft, and Christianity

At 4 A.M. one morning in 1995, I was awakened by a knock on my window shutter and insistent calls of "Hodi, hodi, Katerina." Unlike my previous years in the homeland when I had traveled by foot, I now had the benefit of a Suzuki jeep. I knew that a visit at that hour likely meant that someone was ill and wanted to be driven somewhere. I opened the door to see my neighbors Bura and Samti standing outside, their faces distorted with anxiety. Their one-year-old son was tied to Samti's back and soon began to vomit. They explained that he had fallen ill that night and was getting progressively worse. They wanted to go to the town of Mbulu, so I found the keys to my vehicle and got dressed. We climbed into the vehicle and began the descent from Irqwa Da'aw. About two kilometers down the dirt road, a small black animal leaped out in front of the vehicle and bounded in front of the headlights. I paused and asked Bura, who was sitting in the front seat next to me, what the animal was, as I had never seen it before in the years I had been in the area. He shrugged and looked nervous. Then, after another three kilometers, another of these animals leaped out in front of the headlights again. I was surprised and still puzzled about what animal it was. At this point, Bura and Samti exclaimed, "That's the same one!" I asked, "What do you mean the same one? The same *kind* of animal, right?" "No," Samti said, "not the same kind, the same *one*." At that point, though still very drowsy, I thought to ask why she believed it was the same one and she explained, "The witch sent that

123

animal to make us lose our way to Mbulu." I ruminated on this information and then asked, "So, we are going to Mbulu to go to the hospital, right?" Bura looked sheepish and said, "Well, no, we want to go to a diviner there." "Oh," I said, "but couldn't we have stayed in Irqwa Da'aw and seen a diviner there?" Bura responded, "Well, yes, but they are not nearly so powerful as this diviner. He comes from west of Mbulu and is said to be a great expert at curing witch-craft problems." "Who do you think bewitched your son, and why?" I asked. Samti spoke up from the back seat, "We have people in and out of our house every day. We sell a lot of beer. Sometimes our customers play with our son. I fear that one of them gave him something bad yesterday to bewitch him. People are very jealous these days. No one likes it when people work hard and get ahead. Many are envious of our *maendeleo*." For the past few years, Bura and Samti had been involved in the local beer-brewing business. They sold home-brewed beer in a building just neighboring their house. They also sold, and made a significant profit on, illegal grain alcohol. Their recent success in this business had begun to make them increasingly suspicious of others' be-havior and intentions.

As we neared Mbulu, I asked Bura, "Does the child have to be with you when you see the diviner?" He replied, "No, I don't think it's necessary." So, I suggested that he go to the diviner and Samti and I would go to Mbulu hospi-tal. They agreed, and I dropped Bura off near the path to the diviner's house, and Samti and I drove to the hospital.

Government hospitals in Tanzania are understaffed, often without med-ical supplies, and overcrowded. The hospital compound was in the dark when we arrived, and they would not have generator power until the morn-ing. One of the guards woke up a nurse who in turn woke up a doctor, who came out and looked at the child said: "He does not appear to be dehydrated, and we cannot do anything for him until the morning. In any case, we are out of supplies so I would recommend you go to one of the private clinics where they can test the child for diseases. They will also have medicine." So, Samti and I went back and waited in the vehicle for Bura to get back. Soon, Bura appeared, rushing to the car beaming with relief. He cried, "The diviner found out that it was indeed a witch, and he gave me this powder to give to my son to cure him!"

I was still clinging to a belief in Western medicine and suggested that in any case perhaps they could stay in Mbulu to go to one of the private clinics in the morning and get the child tested. They agreed, and I dropped them off at Samti's sister's house and drove back up the mountain.

The next evening Samti and Bura appeared at my house with their son. I invited them in and gave them tea and listened to their news. They did go to the clinic the next day and the child was tested for malaria, typhoid, cholera, and a host of other things, but all the results came out negative, and the clinic sent them home. Meanwhile, after having ingested some of the white powder prescribed by the diviner, the child had shown signs of quick recovery and was now laughing and playing quite happily.

Modernity, in the form of Western medicine in this case, is not able to address every situation. The state of medical facilities is such that consultations with the diviners remain an important strategy for combating illness. Western medicine, unlike divination, does not give those seeking assistance a sense of control over the frightening circumstances, or the supernatural factors such as witchcraft, that have led them to seek help. Diviners provide a reason for their illnesses and a remedy, giving those affected a sense of relief and a sense of control. Even those who always consult Western-trained medical personnel often seek the assistance of a diviner when bio-medicine fails. Bio-medicine, as has been pointed out by Kwiatkowski (1998) and Howard and Millard (1997), does not treat the social and political-economic causes of distress that people believe contribute to their illness.

Although most people believe in witchcraft and seek ways to protect themselves from it, witchcraft beliefs and faith in diviners are singled out by the Christian churches and government officials as factors that stand in the way of development. The attitude of the Catholic Church is exemplified in this sermon excerpt:

> Now, I have heard that people in this congregation have being going to consult with diviners! You all know that this behavior is sinful! As a Christian, you cannot walk down two paths at once!" the priest exclaimed as he walked down the aisle of the church, his legs straddling an imaginary line. "You cannot have one leg here on the path of Christianity and the other leg headed down the path of paganism and the ways of the devil.

The priest's speech reveals a fundamental struggle between the church and what they term "pagan" beliefs and practices. The attack on "pagan" ways was one I heard in nearly every church service I attended. The Catholic Church, however, is more tolerant of Iraqw traditions than the Pentecostal denominations, who in Karatu, Hagborg notes, are "explicit in their condemnation of traditional customs" (2001:160). The churches frame their attack on tradition in terms of morality and in terms of "progress." Conversion to Christianity is seen by many as an important step in *maendeleo*. Churches offer homeland converts a community that cuts across *aya* membership and descent-group affiliation. Membership in a Christian church confers a sense of belonging to a regional, national, and global—and therefore more modern—community. Since the colonial era, the church has been linked to the West and modernity in people's imaginations. It provides the tools, or the cultural capital, for engagement in modern or Western communities through both its teachings and the institutions it supports. Both the Catholic and Lutheran churches provide education and health facilities and have several of their own development projects.[1] The authority of Catholic priests comes not from the local communities but from the regional church authorities and, in the minds of local Catholics, from Rome.

The priest quoted above targeted diviners in his speech because they continue to have considerable power in Irqwa Da'aw, and their power is perceived as being in direct conflict with the church and its teachings. Diviners are also often opposed to the state and its policies as well. In the Iraqw homeland, diviners are key figures in the struggle over the meanings of tradition and modernity. Their authority, like that of the elders, rests on their knowledge of tradition and the past, together with the power to intervene between people and the supernatural. Although the Christian churches fight a vocal war against the diviners, even some of the priests are rumored to fear them. Interestingly, priests in the homeland resemble diviners in several ways: they communicate with the supernatural on behalf of the community and individuals, and they fight against the devil (who, like the earth spirits, lives "below"). For their service to the community, priests get free labor on the parish plots and a percentage of every household's harvest as a tithe (an obligation due to paramount diviners as well). Priests and diviners alike do not participate directly in political meetings or affairs of the community.

The discourse in the Iraqw homeland about Christianity, diviners, and witchcraft reflects wider concerns and struggles with social and economic change. Embedded in the stories about diviners withholding rain or witches striking out against local entrepreneurs are ideas about power, success, community responsibility, and globalization.

IRAQW DIVINERS: ADVOCATES OF TRADITION

Diviners have long been important, if often behind the scenes, in Iraqw political life. According to oral history, the Iraqw were led into Irqwa Da'aw by the diviner Haimu Tipe. It is diviners who prescribe the proper "medicine" to transform uncivilized bush into the cultural, habitable space that becomes an *aya* community. The Manda clan of paramount diviners who work on behalf of the *aya* and instruct the elders on community rituals have thus been crucial to Iraqw territorial expansion. It is said that the diviner Nade Bea arranged for Iraqw expansion into Maasai territory by providing the pioneers with special medicine to bless the new territory, bring it under Iraqw control, and protect them from Maasai attack. Nade Bea's actions coincided with the British administration's promotion of Iraqw expansion to the north and the development of the region.

There are a number of clans who claim the power to divine, but it is only the Manda clan (*Hay Manda doo Bayo*, or the Manda clan descended from Bayo) who divine on behalf of the *aya* community as a whole. They remain outside of the formal political organization, but this anomalous status allows them to affect local politics. Most Iraqw firmly believe in their abilities to affect the rains and to affect the health of the community. This specialized knowledge, mediating between the spirit and human worlds, in effect gives diviners considerable symbolic power over the economic sphere of Iraqw life, as they have power over the land's fertility. For older Iraqw, in particular, the paramount diviners remain the focus of much anxiety about the rains.

The power and influence of the Manda clan extend throughout Irqwa Da'aw and the whole of Iraqw territory. Although these diviners have the power to affect the rains, I would not call them rainmakers because they do not actually "make" rain through magical means. The Manda clan, as with most of the diviner clans, is not an "original" Iraqw clan but instead traces its origins to an Ihanzu man who wandered into Irqwa Da'aw long ago.[2]

In Murray, the first settlement of Irqwa Da'aw, the number of people from the Manda clan is quite high, as is the number of diviners. In the homeland, Murray has a reputation of being a very closed community with closely guarded secrets. In Murray, there are at least four or five shops, an unusually high number for such a small and remote community. In other equally remote areas, thieves have wiped out shops in a single night, and thus many would-be shopkeepers are reluctant to start these small enterprises. In Murray, however, people claimed that the diviners had put protective medicine around each of these shops, and no thief dared to steal from them. As Murray is seen as a stronghold of Manda clan diviners, homeland residents also consider it the most traditional *aya*. This perception is furthered by its physical remoteness. In 2001, the village government proposed to build a new primary school on Manda clan land in Murray, but the villagers, fearing the wrath of these diviners, quickly rejected this idea and selected another site.

The belief in the power of the Manda clan of diviners is widespread. One ward official, it was rumored, had been made sick and finally run out of the ward because he had somehow offended them. The new official assigned to replace him was so anxious about being harmed by diviners that he initially took up residence in the Catholic parish, where he felt that his water and food would be safe from interference. His choice of the parish suggests the perception that the Church is somehow capable of using its own supernatural clout to combat that of the diviners. Later, when he felt that the threat had lessened, he moved into government housing.

In compensation for protection of the *aya*, the Manda clan diviners receive livestock, a portion of the harvest of the households of the *aya*, and labor on their farms. Iraqw elders stress that this is not payment but a gift of appreciation. To claim that it is payment rather than a gift of thanks would demean the diviners' actions. Diviners are acting selflessly for the good of the community through communication with the benevolent *Looaa*. If a payment is given, the action becomes one of profit seeking. However, the younger generation, particularly Christians and the educated elite, often do not agree with this distinction and state that not only are diviners paid but they demand considerable compensation. The Catholic Church, of course, demands similar "compensation" from its parishioners.

Diviners from the Manda clan have always occupied a significant role in Iraqw society. Nade Bea, the most famous and powerful Manda clan diviner, played an important role in politics throughout the British colonial period. Although he occupied no official position, the colonial authorities consulted him when appointing the Native Authority chiefs. When Chief Mikael Ahho died in 1939, Nade Bea put forward a member of his own clan, Gwassal Nade, as successor. The regional government was not in favor of this selection, but the elders and the district officer supported Gwassal. The District Book (MF/13) reports that the elders supported Gwassal because they wanted to (1) return to the "ruling" family; (2) get a man of substance and position; (3) get a non-Christian; and (4) appoint an elder as opposed to a younger man. They had suffered under Mikael Ahho (a Catholic), who had put an end to female initiation and had been firmly against tradition as an impediment to "progress." In the view of the elders, a member of the Manda clan, and specifically a non-Christian, would be more likely to support Iraqw tradition, particularly as this tradition clearly served the interests of the Manda clan. Gwassal, however, did not remain in office long. He was forced to resign by the British administration in 1942 after it was discovered that he was helping Iraqw men avoid conscription for the war. Elias Sarawat, a Catholic who had been a sub-chief in Kainam under Mikael Ahho, replaced Gwassal. Although Sarawat was a Christian, Nade Bea supported him because Elias showed him considerable deference and visited him frequently to consult him on various matters. He did not present himself as opposed to the elders' beliefs and practices in the way that Mikael Ahho had.

The British recognition of Nade Bea enhanced his power and prestige. Stories of his cleverness and power abound. Iraqw say that even colonial farmers sought him out to ask his help in bringing the rains. One story describes Nade Bea's vengeance when slighted:

The district officer and Chief Sarawat invited Nade to accompany them on a visit to a colonial farmer below the Rift Wall. Nade agreed, and the three of them set off from Mbulu, arriving at the farmer's house in the early afternoon. When they arrived, the farmer came out to greet them but took an immediate dislike to Nade. He said he looked like a baboon and refused to let him in his house (Nade was said to have very frightening and fierce eyes). So, Chief Sarawat, apologizing, explained the situation to Nade, who remained in the Land Rover. On the return journey to Mbulu, the district officer and Chief Sarawat apologized profusely to Nade, who sat silently in the back. When Nade arrived home, he sent one of his sons, with some medicine he had prepared, to return to the farmer's land and apply it to his fields and around his house. Soon thereafter, baboons began invading the farmer's fields, but he told his field hands to leave them alone. The farmer began taking his wife and family on long trips into the bush and grew increasingly obsessed with living in the bush, and, Iraqw claim, began acting like a baboon. After some time, he gave up his farm and returned to Europe. When he left, Nade instructed Iraqw to move quickly and take over his lands for their own farms.

Diviners are able to identify the cause of problems using the power, skill, and inspiration they get from *Looaa*. Thus, the source of their power is a benevolent one, and their work is supposed to be directed toward the positive goal of helping individuals and the entire *aya* community. However, diviners may also turn their power against a community or individual if they perceive that they have been wronged in some way. There are many stories of Manda clan diviners turning their power against a person because they felt that they had been insulted. These stories are told not only by elders but by younger Christians as well. A young Catholic man told me the following story of a Manda clan diviner from Murray:

A Manda clan diviner from Murray came into Mbulu to attend a cattle auction several years ago. On the path outside of the auction grounds, several older women were selling beer. The diviner asked one old woman to give him some beer. She refused to give it to him without payment and began mocking him and complaining that diviners were always taking advantage of people. He replied, angrily, that she "would see him again." Soon thereafter, a pack of hyenas swept through the area and went straight for the woman and mauled her. Her arm was mangled, but she lived.

During my residence in the homeland, there were frequent rumors that Manda clan diviners were sending leopards to attack people or that they were interfering with the rains. Local opinions about what had provoked the diviners ranged from the theory that they were not getting enough respect from community members to the fact that the community had debts lingering from the past.

While the diviners' work is directed primarily at combating the mischief of the earth spirits and the danger of witchcraft, they are also called upon for more practical assistance. They make up specific "medicines" to help a farmer protect his crops from insects and wild animals or to aid clients in making the object of their affections fall in love with them. Each clan of diviners has their own specialty.

The extreme secrecy of diviners has two purposes: to evade disapproving government and church officials and to protect their power from potential competitors. As one man explained: "They don't want anyone to know how they work because they fear the competition. There are many fakes today who pass themselves off as diviners, claiming they bought their power from one of the diviner clans." However, fakes, he claimed, are eventually discovered because they are unable to cure people, or their forecasts are proven wrong. Once they start making mistakes, word travels through the community, and they will no longer attract clients.

Diviners do not participate in the affairs of the elders and never attend meetings or the ceremonies held for the *aya*. They do attend weddings and other public celebrations and often frequent the local bars, where they are given a seat of respect in addition to a great deal of free beer. Their attendance at the bars also provides an opportunity for obtaining clients. Often, someone who has some trouble or worry will coax a diviner out from the crowd inside the bar and ask him for assistance. The diviner accompanies the client outside and proceeds to divine his or her problem and prescribe a solution. He is paid on the spot and returns inside to continue drinking.

Gossip inside the bar can provide the diviner with much information that can assist him with his clients. For these reasons, it is understandable why the diviners have been some of the strongest opponents to the government's attempt to close down or limit the working hours of the bars. They stand to lose a convenient and profitable site for their work. Diviners' resistance to government control of the bars has encouraged elders and juniors alike to oppose bar restrictions. This opposition proves a major headache for local government officials who try to regulate the hours of the bar operations, arguing that young men who should be working are getting drunk in the morning and failing to go to the fields at all.

Many people, young and old, and men and women, when asked what causes _maendeleo_ to falter, complain that drinking home-brewed beer *(pombe)* and hard grain alcohol *(piwa)* is one of the biggest social problems. The economic, social, and health effects of this habit are widespread. More of the farmwork ends up falling on the backs of women and children, and it is hard for many households to achieve food security and to pay for the necessities of life such as school fees, medical costs, clothes, and other needs.

In Irqwa Da'aw, diviners' opinions can be very influential. Both schoolteachers and government officials complained to me that if the diviners opposed something, it was as good as defeated. One government official's strategy was to convince a few important diviners of a particular policy (such as contribution of maize for school lunches), as well as the leader of the eld-ers' council, and hope that they would persuade others, or at the very least, that they would not oppose the plan. Thus, diviners and traditional leaders become, in effect, power brokers, mediating between the local citizens and the government.

In Chapter 2, I discussed the elders' and diviners' opposition to building a new road connecting Kuta, the most remote *aya* of Irqwa Da'aw, to the Rift Valley below. Their objection centered on the fear that Irqwa Da'aw would be invaded by *hoomo* (outsiders). The in-migration of outsiders represents a very real threat to the diviners' authority. Outsiders are less likely to use the diviners' services or to be as fearful of their power. In addition, roads might open competition for diviners' services, as people can more easily travel out of the area and consult with "foreign" diviners. Rekdal (1999) observed a preference for the services of diviners from other ethnic groups. Indeed, the Manda clan was founded by an Ihanzu immigrant from the west of the homeland, and the outside power that he brought was considered more pow-erful than that of local diviners. Elders and diviners are natural allies, as each group supports the power and authority of the other.

Although diviners rarely parlay their authority into positions as govern-ment officials, members of their clan do obtain such positions. In Tsaayo, one diviner of the Sule clan was much respected as well as feared. He would be in-vited to all neighborhood celebrations (such as weddings, farewell parties for men who were going off to study elsewhere, and so on). He was shown special respect at these gatherings by being one of the first guests to be given beer. Everyone referred to this diviner jokingly (in a telling parallel) as the resident "bishop" (*askofu*). Although he had no position in the local government, the son of his father's brother did serve as the chairman of the local neighbor-hood. Often, not diviners but members of their clan occupy many of the posi-tions of power (for example, district commissioner, member of Parliament). Although this may in part be coincidence, it may also reflect the Iraqw attitude of respect and fear toward diviners and, in turn, their clansmen. Also, diviners have greater resources (particularly cattle) and are thus in a better position to assist their relatives in education or entrepreneurial activities.

During a visit I made to Irqwa Da'aw in July 2000, Mbulu District was gearing up for the election in October. The member of Parliament was facing competition within CCM for his seat. Many Iraqw, in both Mbulu and the homeland, gossiped that the MP was seeking aid from his Manda clan divin-ers to ward off the threat posed by his rival. Rumor had it that he filled his Landcruiser with Manda diviners and drove around the district campaigning for his seat. The "truth" of these rumors is not the point but rather the per-ception that even those as modern and well educated as the MP will seek out diviners' aid.

I received a letter from Mbulu in December 2000 describing the election results for that year. The writer went into some detail about how the Manda clan had fallen in line behind their clanmate and vocally supported his candidacy in the 2000 election. In addition, diviners may be hired by candidates to apply medicine to make their opponent fail. One candidate, who worked in an administrative position in the Catholic diocese, competed as a representative from an opposition party for a local seat. He told me that his opponent had hired diviners to place medicine at key points around town to prevent people from voting for him. With a laugh, he explained, "They even put medicine around the church to keep people from voting for me."

As is evident, the power of diviners is highly ambiguous. Theoretically, they are supposed to use their abilities for the benefit of individuals and the entire community. Yet, diviners do turn their power against people and can interfere with the welfare of the whole *aya*. After hearing stories of the diviners' misuse of their power, I asked several elders if the diviners were not in fact the same as witches or sorcerers. None agreed with this suggestion, as they stressed that the magical power that diviners use *(qwaslari'ima)* is not the same as witchcraft *(da'ari)*, in that diviners obtain their power from *Looaa*, a source of good, whereas witches get their power from the earth spirits. Younger Christian Iraqw were less likely to make these distinctions, and often said diviners were doing "the work of the devil."

Today, many diviners have been quick to seek out a new niche for themselves in the ever-changing political-economic environment. A common belief in the area, and throughout Tanzania, is that no one gets rich on his own merit. It is often believed that anyone who has amassed enough capital to invest in a business, and who has become successful, has done so through supernatural means.[3] In the case of the most successful shop owners and businessmen in the district, the common story is that they achieved their success by obtaining powerful medicines, usually from <u>waganga</u> outside of the district, most commonly to the west of Mbulu District. Rumors abound that they had cut off their fingers or toes as payment, or had killed one of their children or relatives or made them go crazy as payment for the powerful medicines. Obviously, this behavior is an inversion of proper behavior and sentiment and illustrates the danger and evil of extreme self-interest. There is definitely a theme revolving around the idea of limited goods running throughout these stories. In other words, if some people become wealthy, others must pay. Resources are limited, and if one person amasses them, others will lose something—a finger, their minds, and so on—to pay the price.[4]

The line between sorcery and divination in these stories of personal success is a blurred one. Some informants would switch back and forth, using the terms *(<u>mganga</u>, <u>mchawi</u>; qwaslarmo, da/alusamo)* for either of these practices, yet most stuck to the term for diviner. I never heard of an Iraqw diviner having the ability to assist someone in getting rich. Rather, only diviners from other ethnic groups in the region seemed to possess this skill.

After meeting a prosperous businessman in one of the villages outside of the homeland, I was told the history behind his success. The story began with his parents. Apparently, eager for financial success, they journeyed west to Sukumaland to seek out the aid of a diviner there. This diviner told them to return home and on the path they would encounter some food that they should eat a bit of. This food would give them the power to succeed in any endeavor. On the way home, the couple came across a dead and rotting hyena on the path. The wife suggested that they cut some meat off of the carcass and eat a bit of it. The husband refused, saying that there was no way a hyena could be considered food. But the wife ripped a piece off and ate it anyway, and upon her return, everything she did reaped great success. Now, she owns a car and has built a "modern" house. Her son owns several lorries, a Toyota Landcruiser, and some shops. All the elements of this story are more usually linked with witchcraft—the hyena, eating food along a pathway, and so on. Yet, in this and many stories, the term for diviner (*mganga* [sing.], *waganga* [pl.]) was used rather than witch. Although these diviners may employ techniques associated with witches, they are still acting to assist their clients, not only themselves. Witches seek to cause only harm.

The fact that Iraqw still frequently describe diviners as capable of harm as well as good reveals the ambiguity that supernatural power has in their belief system. Clearly, power can be used both for individual and community benefit but can also quickly turn around in the opposite direction and be used for harm or for selfish gain. There is no ambiguity about witchcraft, however, which is always viewed as a negative, antisocial, and selfish practice.

WITCHCRAFT

Ready your ears
Here we have a thing
A mother of a child who does not like the children of
  other people or even cattle
Her fertility and her house, let it be lost like the horn
  of a dog
Yes, like the horn of a donkey
And if it is an old woman who does not love children,
or the cows of other people,
let her fall from the roof head first
And if it is an old man,
let him be left behind by his grandchildren while
  tending the livestock

Yes, and let him be abandoned by his grandchildren
and let the white ants play atop his head
and let the jackal steal his stave
If it is a young man who does not love the cattle or
   children of other people
let his cries come from the west
let the stave of another man take him down in combat
Evil, pass far from us

In a conversation about witchcraft one evening, a friend remarked to me on the habit of witches flying through the night on the backs of hyenas: "You know a witch can travel as far as Dar es Salaam and back in the night in a matter of hours. They can fly faster than airplanes." He then paused, laughed, and said: "If there are people here who can accomplish such amazing feats, better than Western science even to travel this fast, you'd think that we would have more *maendeleo* here. I mean we don't even have roads to travel or electricity. But these witches have powers that surpass even *wazungu*! Why don't we have more *maendeleo* here?!"

In 2002, in many of my interviews, witchcraft came up as a major factor in thwarting or stalling development. As one man said: "Witchcraft is the main reason why there is so little *maendeleo* in Irqwa Da'aw. People say there is no point in getting ahead because a witch will just become jealous of your good fortune, bewitch you, and make your life worse than before. So, why bother to struggle to build a better house or have more possessions."

Whereas diviners obtain their power from a benevolent *Looaa*, witches get theirs from the meddlesome earth spirits. Much of the diviners' work in the homeland is directed toward preventing or turning away witchcraft. In previous studies of the Iraqw, most authors have remarked on the low profile that witchcraft has in Iraqw lives. In his experience in the 1970s, Thornton stated that "one must note that witchcraft is very rare" among the Iraqw (1980:7). However, in my research, I found it to be a frequent topic of discussion, and several deaths in the community, as well as illnesses, were attributed to witchcraft.[5] Elders claim that there has been an increase in witchcraft since the colonial era, when a law against killing witches was put into effect. In the precolonial era, a witch was driven from the community or burned, together with his or her family, inside their house. Certainly, since the colonial era there has been greater social and economic differentiation among households, which many claim has led to greater jealousy. Social status and identity is measured in part by modern material possessions such as cooking utensils, chairs, tables, clothes, radios, and so on. Many of the people who complained about witchcraft were those who had these belongings. Those people who do succeed and achieve the goods of the modern prestige sphere are reluctant to live in Irqwa Da'aw for fear of witchcraft. Thus, witchcraft is at the center of conflicts about modernity. Most of those who engage in the wider economy and manage to get ahead have a nagging uneasiness about witchcraft. They may fear witchcraft from jealous neighbors, friends, and others in the community, and they are also themselves sometimes suspected of being witches or of having purchased powerful "medicine" from diviners.

During the time that I did my initial fieldwork, there was a mysterious witchcraft case unraveling in Kilimanjaro District, in which a witch was killing young women, exhuming their bodies, and turning them into zombie laborers who worked for her in a nearby forest. This case went on for months and was reported on frequently in the newspapers and occasionally on Radio Tanzania. News of it reached the homeland and provided considerable entertainment and speculation. Witchcraft accounts continue to be prevalent in Tanzanian newspapers and radio, with Shinyanga and southern Tanzania being featured in more recent reports. In the summer of 2000, there were regular stories in the newspapers about witch killings and the traffic in human skins over the border with Malawi and Zambia. Thus, local imaginations about the veracity and possibilities of witchcraft are fueled by national news.

Witchcraft beliefs among the Iraqw share many similarities with those throughout sub-Saharan Africa. In many of these societies, witches are believed to be active at night. In the dark of night, they venture to rivers or caves in mountains to communicate with the earth spirits to seek their assistance in harming others and in protecting them from the diviners. The Iraqw use one word for these evil practices—*da/ari*—and another name for the practitioners—*daa/aluusmoo* (sing.), *daa/aluusee* (pl.). Witchcraft among the Iraqw is always intentional and premeditated. Both men and women may be witches, but there is a greater incidence, Iraqw believe, of witchcraft among women. Women are believed to be more prone to the emotions of jealousy and envy that lead to witchcraft. Given that women's recourse to nonsupernatural power is rather limited, perhaps it is not hard to understand why Iraqw may think women are particularly prone to witchcraft. Their ability to achieve status, prestige, and economic standing is far more constrained than men's, thus their frustrations may be greater.

Witchcraft is believed to be inherited through the *daa'awi*, but some Iraqw believe that one can purchase the power. If one member of the *daa'awi* is believed to be a witch, it is assumed that all the members are witches. If a woman is reputed to be a witch, her daughters are also certain to be witches. This belief can make it very difficult for the daughters of suspected witches to find suitors, much less husbands. In some instances, usually among Christians, a reputation for witchcraft is sometimes ignored. The Catholic Church takes an uncertain stand on witchcraft. On the one hand, the stated public policy is that it does not exist and furthermore is a backward belief. However, one priest in Irqwa Da'aw took witchcraft very seriously and, it was rumored, even feared that he had become a target of it after his vehicle suffered several accidents.

In one local witchcraft case, the accused family was Catholic, and the church became involved in trying to rectify the situation and make peace. First, the mother, a woman in her late forties and widowed for several years, was accused of killing the young child of a neighbor by giving him poison in a banana. At the burial of the child, her guilt was assumed when the woman did not look the grieving mother in the face. Doctors attributed the cause of death to meningitis, but elders nonetheless were called to mediate the accusation of witchcraft. The grieving mother wanted to brew honey beer and share it with the accused witch, who would then spit out the beer over the grave of the child, thereby proving her innocence. The accused agreed, but the child's father refused to go ahead with this procedure, as he felt it was improper for Christians (all involved were Catholics) to follow a "pagan" procedure. Instead, he wanted to take the case before the church authorities.

Iraqw are reluctant to accuse someone openly of being a witch, because to charge someone wrongly can result in being cursed by the person accused. However, younger Iraqw, particularly Christians, are less familiar with and more skeptical of curses and thus are more likely to be bolder in their accusations.

Awaki's Tragedy

In one case I witnessed, a witchcraft accusation was made, and the young woman who was accused promptly put a curse on her accuser. All the protagonists in this case were Catholics. The history of the antagonism went back several years and escalated when Awaki, a young woman of around twenty-five, lost two children, one through miscarriage and one in stillbirth. Throughout her childhood and until the time of her marriage, she had been close friends with Bo/i, her neighbor. When Awaki began to be courted by her husband, her relationship with Bo/i began to deteriorate. At Awaki's wedding celebration, there was a minor disagreement over some beer that had been brewed by Bo/i's family for the occasion, the payment for which had never been decided upon.

After the loss of Awaki's second child, she and her husband visited a diviner, who attributed her misfortune to witchcraft. After this pronouncement, Awaki began to assign blame to two women. One had lived with Awaki and her husband, Lohay, while they were boarding at a nearby house that took in women and couples who had become pregnant outside of wedlock (Awaki and her husband were married after she became pregnant). The suspected woman was unmarried and had lost a child. Awaki assumed the woman was jealous of her pregnancy and had therefore caused her to miscarry. Soon after she told me about this woman, Awaki began to shift her suspicions to her childhood friend. She began to remember things Bo/i had said to her when she had first announced her pregnancy and impending marriage. She now interpreted these remarks as signs of jealousy and became convinced that Bo/i was responsible for her loss. She began to mention her beliefs to friends and relatives, and finally it got back to Bo/i herself, who was outraged. The situation worsened as Lohay became involved and made public statements that Bo/i's mother and indeed her *daa'awi* all were witches. This crisis escalated, as now all members of Bo/i's *daa'awi,* both male and female, felt that their reputations were being attacked.

Bo/i herself felt deeply wronged. She resorted to cursing Awaki and Lohay at the river where the couple collected their water. Awaki and her husband saw Bo/i at the river and carefully avoided this water source from then on. Yet, they remarked defiantly that the curse would not work, as they were certain they were right about the young woman's guilt. Awaki did go on, two years later, to deliver a healthy son. In 2002, however, I learned that Awaki had separated from Lohay and that Lohay and his new wife were raising Awaki's son. Awaki had also fallen on hard times, having gotten involved in the illegal brewing of hard alcohol. She had been arrested a few times, and when I saw her last I barely recognized her, as she was quite ill and troubled.

Young women like Awaki, who have suffered a miscarriage or have otherwise lost a child, are particularly desperate to find a cause for their misfortune. Their worth as women is measured primarily in their ability to produce children.[6] Thus, they are likely to suspect other women, particularly those without children or those who are unmarried, of jealousy.

To pronounce someone a witch is a very serious matter, both for the accuser and the accused. Although accused or "confirmed" witches are no longer burned along with their families, as they were reported to be in the precolonial era, they may be ostracized or avoided, and to be accused of being a witch can result in a young woman's never marrying. Should a young man fall in love with her and want to marry her, he will meet with very powerful and adamant objections to the union by his relatives. Several of the young women I knew, whose reputations had been in some way tainted by the suspicion of witchcraft, were unmarried and had no likely prospects, even though they were at the age when most young women have either married or have a string of suitors.

The jealousy that is the seedbed of witchcraft targets fertility and outward symbols of economic success, such as livestock, a successful harvest, and material goods. Most of the witchcraft cases that I was told about concerned the deaths of young children or miscarriages. The fear of witchcraft leads expectant mothers to be quite secretive about their pregnancy. There is no joyous announcement of the impending birth, and indeed, often the pregnancy can be successfully hidden for a long time, as women normally wear loose clothes and wrap themselves in _kanga_ or cloaks.

Once a child is born, women are careful to cover their breasts while nursing in a public setting for fear that their milk will be poisoned by the gaze of a witch. If a child begins to throw up regularly after nursing, it is assumed that a witch has harmed the mother's milk. When children are old enough to play with their neighbors and to run about the neighborhood, they are cautioned against eating at other people's houses or accepting food from anyone outside of the family.

Just as women and children are considered more vulnerable to the earth spirits than men, so are they to witchcraft. One man told me that his father, fearing witchcraft when he and his siblings were young children, kept his mother and siblings in virtual isolation from others by handling all matters involving the world outside the household himself. Paying careful attention to one's belongings is another precaution against witchcraft. Iraqw very rarely leave their things lying out. If clothes are left to dry outside, they are brought in at night. In part, they are attentive to their things for reasons of theft, but witchcraft is also a factor. One young man, in addition to being a schoolteacher, was a very hardworking and successful farmer. He was the object of some envy from both his fellow schoolteachers and others in the village and thus was a likely target for witchcraft. After missing a pair of shorts he had put in the sun to dry after washing, he became anxious that a witch might have taken them. He was also careful to eat inside his house with the curtain drawn to avoid being bewitched by the evil eye of a witch who might be nearby.

I myself was cautioned to be careful about my belongings and about eating where people could see me. One friend was forever coming to my door with my soap, which I had left in the bathing stall, saying: "You left this outside again. Someone could disturb it. You really should bring it inside after you bathe." He also cautioned me against my habit of sitting in the open doorway in the sun where I liked to drink my tea. I had assumed that, being an _mzungu_, I would somehow be exempt from witchcraft, but after living in the community for some time, friends began to have some suspicions that I was not immune, particularly after I came down with a few sudden and mysterious fevers.

Witches will attempt to bewitch others by leaving food on the paths and hoping someone will make the mistake of taking it. On my weekly trek to the town of Mbulu for supplies, I once came across an egg in the middle of the path. The friends I was walking with told me not to touch it, explaining that it might have been left there by a witch. That evening, as I returned on the path, the egg was still there.

In the same way that precautions are taken to avoid witchcraft, people behave in certain ways to avoid being accused of witchcraft. For example, if one passes a herd of cows or other livestock on a narrow path, one avoids contact with the animals. I once made the mistake of reaching out to fend off a cow on the path that was headed right into me and was reprimanded soon after by the woman with whom I had been walking. She explained, "If that cow gets sick tomorrow, the owner will think you used witchcraft against it to make it sick." Also, if guests arrive, meals should be eaten together from a common plate, and an even number of cups of tea should be served to them.[7] Throughout Tanzania, if you order a bottle of soda or beer, it will be brought to you and opened in front of you as an indication that no poison has been put in it.

Witches are believed to be people who know their victims, and in many instances, it is neighbors who are the first suspects. Witchcraft beliefs expose tensions and rifts in Iraqw society that undermine the idea or achievement of a harmonious *aya*. In ritual prayers, such as the one cited at the beginning of this section, witches are a chief preoccupation, and the elders pray to *Looaa* to rid them of these evil people in their midst.

As noted earlier, successful people, either those with many children or those who are economically prosperous, are aware that they may be targets for witchcraft. This awareness, although present, was not a constant preoccupation among the people I knew, but it did make them wary of those who were openly resentful of them. One woman, who had ten children, one of the few sheet-metal roofs in the area, as well as larger landholdings, fruit trees, four cows, and a pig, was convinced that one of her pigs had been bewitched (through poison) and killed by a jealous neighbor. Witchcraft looms as an ever-present possible check on anyone's success. Although witchcraft is not a constant preoccupation, entrepreneurial individuals will often assume that it is the source of any sudden illness that might befall them.

THE IMPACT OF CHRISTIANITY

Christianity first entered the Iraqw homeland in the late nineteenth century with the arrival of the Germans. Since that time, the most powerful religion in Mbulu District has been Catholicism. The Lutheran Church has made inroads in the southern and western parts of the district, but the Catholic Church has the greatest numbers of adherents in Irqwa Da'aw. Several evangelical churches have also established churches in the district. In a survey of 150 households conducted in 1994, 51.6 percent of the population were non-Christian, and

48.4 percent were Christian (43.7 percent Catholic, 2.4 percent Pentecostal, 1.8 percent Lutheran, and 0.5 percent Church of God). Most of the households (88.7 percent) had a combination of Christian and non-Christian members. The majority of Christians were individuals under forty years of age, and non-Christians were over forty. Although Thornton (1980) barely mentions the Christian community in his research in the homeland in the mid-1970s, it is most definitely a significant presence in Iraqw communities today. Although figures on conversion were not available to me, it appears from my survey that conversion to Christianity has gained considerable ground in the past twenty years, as the majority of people over fifty claimed they are not Christians.

The Catholic Church, together with the state, promotes a particular vision of *maendeleo* and modernity. In some ways, for many in Mbulu, the Church and state appear intimately linked. The Church is very wealthy and owns schools (which charge tuition), land, petrol stations, guest houses, stores, and other economic enterprises. Government officials of all ranks are often Catholics. The Mbulu diocese collaborates with the government to seek donors and is currently responsible for many of the water and road projects in the area. The district commissioner, members of Parliament, and other local officials meet with the bishop to plan strategies for development and fund-raising. Thus, the separation of church and state is not always easy for the average citizen to distinguish and in the minds of many Iraqw, becoming a Christian, and particularly a Catholic, is to join a community and network of powerful and prestigious people. One close friend of mine began going to the Catholic Church when he was about ten years old. I asked him what led him to this decision, and he explained that it seemed like the modern thing to do and that other children from school talked about going.[8]

Among the younger generation, Christianity serves as an important challenge to the authority of the elders. The Catholic Church and other Christian religions view traditional Iraqw religion as opposed to the public good. This ideology cannot be separated from that of the colonial era or the current ideology of the Tanzanian state, which views precolonial religious beliefs and practices as being opposed to modern thinking and behavior. One young man explained to me that he joined the Catholic Church because, in part, he thought it would free him of many of the restraints and problems of tradition (*mila*), particularly fear of witchcraft and dependence on diviners. Yet, as I have shown, it is often precisely this group of younger, educated, Christian Iraqw who fear witchcraft or visit diviners in times of trouble. What Christianity in effect promotes is, as Howard and Millard noted in their study of the Kilimanjaro area, "individual spiritual salvation over fulfillment of the obligations of community life" (1997:66), particularly if those obligations are of a "traditional" or "pagan" nature. Faced with the request for livestock for rituals or pressure from grandparents to conform to pollution beliefs, individuals can draw on Christian values and rhetoric to reject these "pagan" practices.

Navigating Worlds

Despite younger Christian Iraqw's frequent and public denial of precolonial beliefs and practices, and their denigration of these beliefs as "pagan," this chapter has tried to demonstrate that even Christians do not completely abandon all the beliefs and practices of the past. Many of these practices still have resonance in the environment in which Iraqw find themselves today. In fact, some practices labeled traditional are gaining new salience, as these rural communities are increasingly integrated into wider political-economic frameworks. Yet, it is also very clear that these features of Iraqw culture are constantly undergoing change, as Iraqw seek new methods and new strategies to address some of the problems and choices they confront. What Feierman has noted about discourse holds true for beliefs and practices loosely termed traditional: "Even when forms of discourse are inherited from the past, the peasant must make an active decision to say they are meaningful at this moment, to select a particular form of discourse as opposed to other possible forms, and to shape the inherited language anew to explain current problems" (1990:3). For now, diviners, witches, and the Christian churches remain key players in the struggles and interpretations of tradition, modernity, and development in homeland communities.

Notes

1. See Green 1995 and 2003 for more on the Catholic Church and development in Tanzania.

2. Fosbrooke states that he appeared "two or three generations after the Iraqw had established themselves in Murai" (1955:62). For greater discussion of the Manda clan origins, see Thornton (1980:215–217).

3. See, for example, Geshiere 1997; Sanders 1999.

4. In her discussion of a "global witch-city" in Sierra Leone, Shaw reports that people are clear about "what constitutes payment for this privileged access—the lives and wealth of others, misappropriated from an everyday African world" (1997:869). Clearly, as Lambek has observed in Madagascar, the discourse on sorcery is a "critique of power and the powerful" (1993:241).

5. Thornton also worked in Irqwa Da'aw, in the *aya* neighboring the one in which I resided. Thus, the difference of view is probably not attributable to locality but rather to time and other factors.

6. The Iraqw have a saying—"*hhoohhaarta' /aamena' na/aay*," or "the beauty of a woman is children."

7. The Samburu have similar ideas about odd and even numbers. Fratkin states: "Even numbers represent the moral order of human society, where humans engage the blessings and protection of *Nkai* the creator. Odd numbers represent supernatural power outside the moral order, particularly those forces used to harm someone" (1991:326).

8. As Beidelman has observed, "for most Africans conversion to Christianity is associated with securing access to modern skill and superior status" (1982:12).

CHAPTER NINE

POLLUTION AND RITUAL

Making and Reinforcing Boundaries

A s I sat outside in the warm sun one day, shucking corn with an older woman in her sixties, she told me of the time she lost a son when he was about nine months old, and she had to go into quarantine because of the ritual pollution caused by his death:

My husband was away studying agriculture in Mwanza (in western Tanzania), and I lived in *meetaa* together with my other children. No one visited my home. If friends or relatives passed near the house, they would sit at a "safe" distance away and would turn their heads away from me while speaking to me. It was very difficult. I lived like this for three years, until my husband returned from his studies and we were able to have another child.

Many Tanzanians, especially government and church officials, see Iraqw pollution beliefs and practices *(meetaa)* as indicators of Iraqw conservativeness and lack of interest in progress.[1] Iraqw from expansion areas such as Karatu in the north, and even in the town of Mbulu, view *meetaa* as a mainstay of life in the homeland. In Karatu, one young man expressed this rather common perception: "Those people in Irqwa Da'aw are very backward. They still believe in *meetaa* and are very wary and suspicious of outsiders there.

You will have a hard time living there." I have heard similar views expressed throughout the expansion areas regarding homeland residents. Most people seem to assume that Irqwa Da'aw is the seat of pollution beliefs. While residents of expansion areas may use this perception as a way of asserting their own modernity, there are Iraqw in these regions as well who still follow these beliefs and practices. Iraqw pollution beliefs contribute to the notion of Iraqw as "tribal" people. Several people I interviewed outside of the homeland claimed their families originally moved from Irqwa Da'aw to avoid the restrictions of pollution quarantines. In the 1930s, according to an account by E.C.L. Lees, who was traveling through Mbulu District at the time, it appears that pollution beliefs were still quite powerful. One of Lees's Iraqw porters requested leave to be at his sick wife's side. News came soon thereafter that the woman had died in childbirth, and the local Iraqw sub-chief at the time requested that the porter be given a longer leave. When the man did finally come back to take up his work again, the other Iraqw in Lees's service threatened to abandon him. As Lees writes, they told him that "owing to their tribal customs they could no longer remain with me if I retained the bereaved husband; especially they could not, on any account draw water with him, as, in this event, their own wives would most certainly die also" (1936:106).

The degree to which younger people, particularly women, are rejecting pollution beliefs and practices in the homeland today is a source of considerable discussion and disapproval by both male and female elders. In several of their meetings, elders cited the decline in these practices as the reason for the community's lack of rain. Iraqw pollution concepts revolve around concern for fertility and prosperity for the *aya* community. The quarantine created to contain pollution isolates individuals for the benefit of their neighbors and others within the *aya*. Pollution arises from specific types of misfortune. Pollution itself is not morally wrong, but failure to observe quarantine practices is. Thus, the relationship of pollution itself to morality is an ambiguous one. To live in quarantine is to suffer isolation and unhappiness. But as one Iraqw man stated, "the household suffers for the benefit of the rest of the *aya*."

A person who has suffered a polluting misfortune may choose not to follow quarantine practices but risks being ostracized by neighbors and the rest of the community if she or he refuses. In the view of elders and non-Christians, to reject the rules of quarantine is viewed as an aggressive, antisocial act against the community. Yet, today, practices regarding pollution are becoming increasingly relaxed as the Christian churches offer an alternative worldview that rejects pollution beliefs. In fact, it often singles out these particular "pagan" beliefs as _mambo ya shetani_, or things of the devil. It is impractical for many Iraqw to follow quarantine rules today, as they depend on travel away from home for a variety of social and economic reasons. For women, the rejection of the practices surrounding pollution carries both advantages and disadvantages. Although they are less confined to the homestead if they choose not to adhere to quarantine practices and pollution avoidance, freer movement seems to have added considerably to their work burden. In sum, when so much of a household's economy revolves around trade and travel to Mbulu and elsewhere, and when children must travel to school, it is very difficult in the current context to follow many of the pollution containment practices.

QUARANTINE

Quarantines are designed to prevent polluted individuals from coming into contact with the earth spirits. These spirits become angry if an individual in a polluted state approaches their home (any water source) because they fear that the pollution will affect their family. If a person should break the quarantine, then the earth spirits will strike out against that individual's household first, followed by their neighbors and finally the entire *aya,* either by moving and thus drying up the water source, by interfering with the rains, or by sending leopards to attack. If someone has suffered a polluting misfortune but has kept it secret, Iraqw say that river grass (used for roof thatch) will start to sprout suddenly near the person's house. This sign is put there by *neetlaamee* to announce the person's pollution.

Pollution results from a variety of misfortunes that threaten fertility and prosperity. Chief among these events is death and/or the shedding of blood, both of which represent the breakdown of boundaries. Death involves crossing the boundary from this world to the afterlife, whereas the shedding of blood involves a violation of the boundaries of the human body and the loss of a vital fluid. The most powerful forms of pollution are those that affect the family unit, and most importantly, the offspring of (and hence the perpetuation of) the household. The following misfortunes are of the greatest concern: (1) miscarriage or the birth of a stillborn child, (2) the death of a child while still at the breast, (3) an unmarried woman becoming pregnant out of wedlock, and (4) a woman giving birth inside her parents' home. In the past, a death of a spouse, any shedding of blood, and attack by wild animal all elicited quarantine practices and cleansing rituals. Today, these are very rare. Although practices regarding quarantine are changing today, particularly through the influence of the Christian churches, *meetaa* still permeates Iraqw perceptions of the world.

Quarantine After the Death of Child

It is difficult to know whether people still adhere to the practice of quarantine established after the death of a child (through miscarriage, stillbirth, or while still nursing), or *meetaa xawir naao/ qawri.* Certainly, throughout my time spent in the homeland I heard of families who were in such states of quarantine, but the degree to which they strictly followed the practices is impossible for me to determine.

The death of a child is particularly tragic. There are numerous reasons thought to cause these deaths (cursing, witchcraft, as well as the earth spirits). For a couple to lose a child strikes at the fertility of the household, the lineage, and the clan but also is thought by many to endanger the neighboring households and finally the entire *aya*. If a household should suffer this misfortune, they are expected to follow certain prescribed behavior until the pollution is cleansed through the birth of another child. Until another birth, the household members will be in quarantine. In addition, their livestock will go into quarantine and cannot be herded together with those of their neighbors. If they have other children, they will be instructed to stop fetching water and not to bathe in the river. Often a neighbor's child or a relative will fetch water and place it at a safe distance from the house. Or, another family member or neighbor may construct a ditch to channel water from a spring or stream so that the family can use it and thereby not come into direct contact with the earth spirits and spread the pollution to the water source of others.

Men are less restricted under quarantine than women. Although they are not to eat or drink with others, as they may pass the pollution through food or drink, they can go outside of their household and interact with others. Men are thought to be stronger and thus less susceptible to attack by the earth spirits than women. Women are advised to avoid water sources once they become wives and are expected to limit their contact with others outside of the household in order to avoid pollution. Thus, quarantine is designed, Iraqw say, to protect women from attack by *neetlaamee*. While I lived in the homeland, I met a number of people who were, or had been, in quarantine.

My neighbors to the west, Baha and Sakri, a young couple married for only three years, had lost two children, one through miscarriage in the final months of pregnancy and one in stillbirth. Although Baha and Sakri were Catholic, they still observed some of the customary prohibitions of this form of *meetaa*, though they had not conducted the customary rituals to establish the quarantine. For example, they gathered their water from a source separate from that of their neighbors, they did not visit friends or families at their homes, they did not eat with others, nor did they participate in communal work projects. When I asked Sakri if they believed that quarantine was necessary, she explained:

> We are Catholics and do not believe in *meetaa*, but many people here still do, so we have to follow the rules or people will be angry with us. Many of our friends who are Catholics live with their parents or grandparents and do not want to anger their relatives by refusing to observe the quarantine.

Their relatives are afraid that they'll bring the contamination into their households.

Sakri resented the quarantine bitterly because she felt terribly isolated and alone as well as stigmatized. She called pollution beliefs "foolish" and "uncivilized." Although suffering a misfortune is not considered morally wrong, living in a state of quarantine in effect makes the affected person feel as though they committed a wrong, because they are avoided by others. In Irqwa Da'aw, if a neighborhood or *aya* comes to a consensus regarding deviant behavior on the part of an individual or household, the members will ostracize the household, refusing to talk to them or assist them in any way *(bayni)*. Thus, if a person refuses to follow the rules of quarantine, they risk this punishment or, worse, a curse. In a rural community where people rely on one another for assistance, this is a powerful sanction.

Neither Baha nor Sakri visited other households except that of Baha's mother, herself a Christian and past childbearing age. Occasionally, Christian friends, or women who were living in the neighboring house for unwed mothers, would visit them at their home. Their Christian friends shared Sakri's assessment of *meetaa* and viewed these practices as an impediment to progress. Out of conformity to tradition (women are not supposed to fetch water after they marry), and because of her quarantine, Sakri never fetched water but left it to Baha (for men to come into contact with water sources is less dangerous, but, under quarantine, they should draw water from a source not used by other people). However, Sakri did go to the river to wash her clothes but believed it was more or less safe, as she felt hidden from the view of others by the tall rushes. As husbands are freer to move outside of the household, Baha would spend a certain amount of time every day at what residents jokingly referred to as "town," a collection of small shops and beer stalls that make up Kuntay, a central gathering area in the ward. There he played cards and draughts with his friends and joined in an occasional soccer game. However, he was careful not to eat or drink with others.

When I returned to Irqwa Da'aw in 1993, the couple's situation had improved because Sakri was again pregnant. Although she still did not visit people at their homes, she was able to brew beer and sell it, as her pregnancy made her less dangerous. Often, people are more lax about *meetaa* at places where beer is sold. Certain locations, such as bars, hospitals, and dispensaries, and even schools, are seen as falling somehow outside of social space, and traditional codes of behavior lapse. Rekdal (1996) observed this attitude toward modern spaces in his research in the region to the southwest of the homeland.

In 2001, I went to visit a family I have spent a lot of time with over the years. The daughter-in-law, who takes care of her in-laws while her husband is away working as a schoolteacher to the north, had given birth to her fourth child a few months earlier. She is a Catholic, as is her husband, but her husband's parents are not Christian. We sat together over a cup of tea, and she described to me the difficulty of her past year and a half. Her third child had died at the age of nine months, and although she did not subscribe to pollution beliefs and practices herself, they were forced upon her by her in-laws, who rigorously followed the quarantine practices. Fortunately, her husband came home for a time, and she was able to conceive and deliver another child, thus removing her from *meetaa.*

Pollution resulting from a death is known as *xaw'i* and is used to refer to both men and women, and even children, who have lost a household member. When a woman suffers a miscarriage or loses a child at the breast, she suffers the additional pollution of the milk in her breasts, which is known as *marwi.* Unlike *xaw'i*, which can fade over time and eventually be considered dissipated, *marwi* does not end until another child is born, and the mother's milk flows again. *Marwi* is found not only in humans but among cattle as well. If a cow loses a calf that was still suckling, the milk from that cow will not be used for family consumption, and the mother of the household must maintain a distance from the cow and most certainly may not milk it. If the cow is slaughtered for some reason, many Iraqw will not eat the meat.

Most Iraqw, including many Christians, still follow these prohibitions regarding the milk and meat of livestock. Kareri, a young Catholic woman in the town of Mbulu, had a European-breed cow who delivered a calf in May of 1993. When the calf was about two months old, it contracted pneumonia and died. Kareri had been selling the milk from the cow in town, but was then limited to selling to mostly non-Iraqw, as most Iraqw refused to buy "contaminated" milk.[2]

Before buying an animal, its history is sought to be sure no pollution exists either directly from the animal or from its living in a household that was under quarantine. It is informally assumed that anyone selling meat would not attempt to pass off meat from a polluted animal. However, some more conservative elders remain suspicious and refuse to eat meat at the *mnaada* (livestock auctions and markets where meat roasting is a big business). One man, whose sow had lost its piglet, complained: "I can't sell her until she gives birth again. No one would buy her now."[3] Elders' suspicions of meat sold in markets are not without justification, as I know of people who, although their household was in quarantine, sold their pigs for meat in the village anyway. They did not do this directly but went through a middleman who sold the meat at the butchery. Although the animals themselves were not in a state of pollution, they were affected by the pollution suffered by their owners with whom they shared the same space. Only "clean" animals may be used for ritual purposes, thus the history of any animal to be used must be known to assure it has no pollution.

Women who have already suffered the death of a child are, together with their recently born child (particularly if the child is the same sex as the one who died before it), more susceptible to contracting this misfortune again. Thus, until her child is weaned, the mother may take extra precautions to avoid contact with people. One man in his late twenties related the story of his own mother, who had lost one of his brothers in a miscarriage when he, Neema, was about eight years old. She went on to conceive again soon after and gave birth to a healthy boy. When women came to visit her, she would sit at a distance from them, and all conversations would be conducted through Neema. Although they did not sit far enough away to prevent themselves being heard, each used Neema as a mouthpiece. In this way, a barrier was established between the women, which provided protection for Neema's mother and his new brother. Women are particularly dangerous to new mothers, as they may themselves have suffered a miscarriage or the death of a child and may transmit the contamination to the new child.[4] Obviously, there are reasons why a woman might not want to have her misfortunes made public, chief among them being the restrictions of *meetaa*. So, while women are more vulnerable to pollution, they are also potentially dangerous for transmitting the pollution that they themselves are carrying.

Quarantine of Pollution from a Pregnancy Out of Wedlock

In the past, if a girl became pregnant out of wedlock and had no fiancé to marry her, she was banished to the bush to build her own shelter and deliver her child alone. Often, she fled instead to marry someone from another ethnic group who did not share these concepts of pollution. Or she may have chosen to leave the child with a family from a neighboring ethnic group and return to her own family later.

If the young woman did have a fiancé (not necessarily the father of the child), he would promptly marry her, but the fact that she had become pregnant before the marriage still placed her in a state of pollution. Once she reached the latter stages of pregnancy (anywhere from the sixth to eighth month), her husband would build two small huts in the bush, far from the village. One hut was large enough for two people and their possessions. The other was a small structure inside of which the woman would give birth.

Once the child reached perhaps four or five months, the husband shaved the head of the mother as well as that of the child. Then, the couple slept together, after which their quarantine ended, and it was possible for them to return to the home of his parents, or to their own home, to live.

Today, variations of these practices, known as *meetaa dasir doroway*, continue among both Christian and non-Christian Iraqw. As finding any bush suitably removed from habitation has become difficult, it has become the practice to find the young woman lodgings in town. The town of Mbulu, as it is a mixture of ethnic groups and is not a community of Iraqw in the way that a neighborhood or *aya* is, serves as a neutral area to which people flee.

The growing incidence of unwed mothers has become one of the most lamented social problems of the Iraqw, both by the older generation and by church and government officials. There is such a high frequency of unwed mothers that a whole section of Mbulu has become their ghetto. There, these women find lodging through other women in similar circumstances or through family members. Several people have set up boardinghouses and charge the women for food and lodging, for which their families (or the father of the child) provide them with cash.

In the neighborhood where I was living, an old, childless Christian widow converted her home into a boardinghouse for women who had become pregnant out of wedlock. During my residence, she was never without boarders, often single women, sometimes women and their husbands (they had married after the woman became pregnant). Most of the women themselves were Christians, as were their husbands, yet all of them followed (and indeed the old woman herself laid down the rules accordingly) the codes of behavior concerning the fetching of water and the separation of various water and cooking vessels. A few women who had lost their children through miscarriage or stillbirth lived there as well. The house, which was one of the few in the area with a sheet-metal roof, had been built during the British colonial era, and the woman's husband had been a clerk in the colonial court. There was considerable land around the house, so it was able to remain somewhat isolated. A small grove of trees contributed to its seclusion. This physical location, together with the observance of quarantine practices, served the function of the "bush" within an inhabited area. Most of the other residents of the area carefully avoided contact with this quarantined household, giving it a wide berth and only communicating from a safe distance. The widow, herself past childbearing age, and having no children of her own, used her anomalous status to create an important niche in the community. Because she is a Catholic, and because her husband had been one of the wealthier and respected members of the community, the usual fears of a childless woman (associating her with witchcraft) seemed to be absent. She was feared for her constant contact with unwed mothers, and for her rather bawdy and aggressive nature, but I heard no rumors of her being a witch.

To board in this house is a public acknowledgment of one's disgrace at becoming pregnant outside of marriage. Yet, for many young women it is the only option available, as their families cannot afford to send them to Mbulu, where they could maintain some anonymity. In a few cases, unwed mothers found Christian families who agreed to take them in and care for them through their delivery. One Catholic family, during my period of fieldwork, took in three such unmarried women from other *aya* for a small fee. This family was one of the wealthier households in the area, as both the husband and wife had government jobs. These women resided with the family for a few weeks prior to their delivery and then again for about a month after they delivered their children. Usually, they returned to their parents' home after this period.

With the exception of some Christian families, most Iraqw still subscribe to the belief that unwed mothers are somehow polluted. Because cleansing oneself of pollution often requires sexual intercourse, young men (even Christians) are highly suspicious of any woman who has migrated to the town for purposes other than a job. If a young woman happens to be unusually forward and propositions a man, he will be particularly wary. I was told of one case in which a young woman who, discovering herself pregnant, married a man who was not the father in order to rid herself of pollution. Right after the wedding, she rejected her new husband to return to the man who had fathered her child. All the people involved in this drama were Catholics, so the duped groom fought for an annulment from the Church so he could wed again.

Christian and non-Christian, old and young, men and women, all expressed dismay about the incidence of unwed mothers. Non-Christians blame the modern leniency toward these mothers, which they feel the churches promote. Many people say that, because the punishment was so harsh in the past (of being banished to the bush), young women and men were reluctant to take chances with getting pregnant. Also, some older women cite the lack of proper training of young women that had formerly occurred during *marmo,* the period of seclusion during which young women were initiated into adulthood. Older men and women criticized young men for their lack of responsibility to the mothers of their children and to the children themselves. Increasingly, parents are raising the children of their daughters, but the child still remains *doroway,* born out of wedlock and without a clan. Although the child's grandparents may raise the child, he or she is not adopted into the maternal grandfather's clan.

Children born out of wedlock and to mothers who remain unmarried are not considered the social equals of those who have fathers (not necessarily the biological one) because they lack a clan affiliation. They become known as the children of their mother and bear her name, not one from a man, and are thus singled out from others. Because the Iraqw are patrilineal, the child will not be considered a member of the mother's clan. Without a clan, the child will have an anomalous status, not fully incorporated into Iraqw society. This affiliation is of most significance at marriage when a person's clan and *daa'awi* history is carefully assessed in determining whether a couple can marry. Often these individuals marry people from other ethnic groups.

What happens to unwed mothers who have no prospective husbands varies. In many cases, they never marry but continue to have children out of wedlock. Some informants claimed that it is hard for a young woman to find a man to marry after she has borne a child out of wedlock because she will be considered unclean and less desirable than a woman who has not had such misfortune. On the other hand, others said that men will be happy to marry her because they are certain of her fertility. However, most agreed that although these young mothers may receive proposals, often these come from young men who are somehow less desirable husbands (either due to their family history or their personality). Those who remain unmarried and who do not return to their homes sometimes take refuge in the Catholic Church, doing household chores for the priest and parish in exchange for room and board. Others who remain in town take up wage labor if they can find it but also may enter into prostitution or into a series of liaisons with men who will support them while they are their lovers.

A connected form of pollution, and one that is scrupulously avoided, is for a woman (married or not) to give birth in the home of her parents. This pollution is considered very dangerous and can result in the death of the woman and everyone in the household. Fortunately, this pollution is fairly easily avoided. If it does occur, the only way to prevent the destruction of the household is to sacrifice a sheep to "cool" the woman's water that broke inside her parents' house. The water from the woman's womb is of concern here, because it is feared that the cattle and other livestock pass through this water and carry the pollution from it to the river where *neetlaamee* will become angry and set out to destroy the household. This form of pollution is based on Iraqw ideas surrounding incest. For a woman to give birth inside the house of her father implies that her father is the father of her child. Although everyone may know that the woman's father is not the father of her child, it is the symbolic association of her giving birth inside her parents' house that matters. Because her father is the head of the household, any children born within are, symbolically at least, considered to be his.

Pollution associated with childbirth emphasizes the primacy of the marriage bond and the establishment of household autonomy. In discouraging illegitimate children, pollution reinforces the marriage system in which elders have considerable control over juniors. The quarantine that couples enter after the death of a child is intended to reaffirm and strengthen the conjugal bond. In this way, it reestablishes their fertility without endangering the fertility of the *aya* and maintains control over women's fertility.

PRECAUTIONS AGAINST POLLUTION

Many Iraqw follow some precautions to avoid bringing pollution into their homes by mistake. Even Christians who claim not to believe in pollution and not to follow quarantines follow some of the basic precautions, perhaps out of habit, or perhaps as part of a general concern to avoid contamination from outside the household. In many of households I visited, vessels and eating utensils were kept separate for the mother and her children. The husband has his own things for eating and drinking, and these are used for guests should they appear.[5] As the husband comes into contact with more people in his day-to-day life through cattle herding and through travel to other villages, his utensils must be kept apart for fear that if he shares them with his wife and children, he may transmit the pollution to them.

Although Christians and the educated elite frequently denounce pollution and quarantine practices as "primitive" and "uncivilized," many admit that certain of these practices are hard to, as one man put it, "cast out of one's mind." Young men, even those who are Christian and who may have studied and lived outside of Iraqw territory for long periods of time, admitted that some of the beliefs about pollution have influenced their behavior. For example, a few young men told me that they are wary of sleeping with women whose backgrounds they do not know, as they fear traditional pollution as well as the more modern pollutions such as sexually transmitted diseases and in particular HIV/AIDS. Fear of these diseases has meshed with traditional notions of impurity. That said, as the increase in HIV/AIDS cases in Mbulu attests, these pollution beliefs are not perhaps in the minds of many of today's youth, particularly those residing in towns.

Pollution beliefs and quarantine practices, although contested, are central to Iraqw cultural identity. Many of the ethnic groups neighboring Iraqw, and non-Iraqw living among them, identify pollution beliefs as a key cultural characteristic of the Iraqw, one that younger Christian Iraqw grudgingly admit is a part of their "custom and tradition." During the villagization program of _ujamaa,_ Iraqw both in the homeland and in the expansion areas were strongly opposed to moving their houses in a line, one house next to the other. As one man, who himself had fought against moving, stated: "It was crazy. The government made us tear down our houses and live side by side with people in _meetaa._ They also made us move into polluted areas that had been abandoned." Living in close proximity endangered the entire community, as the pollution would spread rapidly and be carried to the river and springs by contaminated persons. When the government slacked off on using force to hold villagization together, people quickly moved apart and, where possible, returned to their former lands.

Pollution beliefs and practices are denigrated by the Christian churches, and many younger Iraqw find them too great a burden to follow in a world where mobility has become a more common feature and necessity of everyday life. _Meetaa_ is clearly changing today. Although abandoning quarantine and practices of avoiding pollution permits women greater freedom of movement outside of the household and thus greater participation in economic activities, doing so increases the daily burden that women carry. For example, when women stayed close to home to avoid pollution, men were responsible for traveling to other villages to trade in foodstuffs. Today, women are increasingly involved in this trade, while men stay at home. Thus, women's workloads are often doubled. In a government meeting in 1992, a ward official remarked that "women have become the donkeys of the household." Every morning as the cool fog clinging to the valley bottoms begins to burn off, the paths grow busy with women carrying heavy loads of charcoal, firewood, potatoes, maize, tomatoes, or fruit to the market in Mbulu many kilometers away. They return late in the evening and must then face all the chores awaiting them.

Attitudes toward pollution and quarantine practices vary according to gender, age, religion, and education. Rejection of pollution beliefs is a feature of Iraqw social life today, as no doubt it was in the past. This rejection leads young women in particular to convert to Christianity, giving them license to dismiss the restrictions and stigma of pollution. One woman who was living in quarantine after a miscarriage converted to Pentecostalism because the church promised her relief from her misery. Her husband had refused to live with her but insisted she remain in quarantine, so she saw no way out of her situation. Her conversion to Pentecostalism, which denounced such "pagan" beliefs, allowed her freedom from quarantine and, she felt, hope for a better life.

RITUALS TO PROTECT AND
CLEANSE THE COMMUNITY

No matter what precaution is taken to contain pollution, inevitably individuals, even unintentionally, violate the norms of quarantine. The entire community suffers because of these and other breeches of proper moral conduct, particularly disruptions in harmony. Thus, action must be taken to cleanse the *aya* and restore it to harmony. Rituals are undertaken to appease *neetlaamee* for these moral violations. Appeased, *neetlaamee* will not interfere with the proper falling of the rains on which the community depends. These rituals, known as *masay* (which translates as "medicine"), are organized and orchestrated by the male council of elders in consultation with a paramount diviner. As I have discussed these rituals at length elsewhere (Snyder 1997), I provide only an overview of them here to illustrate how these rites have been affected by incorporation into the Tanzanian state.

The elders claim it is necessary to hold the *masay* ritual to cleanse the *aya* of pollution, restore community harmony, and so rid the land and its inhabitants of misfortune and bring on the rains. The *masay* ritual emphasizes the connection of a specific group of people to a bounded territory. When elders perform the ritual, it affects everyone within its borders, Christian and non-Christian alike. The ritual also underscores the value of the Iraqw elders' concepts of moral conduct and community responsibility. Elders claimed that in

Figure 9.1   Youth being instructed on how to perform the *masay* ritual.

the past they performed this ritual regularly. Today, it is becoming rare, and the *masay* ritual is conducted only when the community is in an obvious crisis, such as a drought or a series of wild animal attacks.

In the precolonial and early colonial era, the performance of *masay* may have reaffirmed the elders' role as guardians of the community and its well-being and legitimized their authority over juniors and women. In this way, as Thornton (1980) has argued, they also asserted their authority over the material aspects of Iraqw life by guarding the health of land and livestock. However, with changes in the political-economic context and in everyday life, the ritual is not effective in demonstrating and consolidating their power and authority in the world outside of ritual. Today, there are alternatives to the elders' ideology. These alternatives, found in the discourse on *maendeleo* and in the Christian churches, offer younger people a way to reject the elders' dictates and to pursue their own objectives.

Many homeland residents care little about the performance of *masay* and often ignore the restrictions on behavior that elders claim are necessary for the ritual's success. Thus, the struggle over cultural politics is one in which the lines are drawn around tradition and modernity, and the protagonists shift their positions along this continuum, giving rise to what Williams (1977) and later Donham (1985) called an "emergent" cultural politics. In the

Figure 9.2   Performing the *masay* ritual.

Iraqw homeland, elders have been, since the colonial era, marginalized from public life. The state's political organization is dominated by younger, educated, and often Christian men. Elders may play a role in local government, but usually in a limited advisory capacity. By continuing to perform the *masay* ritual, elders are refusing to accept the state's dominance over all the affairs of the community. They are reasserting their right to claim authority over the moral health and physical well-being of the local *aya* residents. In this role, the male elders receive necessary and validating support from elder women. Women's protest marches call the community's attention to the need for action on the part of elder men.

Whereas women march openly in public and entreat the elders to take care of the community's problems, the men's elder council prefers to keep a low profile on its activities, fearing perhaps that the state (whether colonial or independent) will interfere and perhaps ban their activities (Winter 1966; Thornton 1980, 1982). Similar to what Winter observed in the 1950s, elders maintain a climate of secrecy, not discussing their affairs with junior men and hiding their activities from the government. Although this secrecy may enable elders to maintain authority over the domain of ritual, it may also serve ultimately to undermine their authority and contribute to their marginalization in the political-economic domain, as younger men, feeling themselves excluded from male elders' councils, look elsewhere for power and influence.

In the elders' council meetings leading up to the *masay* ritual, elders spent considerable time bemoaning the lack of regard for tradition that young people and all Christians display. They suggested that these divisions, and the disharmony that it produces, may in fact be the root cause of lack of rain, poor harvests, and sickness. For the *masay* ritual, the sacrificial animals are supposed to be obtained from community members after the Manda clan diviner has prescribed the color and sex of the animals to be used. In the past, elders would then approach owners of such livestock by holding *barsi,* a symbolically important pasture grass, high over their heads upon approaching the homestead. This grass is used for many occasions to indicate peaceful intentions and to make a request. When *barsi* is used, a request should not be denied. Elders complained often that "no one respects *barsi* today," and it is becoming increasingly difficult to get people to give up animals for the ritual.

During one elders' council meeting I attended, a few elders began discussing what they perceived to be a serious threat to the community's welfare. They explained that the Pentecostal church in the area was baptizing its new members in a local stream. As one elder declared, as he stood before the group to state his views: "They take women with *meetaa* (pollution) to the home of *neetlaangw. Neetlaangw* is angry, and that is why we are not getting any rain." Apparently the elders had complained to the local government, but nothing had been done. While the elders were discussing this issue, two young men and a young woman came up the path. They were carrying Bibles and were coincidentally just coming from the Pentecostal church. They greeted the elders and began to joke with them. One elder told them that they should have more respect for the ways of the past, to which one of the young men replied laughingly, "Your pagan ways are foolishness old man." This retort by the younger man is a flagrant violation of the respect that elders should receive. Discussions continued after the youth left, until finally about half of the elders gathered there became so agitated that they rose to take action. One announced: "Let's go to that church and tear it down. That will stop them from violating the rules of *meetaa.*" Many rose to follow him, grabbing their staves and tying up their capes, but a few elders moved to stop them. One man said: "If we tear down that church, the government will arrest us, and the church will simply be rebuilt. What will that accomplish?" Realizing the wisdom in this, the disgruntled group of men eventually sat down. This incident illustrates not only the different attitudes of elders and youth toward tradition but also the elders' awareness of the limits to their authority. The local government, in respect of the elders, did in the end take some action on their behalf. Officials told the Pentecostal church to build a cement pool in which they could baptize their converts and so avoid the local streams.

The *masay* ritual usually involves three days of rites, one to expel misfortune, disease, and pollution; one to establish a protective barrier to prevent evil and misfortune from entering; and one to reopen the borders. During the rites, the borders to the *aya* are reinforced and also, in theory, closed. Today, however, it is essentially impossible to keep people from leaving or entering. Various prohibitions also are set to prevent people from farming or using any metal tools, the use of which could result in their getting cut and shedding blood upon the land. Fighting is also prohibited. These days it is hard for elders to prevent people from violating these rules, with the exception of fighting, which most people, Christian and non-Christian, do not approve of in any case.

When I lived in Irqwa Da'aw, it was the protest marches of the women's council that prodded the male elders' council into performing the ritual. Late rains and a series of leopard attacks in the area led the women to mobilize and demand that the men take action to handle the crisis. Elder men claimed that the prompting of women was not always necessary in the past, but they admitted that more recently *masay* was rarely performed without the women marching in protest first. Men explained to me that women are like *Looaa*, and like *Looaa*, who cares for the things she created, women, as mothers, care first and foremost about the welfare of their children and thus the entire community. So, women spur men to take action for the community in the same way they push their husbands to attend to the needs of the household. Women, many men admit, have a better understanding of the health of their children and the state of their households. The leader of the women's council, a fiery old woman, was emphatic when I asked her about the women's role in the *masay* ritual: "Men would not know anything about what is happening in this community unless we told them."

In 1992, I participated in a women's protest march. The elder men had agreed to meet the women's council at a designated spot near the western border of the neighboring *aya*. All the participants on both the men's and women's sides were non-Christian. When everyone was seated, with the women's group facing the men's, the women's leader stood up and began to list the grievances she had. She complained: "The men have become lazy. You can see there are problems in the community. Look at the state of the pastures and of people's farms and livestock. Why don't you do something about these problems?" When she had finished, the men's council leader stood up and told the women: "These are matters best left to the care of men. You women should return to your homes and care for your children. You know nothing of these matters." When women march in protest, they threaten to leave their homes and "sleep in the bush," leaving their husbands alone to take care of the household. The women decided not to sleep in the bush at this juncture but pressed the men to take their requests seriously.

While women's protest marches appear to mock male elders' power and ability, their actions actually serve to reinforce male elders' authority as the moral guardians of the community, for it is men who ultimately take action on behalf of the community. Yet, as women's protest marches are becoming increasingly important to spurring men to perform their duties, it appears that men rely more on women to legitimate their authority in the community. This legitimization can be clearly seen in the protest discussed earlier, in which the male elders' council was pressed to intervene when a widow protested the seizure of her land. While women's protest is important in prompting the performance of the *masay* ritual, women themselves cannot participate in the ritual. Their absence is explained by the concern that they may carry pollution within them that will harm or spoil the medicine and so damage the efficacy of the ritual.

More recently, women have turned their protest marches to other social issues and in so doing are expanding their moral authority and separating it from men's authority. They are seeking to claim some authority in the public sphere, which in both the colonial and postcolonial era has been the domain primarily of men. In the late 1980s, women marched to protest the head tax for women (and it was overturned). In 1998, in Bashaynet village, women demonstrated against the problems of schoolgirls getting pregnant, often from schoolteachers. They succeeded in getting teachers removed after they marched from Bashaynet to bring their complaint to the prime minister in Katesh, his hometown. Also that year, again in Bashaynet, women demonstrated against the problem of drunkenness in the village, particularly as a result of the illegal grain alcohol known as *piwa* or *gongo*. They were successful in shutting down the establishments that sold the brew.

Praying for Rain

The Christians in the Iraqw homeland also attributed the lack of rain and other misfortunes to human transgressions. Rather than *neetlaamee,* however, it was the Christian God that was delivering punishment. Christians, like non-Christian elders, often pointed to selfishness and disharmony in the community. One afternoon, I was sitting with a group of young people outside the local cluster of shops in what makes up Kuntay. One young man brought up the Gulf War, which had recently begun. He said he thought that God was angry about the war and was delivering punishment for this moral offense by withholding rain. Another man chimed in and said: "I think it might be because of all those bombs and chemicals used in the war. Maybe they have caused the rains to fail. The weather has been very odd since the beginning of that war." Others grumbled about how they were suffering because of a war that did not concern them. Although younger Iraqw appear to espouse modernity in emphasizing education, conversion to Christianity, possession of Western goods, and other markers of a global economy, their desire for modernity is not without limits. They see violent political conflicts, selfishness, greed, and other motivations as the products of a *maendeleo* that has gone too far. Thus, *maendeleo* should have its limits.

Community harmony is not the ideology of elders and tradition alone. Peace and unity have been guiding themes in political ideology since independence, and Tanzanians pride themselves on their peaceful history as compared to most of their neighbors in East and Southern Africa. Pursuing harmony requires, on all sides, a constant negotiating of boundaries and positions. While elders often appear disgruntled and make reference to a past in which their roles were respected, in fact they are still important moral authorities in the local community. It is the elders that many turn to when having trouble with neighbors, or with spouses, or when witchcraft or a curse may be suspected. However, while their moral authority is valued in land cases and the settlement of personal crises, their opinions on pollution beliefs and the *masay* ritual are more frequently coming to be ignored. The attitude toward pollution beliefs and the *masay* ritual has been deeply affected by the Christian churches' opposition to such "pagan" beliefs and practices. Yet, other such beliefs and practices, such as witchcraft and divination, remain strong, if often shrouded in secrecy.

Pollution beliefs and the *masay* ritual reinforce the idea of a very specific, bounded, and *local* idea of community in which senior men have authority. Yet, this emphasis on the local community does not resonate with people's experience in the postcolonial state in the way it may have done in the precolonial past when the Iraqw were hemmed in by the Maasai and Datoga. Today, relationships with kin and friends outside the homeland are vital for a host of economic and practical reasons. Loans or purchase of land, places to loan out your livestock, markets for tree products, and employment and education opportunities are all sought outside of home communities. The Tanzanian state, through political participation and education, and the Christian churches have emphasized membership and participation in wider communities, both national and global. The sense of national unity forged by the state, rather unique in sub-Saharan Africa, is built on the formation of a national, as opposed to ethnic or local, identity. For younger Iraqw, in even the most hard-to-reach locations like the homeland, their day-to-day lives involve negotiating and trying to make use of the resources in all these communities, from local to global. Through these negotiations, an emergent Iraqw culture is forming. It is difficult to predict whether pollution beliefs and the *masay* ritual will eventually be abandoned and forgotten. As younger Iraqw eventually become elders, they may seek to reconnect with traditions that emphasize the local as a way to assert their authority, in the same way that elders do today. The form that this tradition will take will no doubt be different. _Maendeleo_ has yet to provide Iraqw with the ability to control the rains, prevent attacks by wild animals, check the spread of disease, or avoid other natural misfortunes, so perhaps the *masay* ritual will continue well into the future. The traditions that younger people and Christians continue to rely on are ones that address their individual, rather than the community's, needs and problems. These traditions in particular are being reinvented to address the problems that arise in people's lives as they grapple with local and global problems.

Notes

1. As Thornton observed, "practices that have resulted from the Iraqw concept of pollution . . . have been regarded as barbaric by colonial and independent government officials alike" (1980:6).

2. Rekdal (1996) found that in instances concerning the consumption of products from so-called "modern" cows (European breeds) rules of *meetaa* did not apply, as they, like schools, beer halls, and other modern spaces, were somehow outside of the traditional rules. Yet, in my own work, as described in the cases above, the cows were modern cows, and similar rules of pollution were applied to them. These cases may have been exceptions, or they may reflect different interpretations held in different Iraqw areas.

3. Fosbrooke, writing in the 1950s, noted that "an Iraqw hesitates to purchase food of which he does not know the origin in case at some time it has been handled by a person whom the Iraqw would regard as in a state of uncleanliness" (1955:6).

4. As it is possible for a woman to hide the fact that she has had a miscarriage, women are never completely trusted to be free of pollution.

5. The neighboring Wambugwe seclude themselves during mealtimes for fear of witchcraft (Gray 1963:182–165).

CHAPTER TEN

PRAYING FOR HARMONY

Tanzania and Globalization

The World Bank has done research and found that 50 percent of Tanzanians live below the poverty line. That means they make less than
one dollar, or 975 shillings a day. Do you know why this is? One reason is that too many people wake up every day and go to the *kilabu*
(beer hall) instead of working in the fields.
—District Commissioner of Mbulu, in speech
to Kainam residents on April 18, 2002

No doubt, this news from the district commissioner concerning income
levels did not come as much of a surprise to the inhabitants of the
homeland, who while they grow their food also struggle to earn cash to pay
for the many financial demands of their households. Whether they would
agree to beer drinking being the reason for their low incomes is another matter. A solution to this economic problem, the government argues, is to embrace global markets through the cultivation of *mazao ya biashara* or cash
crops, which in the homeland means coffee and pyrethrum. Indeed, in another ward meeting, this time in Murray, the district commissioner announced that every farmer must plant one quarter-acre of pyrethrum and
one quarter-acre of coffee. Yet most farmers in Irqwa Da'aw, old and young
alike, are rightly wary of being at the mercy of the vagaries of global markets,
knowing full well that they are not equal participants in this economy. Their
experiences with cash crops such as coffee and pyrethrum in the past have

not been enormously positive. In the case of coffee, when the crop was controlled through the state marketing board, farmers rarely saw any money, much less any profit for the harvest they gave to the cooperative board to sell. With liberalization, the situation looked as if it would improve, and farmers' hopes were raised. However, falling prices on the world markets for coffee have deflated many farmers' hopes. A similar situation is found with pyrethrum. At the moment, farmers are getting a good price for the crop, but in the 1960s and 1970s they had also experienced a boom period for this commodity, which was followed by a bust, leading many to stop cultivating the crop altogether.

Tanzania's historical place in the global economy has, from the colonial period to the present day, always been a marginal one. Unlike neighboring Zambia, which Ferguson (1999) argues feels a loss of membership in the "world society," Tanzania is undergoing a process of entry into this global system after years of being largely cut off from other countries during the *ujamaa* era of self-reliance. Today, Tanzania is held up by the World Bank and IMF as a promising example of development. It is undergoing privatization of all its major industries and welcoming foreign investment. However, these changes have not yet resulted in great gains in employment or income for the majority of citizens, and many Tanzanians feel the state is selling the country's assets to foreigners.

There are certainly significant changes in Tanzania from when I began doing research in the country. Where I used to spend an entire day looking for a working telephone in Dar es Salaam, there are now functioning paycard phones everywhere. In addition, mobile phones have become commonplace in the cities and continue to spread throughout the country. In January 2004, a mobile phone provider began construction of receiving towers in the town of Mbulu. Where there were only government newspapers in 1990, now there are literally hundreds of independent publications, and many of them can be bought daily in Mbulu today. Roads have been improved, and transportation to Mbulu is not limited to the one daily bus that was the only option when I first began fieldwork. In the Iraqw homeland, there are increasingly more sheet-metal roofs, more people wearing shoes, and many more bicycles in use. More people have planted timber trees, coffee, and pyrethrum. Others market their food crops or grow tomatoes, tobacco, cabbages, bananas, and other more perishable crops to take to traders in Mbulu. Yet, while these changes mark a certain *maendeleo*, it is also true that farms are becoming increasingly smaller as they become subdivided, yields continue to decline, and markets for selling produce and goods are hard to reach. The nation's move away from *ujamaa* socialism and embrace of free markets, privatization, and a multiparty system has yet to be perceived as a significant benefit to the average resident of the Iraqw homeland or other areas of rural Tanzania.

Structural adjustment policies designed to encourage repayment of debt and to liberalize the economy were accompanied by the state's withdrawal from the social service sector, inaugurating an era of school fees and payment for health services and medicine. In addition, Tanzania opened its markets to goods from the West and from neighboring countries. With these changes has come both a national-level and village-level discourse of skepticism and caution. To many, the economic changes taking place are viewed as a way for a few individuals to get rich and the remainder to remain poor or grow poorer. This situation, often referred to locally as _ubinafsi,_ or selfishness, is seen as a growing social problem by many homeland residents, particularly older Iraqw who are not well equipped to take much advantage of these economic and social changes. And indeed, throughout Tanzania there is a growing division of wealth that, in the era of _ujamaa,_ was held in check.

At the level of national discourse, President Mkapa himself has registered caution in the national press against the effects of globalization and world trade. In a meeting of the World Commission on the Social Dimension of Globalisation, of which he is co-chairman, Mkapa stated that there is a "growing danger of an economic and social system that is neither fair nor at peace with itself. Examined closely, these present some of the unacceptable faces of globalisation" (_Daily News,_ March 25, 2002). In particular, Mkapa criticizes the West's stance of protecting of its own markets while calling on the developing world to remove their restrictions to international trade. In an editorial in the _East African_ (December 9, 2002), it was reported that President Mkapa "told several international conferences held in Dar es Salaam that his government had realised that accolades from the donor community were not translating into food on _wananchi_'s (people's) plates." While the World Bank and IMF have "showered praise" on the Tanzanian government for its success at the macroeconomic level, the editorial asks: "[When] will this success trickle down to the people? Their tables are without food, and they have to pay for education and meet hospital bills, all this at a time when unemployment is high and the agricultural sector neglected."

The changes brought about by globalization are not seen only as economic. In the Culture and Arts section of the _Business Times_ on April 19, 2002, writer Gama Mwanga decries what he sees as a cultural "vacuum" created by the sudden rush into Tanzania of "Western" culture. Even the ward of Kainam in the homeland now boasts a satellite dish that brings television programs from Africa and the West to a rural area that in the early 1990s had fairly few radios. Mwanga claims that the "Tanzania way of life" is in "utter chaos": "The youth are busy aping the Western culture, Arab culture or other foreign cultures . . . they diligently cram the American race-hate rape [_sic_], smoking dope or flying the Union Jack, the French, Canadian and American flags and even the Nazi Swastika."

This viewpoint is not an uncommon one and is expressed not only in the media but by many rural and urban residents alike. The picture that accompanied this article was of three contestants in a beauty contest. The caption reads: "Traditionalists and moralists in Tanzania argue that even beauty contests are un-African while modernists stridently support such events." This caption brings us back yet again to that ever-present dichotomy of tradition and modernity, which, in nonacademic circles, still stubbornly holds and is lodged firmly in people's imaginations. Even so-called modernists have reservations about many changes they are witnessing, and I often heard both young educated men and women as well as male and female elders express the opinion that "_maendeleo_ can go too far." This view was usually pronounced in hearing about either American or European modes of behavior (divorce, clothing styles, and so on) or in response to various social, cultural, and political changes taking place in the country.

The struggles with development and globalization are often framed in moral terms. Witchcraft, sorcery, and divination are intertwined with ideas of success and failure. These beliefs serve as a moral discourse about power and inequality. This situation goes well beyond the boundaries of the Iraqw homeland and indeed Tanzania. In neighboring Malawi, it was recently reported that a "rumor that Malawi's government is colluding with vampires to collect human blood for international aid agencies in exchange for food has led to a rash of vigilante violence" (*New York Times*, December 24, 2002, p. 4).

PERSPECTIVES OF THE ELDERS

In Iraqw communities, the tensions brought about through social and economic change are often expressed as a conflict between maintaining traditions or embracing _maendeleo_ and Western models. Furthermore, this conflict is often perceived as being a generational one. As one elder said in a speech at a harvest festival, "The youth of today are our children but they run from us." He followed this with a plea: "Things from our past, return to us!" Elders view the changes pursued by younger Iraqw, in their desire to seek _maendeleo_, as threats to community harmony, which they assert is crucial to the well-being of animals, land, and people. Although harmony is clearly a stated ideal, as we have seen in the previous chapters, there are many areas where conflicts emerge and destroy any notions of unity. The tradition/modernity dichotomy simply adds a new layer of negotiation and gives a new meaning to these tensions, struggles for authority, and conflicting visions of the world.[1]

The concerns of elders, and what they see as community problems, come across quite clearly in the prayers recited at ritual occasions and at elders' council meetings. In particular, in *firoo*, or prologue prayers to the main *sluu-fay* prayer, speakers highlight "the issues currently at stake in the respective community" (Lawi 2000: 131n). These prayers are recited at public events

Figure 10.1   Youth, elder, and anthropologist.

such as weddings, harvest celebrations, and elders' meetings. Prayers are directed toward *Looaa*, asking for her protection, thanking her for a good harvest and the health of the people and livestock of the community, and enlisting her aid in removing the influence of evil. When reciting a prayer, the speaker stands, and everyone seated participates as a chorus at key junctures in the prayer, humming in unison during pauses between lines. A common theme in these prayers is decline: of morality, of health, of production, and so on. This decline is generally attributed to the failure of younger people and others to follow the ways of the past and, in particular, to listen to and obey elders' advice and directives:

> I believe you have seen the way in which things have declined. Disease is everywhere, and the people are ill, even the cows are sick, there is nothing which is whole and well. . . . Let us come together to cure the hide of our country, to cure the disease that has stricken the bodies of the people and the livestock. Everyone, with a white heart and with mutual intention. And if everyone prays with one heart, certainly *Looaa* will listen to our pleas. . . . Everyone together! The entire country, be cured of your problems!

Here, the speaker paused to allow those present to respond:

> Let it be cured, let it be cured!

The focus on community misfortune reflects very real problems in Iraqw communities, not simply elders' grousing about the youth's bad manners. Food security, disease of both people and livestock, and witchcraft and theft are issues in all Iraqw communities, and no doubt throughout Tanzania. From many elders' point of view, to be of "one heart" is necessary in order for *Looaa* to hear their prayers and respond to their problems. The unity or consensus that elders emphasize is one in which young people come around to agreeing with and obeying the elders' point of view. The harmony/unity/consensus motif is evident in most gatherings involving *aya* or neighborhood residents. In elders' own council meetings, coming to a consensus is critical, as no action can be taken without agreement. In the excerpt below, the speaker returned to the subject of disease, specifically the realization (in 1990) that HIV/AIDS had come to Mbulu District:

> Let me tell you this, I believe you all have listened, and now there has come about a disease that we never knew here in the past, and it is very bad for the people. So let me say to the young people, go ahead with your lives of today with caution. Let me say that it is for you people to decide, each person can choose whether to live or die, but with this disease there is no turning back, there is no cure, only death. We are told every day to beware of this disease, but we do not listen. And again let me say, every woman and every man, beware of this disease. I am saying this now, as though we have only heard of this disease just now, but truthfully, it has already entered our midst.

The youth's lack of respect and obedience to elders and the issues of alcoholism and theft are addressed in the following excerpt.

> And thus, I thank you all, this drink which was prepared for us, and this, our young man. This drink can make a fool of young men until they walk all night. These days, young men walk around in the middle of the night searching for beer, breaking into the homes of people, even their parents, taking things of wealth to get money for beer. In no time at all you will see that a young man has taken people's property, even their harvest and their livestock, and our people are poor, they do not have enough possessions, they are not rich. Together with this, our children have contributed to our poverty, as they steal a little from us. So I beg you young people, stop this sabotage, this stealing from your parents, and taking the things of people.

Eat or use your own property, your cows. I believe, a few days past, all of you heard how a certain person was robbed (I do not want to say his name out loud) of all the maize from his field. It was stolen in the night. After leaving the field, the thief entered into the storeroom of another person and stole his maize. People, is this civilized behavior? Is this a good life? Thus I am telling you, this mischief has no meaning. I am telling you, this thievery does not help. A thief's throat is like a pit that cannot be filled. Every day it demands that more things pass through it to the stomach. It is like a grave that will not be filled. Thus I beg you, I coax you, again and again, I remind you, do your work by your own hands. If you continue in this attitude, with this thievery, you will be captured and locked up. Look at the many young men who have given up farming, and their fields have turned to bush. Tomorrow, you will see these young men creeping up and stealing the people's harvest. What? Has *Looaa* made you less than normal? Do you have some disability, do you not have intelligence and health, are you not able to do work like anyone else without wasting your time on street corners? Is it right for this sort of person to steal the things of his fellows? Me, I do not know. If he is able to do this, he is able to steal from anyone.

Iraqw say that the format for these oral performances has been handed down from "the time of our forefathers." However, the content, though it contains certain standard themes, varies according to the speaker and the context. This flexibility is apparent in the speaker's reference to HIV/AIDS, or in his words, the disease for which "there is no cure."

The elder in his prayer is pointing to very real social problems, not only exaggerations of the tensions between elders and juniors. There is increasing theft and drunkenness among young people, as they reject farming and what they see as the "backwardness" of the lives of their parents. They flee their homes and go to the towns in search of a better, more modern life, only to find that no jobs are available. However, there are many elders who also evade farmwork and spend much of their time at the *kilabu*, so the problem is not simply a generational one. In 2002, in the meeting described in the opening of this chapter, the district commissioner began a district-wide campaign against drinking. He asked for two elders to stand up and deliver *firoo* against *gongo* or *piwa*, the illegal hard alcohol that increasingly has become a significant problem in the area. Elders proved reluctant to take up the task, but finally two did so and went into detail about the problems brought about by this drink. They cursed the brew, and everyone gathered joined in the chorus. Afterward, however, elders told me they thought it would not do much good, as it was doubtful that all those who were gathered there agreed or had come to a consensus about the evils of *piwa*. Without this consensus, it is doubtful whether *Looaa* would hear their prayers.

In another *firoo* I recorded in 1990, an elder introduced new topics: youths avoiding marriage and women going to the hospital to deliver. He urged a "return to the ways of the past."

> These days, people have become very bad. Even we parents get no assistance from our children, even to send them on an errand. We have prayed because we see no other way, and our cattle and our people are dying. So, we beg of you to help us reduce our problems. Another problem is that many of our young people refuse to marry, and our girls have filled the town. This attitude is very bad, it is not right for our young men to refuse to marry, leading the girls to run off to the town. This is the root of the disease that has even entered our villages. These days, the traffic is increasing between the villages and the town, and this is leading to an outbreak of disease in the villages. . . . My friends, let us pray to *Looaa* on behalf of our pregnant women who go to the hospital to deliver their children. This means that today, giving birth in your home is dangerous, it has refused our women. They fear to deliver at home because many have serious problems in delivery, even death. Let us pray: my friends, let our births take place in our homes like the past.

The refusal of the young to marry is seen by elders as a rejection of their authority and a lack of attention to the fertility and prosperity of the household, lineage, clan, and entire Iraqw community. Because fathers assert their authority over their adult children and establish alliances with other families through marriage negotiations and bride wealth, evasion of marriage denies them a powerful role both in their children's lives and in intraclan relations.

Objection to hospital births centered on the perception that giving birth outside of the household implies that the birth is illegitimate.[2] In other words, going to the hospital to deliver a child is seen as equivalent to going to the bush, or to Mbulu, when the child is the product of a union that has taken place prior to marriage *(meetaa doroway)*. Elder women are also often opposed to hospital births. A year or two before my first fieldwork, a group of older women went to the hospital to protest hospital deliveries. They object to hospital births because of its association with *meetaa* and because they believe one of their most important and prestigious areas of expertise is being usurped. Midwives have always been respected among the Iraqw, and they are highly secretive about their methods (as secrecy maintains their power). When a woman gives birth, her husband and all men are banished from the house. Delivery and female circumcision are the only areas in which women have complete authority and men are excluded. As they have already lost one important cultural practice in which they had considerable authority and respect (female initiation rites, or *marmo*), it is not surprising that many elder women should object to hospital births.

In the *sluufay* that follows the *firoo*, speakers repeat themes of unity and harmony and emphasize various pairings that promote complementarity. The lines from a *sluufay* below illustrate these themes.

> *Let our elders eat together*
> *Even more, those who appreciate love*
> *Let us follow that which we have heard passed down to*
>   *us from the origin of our tribe*
> *Let our women and girls agree in their discussions*
> *Let our young men listen to the words of their elders*
> *Among ourselves, let us agree in our discussions*
> *Let those people from other tribes agree with our words*
> *Let our leaders have good health and grow fat*
> *And agree with our words and our advice*
> *Let the woman from far away deliver us a child*
> *Let the cow from far away give birth among us*
> *And truly, let it give birth in our country*
> *Let the evil vanish and let us love one another*
> *Like water and the razor*[3]
> *Let us get along like sleep and bedtime stories*
> *Let us get along like the mouth and the hand while eating*
> *Like water and honey*[4]

These prayers depict hope for ideals in Iraqw life, one in which girls obey their mothers, boys their fathers, witches and other evil people are banished or die, and immigrants marry into Iraqw society, contributing to its fertility but conforming to its customs and traditions. This ideal world is one in which clear lines of authority and power are drawn.

Through the performance of ritual prayers at public gatherings, elders attempt to relate practices and conceptions of the past with the present. While elders admonish young men and women to be independent and self-reliant, they also clearly want them to defer to elders' authority in marriage and in everyday behavior. The fertility that they wish for, however, is also the very means by which younger Iraqw get out from under their fathers' control. In bringing up their own children, they establish their independent households and their own dependents.

As a local stereotype goes, many older people in Irqwa Da'aw prefer to go along "as they always have": planting the crop varieties they grew up with, tending their livestock to increase the family herds (rather than buying and selling to obtain a profit), performing the rituals for the land and for protection of their household, honoring their dead, and marrying their children. Although there are elder men and women, mostly Christian, who have embraced cash crop production, become involved in regional networks, and abandoned participation in local elders' councils, the orientations of many older Iraqw are primarily local. They revolve around farming, livestock, and relations within their families and the local community. The reasons for this emphasis on the local are varied. For one, as Winter (1968) and Thornton (1980, 1982) have shown, Iraqw ideology has always emphasized relationships within shared space as crucial to the fertility and health of the community. For another, it is within more local arenas and with practices labeled traditional that elders' authority and prestige rests. Many older Iraqw do not have the "cultural capital" to operate in the expanded economic and political arena that encompasses the local. While elder men and women may understand Swahili, they speak primarily Iraqw. Many do not read or write. They are often not Christians, and they have had little or no formal education. So, when government officials come and explain, in Swahili, government policy on *demokrasia* (democracy) and the multiparty system *(mfumo wa vyama vyingi),* or price fluctuations of coffee on the global market, many older Iraqw have a limited interest in these national initiatives.

CONCERNS OF THE YOUTH

In schools, the youth are taught about the world outside of the Iraqw homeland. They learn about global institutions like the World Bank and the IMF, the United Nations and the African Union. They are taught about the free market *(soko huria)* and political systems around the world. In Kainam today, they can even watch television programs and videos from around the world. Still, this education and exposure does not necessarily equip them with the ability to participate in this globalized world. In Tanzania, though secondary schools have increased significantly all over the country, and Irqwa Da'aw now has a secondary school in each ward, the percentage of young people who go on to study in secondary school and then university is still very low. These local schools are generally not well equipped: they lack books, lab equipment, and often even desks. Learning English remains a hard struggle for many students. When students finish Form 4, they may go on to study Forms 5 and 6 and eventually to university, or they may go to teacher's college or pursue a trade. Many return home, full of hopes for a different life from the farming of their fathers, but with little means to pursue this more modern life. Many young men become discouraged, give up, and end up donning their *mgorori* and heading out to the beer hall every morning to "reduce their thirst." The youth are not a uniform category of people, however. Many shun education and prefer instead to stay home, marry young, and try to survive on farming and herding. Others remain determined to forge ahead with education and eventually find some kind of job. They go to church and seek multiple ways to pursue *maendeleo.*

Figure 10.2   Student in local school.

Those individuals who strive to further their education and to seek economic opportunities that will provide more than basic subsistence face myriad obstacles. Many of these younger people run into resistance from their parents, who cannot fathom why they are not satisfied with staying home and carrying on with their lives as their parents did at their age. A complaint I heard fairly often, particularly from young men, was, "My father cares more for his cows than for his children. He does not see any need for me to get an education." Some of the resistance parents may have to their children's education may be related to the fact that, once educated, many come to view their elders as obsolete characters clinging to an impractical past. In other instances, parents desperately want their children to get an education, as they know that only further study can open doors to greater economic possibilities.[5] Yet, many parents have no money for school fees and are faced with enormous financial responsibilities in providing for their households.

Some parents, while supportive of education, are still dubious about it leading to jobs for their children. In 2002, I attended a meeting in Dongabesh village at which the local member of parliament addressed the villagers. The subject of a new secondary school came up. One man stood up and, after

Figure 10.3   Children on the back stoop of a schoolteacher's house.

saying he was in favor of a new school, added that he did not understand why students who finished Form 4 did not get employment and instead ended up coming home to live. "I don't see much point to paying these school fees if my son just returns home and farms. He does not need to go to school for that." In an article titled "Forty Years On, the Promised Land Is Not in Sight!" in the *Business Times* (December 14, 2001), Robert Mihayo reported that secondary school enrollment "stands at a low 6 percent of all primary school leavers!" He added that "among the youth, unemployment stands at a dangerously high 30 percent." Tanzania's economy is primarily an agricultural one, and depending on agriculture means depending on the weather and the constant fluctuations of the markets. This situation does not lend itself to rapid <u>maendeleo</u> or economic security.

The residents of Irqwa Da'aw have little opportunity for economic development at a significant level. Their farms are small, their livestock holdings are similarly small, and their ability to purchase inputs to increase production is limited, as is the opportunity for off-farm income. Their access to markets, such as decent roads, is also poor. Yet, there is still room for an improved standard of life in terms of greater food and economic security in Irqwa Da'aw. However, these small though significant improvements will be unlikely to produce a lifestyle that resembles what young people see of life in the cities of Europe or Africa when they watch ITV television in the tea shop in Kainam. One expatriate development official told me: "People want to jump from a hand hoe to a computer. It is simply not possible."

Claude Ake has argued that the reason for the lack of development in Africa has been the top-down fashion in which development projects are implemented. Furthermore, he asserts that the development paradigm itself has a "negative view of the people and their culture" in Africa and that it "focuses on the possibility of Africa becoming what it is not and probably never can be . . . and offers the notion that African societies can find validity only in their total transformation, that is, in their total self-alienation" (Ake 1996:15–16). At independence, Tanzania forged a policy for _maendeleo_ that ideologically and rhetorically placed emphasis on development from the grass roots. Yet, as has been widely documented, the state never managed to achieve this goal and instead fell back into the typical state-driven, top-down approach (Coulson 1982; Cliffe and Saul 1973; Raikes 1986).

In part, the failure to develop a grassroots development plan was based on the assumption that the "peasants" really did not know what was in their best interests and that they stubbornly clung to backward tradition.[6] As James Scott has pointed out, Tanzania's development agenda, built around _ujamaa_ and villagization, had a religious quality to it: "What these planners carried in their mind's eye was a certain aesthetic, what one might call a visual codification of modern rural production and community life. Like a religious faith, this visual codification was almost impervious to criticism or disconfirming evidence" (Scott 1998:253).

This idea of development resembling a religious faith is very apt for Tanzania even today. Not only does development ideology come with a host of associations—that modern is good, that tradition is backward—but in the minds of many in Irqwa Da'aw, development and Christianity go hand in hand, and both dictate a rejection of the past and its associated "pagan" beliefs and practices. Yet, while many Iraqw in the homeland carry these schema in their imaginations, their lived experience suggests a more complicated picture. Tanzanians are grappling at many levels with how to pursue development and how to shape it to meet their needs. There is an ongoing discussion, at both local and national levels, about the benefits and dangers of a course of development modeled on the West. For many Iraqw, _maendeleo_, with its associated beliefs and practices, has its limits for addressing the realities of life in Irqwa Da'aw, where responsibilities are many and the means to achieve a more modern life are severely limited.

The stance of the Tanzanian state on "local culture" has always been a bit ambivalent. On the one hand, _ujamaa_ was supposed to be an "African socialism" based on "traditional" African values of egalitarianism. Yet, the policies and practices of the state continually and routinely set up "local culture" as an impediment to the development of the nation-state and its economy. At government events, various "local" cultural dances and songs are often encouraged, and local forms are modified to address the agenda of the day—children's rights, adoption of new technologies, and so forth. However, when cultural practices are seen to get in the way of state development initiatives, they are discouraged and even banned. Yet, it is often the state's failure to address the problems people face that leads them to pursue more "local" cultural traditions such as cursing, consulting diviners, and honoring the dead.

The degree to which something is local or traditional is obviously impossible to determine and in fact is not that terribly interesting. What is interesting is that people continually draw upon these imagined categories of traditional and modern to explain the world around them. When individuals turn to kin for help with school fees or try to strike it rich by paying a diviner for the magic needed to make their endeavors a success, they are acting in not only a "local" idiom but also, judging by evidence in both the academic literature and the press, a regional and global one. Many Iraqw traditions, such as curses and wedding rites, remain salient today, as they are molded to fit current circumstances. Iraqw, and indeed all Tanzanians (as Tripp's [1997] work in Dar es Salaam shows), exhibit enormous creativity and resourcefulness in response to difficult and demanding circumstances. In the Iraqw homeland, cultural practices continue in modified form to endure in new circumstances and are deployed in novel ways to fit current problems, thus continually blurring the divide between past and present, traditional and modern.

Notes

1. Bravman (1998) has similar observations of Taita communities in Kenya.

2. Iraqw definition of illegitimate refers to a child that has been conceived before marriage. Even if the child has been conceived by an adulterous union, it is still legitimate, as the woman is already married (and thus the child is the husband's).

3. As in shaving.

4. Water and honey, when mixed together, form one substance. The elders, through this symbol, exhort individuals to merge together into a harmonious community.

5. See Hodgson (2001) for similar views among the Maasai.

6. See Crewe and Harrison (1998) and Gardner and Lewis (1996) for discussions of how the aid industry views culture as an impediment to development.

References

Ake, Claude. 1996. *Democracy and Development in Africa*. Washington, D.C.: Brookings Institution.

Arens, William. 1987. "Mto wa Mbu: A Rural Polyethnic Community in Tanzania." In *The African Frontier: The Reproduction of Traditional African Societies*, edited by Igor Kopytoff. Bloomington and Indianapolis: Indiana University Press.

———. 1979. *On the Frontier of Change: Mto wa Mbu, Tanzania*. Ann Arbor: University of Michigan Press.

Arens, William, and Ivan Karp. 1989. *Creativity of Power. Cosmology and Action in African Societies*. Washington, D.C.: Smithsonian Institution Press.

Barkan, Joel D. 1984. *Politics and Public Policy in Kenya and Tanzania*. New York: Praeger.

Beidelman, T. O. 1993. *Moral Imagination in Kaguru Modes of Thought*. Washington, D.C.: Smithsonian Institution Press. First published 1986 by Indiana University Press.

———. 1982. *Colonial Evangelism: A Socio-Historical Study of an East African Mission at the Grassroots*. Bloomington: Indiana University Press.

———. 1980. "The Moral Imagination of the Kaguru: Some Thoughts on Tricksters, Translation and Comparative Analysis." *American Ethnologist* 7(1):27–41.

Bernstein, Henry. 1982. "Notes of Capital and Peasantry." In *Rural Development*, edited by John Harriss. London: Longman.

Blystad, Astrid. 1992. The Pastoral Barabaig: Fertility, Recycling and the Social Order. Master's Thesis, University of Bergen, Norway. Unpublished manuscript.

Boddy, Janice. 1989. *Wombs and Alien Spirits: Women, Men, and the Zar Cult in Northern Sudan*. Madison: University of Wisconsin Press.

Bourdieu, Pierre. 1977. *Outline of a Theory of Practice*. Cambridge: Cambridge University Press.

Bravman, Bill. 1998. *Making Ethnic Ways: Communities and Their Transformations in Taita, Kenya, 1800–1950.* Portsmouth, N.H.: Heineman.

Cliffe, Lionel, and John S. Saul. 1973. *Socialism in Tanzania: An Interdisciplinary Reader.* Dar es Salaam: East African Publishing House.

Comaroff, Jean, and John L. Comaroff. 1997. *Of Revelation and Revolution: The Dialectics of Modernity on a South African Frontier.* Vol. 2. Chicago: University of Chicago Press.

_____. 1993. *Modernity and Its Malcontents: Ritual and Power in Postcolonial Africa.* Chicago: Chicago University Press.

Coulson, Andrew. 1982. *Tanzania: A Political Economy.* Oxford: Clarendon Press.

Crewe, Emma, and Elizabeth Harrison. 1998. *Whose Development? An Ethnography of Aid.* London: Zed Books.

Crush, Jonathan. 1995. *Power of Development.* London: Routledge.

Donham, Donald. 1985. *Work and Power in Maale, Ethiopia.* Ann Arbor: University of Michigan Press.

Ehret, Christopher. 1974. *Ethiopians and East Africans: The Problem of Contacts.* Nairobi: East African Publishing House.

Englund, Harry, and James Leach. 2000. "Ethnography and the Metanarratives of Modernity." *Current Anthropology* 41(2):225–248.

Ergas, Zaki. 1980. "Why Did the Ujamaa Village Policy Fail—Towards a Global Analysis." *Journal of Modern African Studies* 18:387–410.

Escobar, Arturo. 1995. *Encountering Development: The Making and Unmaking of the Third World.* Princeton: Princeton University Press.

_____. 1991. "Anthropology and the Development Encounter: The Making and Marketing of Development Anthropology." *American Ethnologist* 18(4):658–682.

Feierman, Steven. 1990. *Peasant Intellectuals: Anthropology and History in Tanzania.* Madison: University of Wisconsin Press.

Ferguson, James. 1999. *Expectations of Modernity: Myths and Meanings of Urban Life on the Zambian Copperbelt.* Berkeley: University of California Press.

_____. [1990] 1994. *The Anti-politics Machine: "Development," Depoliticization, and Bureaucratic Power in Lesotho.* Cambridge: Cambridge University Press.

Fleuret, Patrick. 1980. "Sources of Material Inequality in Lushoto District, Tanzania." *African Studies Review* 23(3):69–87.

Fortes, Meyer. 1949. *The Web of Kinship among the Tallensi.* London: Oxford University Press.

Fosbrooke, H. A. 1955. The Mbulu Highlands: Problems of People, Land and Cattle. Unpublished manuscript.

_____. 1954. "The Defensive Measures of Certain Tribes in North-eastern Tanzania: Iraqw Housing as Affected by Inter-Tribal Raiding." *Tanganyika Notes and Records* 36:50–57.

Fratkin, Elliot. 1991. "The *Loibon* as Sorcerer: A Samburu *Loibon* among the Ariaal Rendille, 1973–87." *Africa* 67(3):318–333.

Fukui, K. 1970a. "Alcoholic Drinks of the Iraqw, Brewing Methods and Social Functions." *Kyoto University African Studies* 4:41–76.

_____. 1970b. "Migration and Settlement of the Iraqw in Hanang Area." *Kyoto University African Studies* 5:101–123.

_____. 1969. "The Subsistence Economy of the Agro-Pastoral Iraqw." *Kyoto University African Studies* 4:41–76.

Gardner, Katy, and David Lewis. 1996. *Anthropology, Development and the Post-Modern Challenge.* London: Pluto Press.

Geshiere, Peter. 1997. *The Modernity of Witchcraft: Politics and the Occult in Post-colonial Africa.* Charlottesville: University Press of Virginia.

Gewertz, Deborah, and Frederick Errington. 1996. "On Pepsico and Piety in a Papua New Guinea 'Modernity.'" *American Ethnologist* 23(3):476–493.

_____. 1991. *Twisted Histories, Altered Contexts: Representing the Chambri in a World System.* Cambridge: Cambridge University Press.

Giddens, Anthony. 1991. *Modernity and Self-Identity.* Stanford: Stanford University Press.

Gray, Robert F. 1963. "Some Structural Aspects of Mbugwe Witchcraft." In *Witchcraft and Sorcery in East Africa,* edited by John Middleton and E. H. Winter. London: Routledge and Kegan Paul.

Green, Maia. 2003. *Priests, Witches and Power: Popular Christianity after Mission in Southern Tanzania.* Cambridge: Cambridge University Press.

_____. 1995. "Why Christianity Is the Religion of Business: Perceptions of the Church among Pogoro Catholics." *Journal of Religion in Africa* 25(1):26–47.

Grillo, Ralph D. 1997. "Discourses of Development: The View from Anthropology." In *Discourses of Development: Anthropological Perspectives,* by R. D. Grillo and R. L. Stirrat. Oxford: Berg.

Grillo, R. D., and R. L. Stirrat. 1997. *Discourses of Development: Anthropological Perspectives.* Oxford: Berg.

Grinker, Roy R. 1994. *Houses in the Rainforest: Ethnicity and Inequality among Farmers and Foragers in Central Africa.* Berkeley: University of California Press.

Habermas, Jurgen. [1981] 1990. "Modernity versus Postmodernity." In *Culture and Society: Contemporary Debates,* edited by Jeffrey Alexander and Steven Seidman. Cambridge: Cambridge University Press.

Hagborg, Lars. 2001. Silence: Disputes on the Ground and in the Mind among the Iraqw in Karatu District, Tanzania. Ph.D. Dissertation, Uppsala University, Sweden.

Hatch, John Charles. 1972. *Tanzania: A Profile.* New York, Praeger.

Heald, Suzette. 1990. "Joking and Avoidance, Hostility and Incest: An Essay on Gisu Moral Categories." *Man* 25(3):377–392.

Hobart, Mark. 1993. *An Anthropological Critique of Development: The Growth of Ignorance.* London, New York: Routledge.

Hodgson, Dorothy L. 2001. *Once Intrepid Warriors: Gender, Ethnicity, and the Cultural Politics of Maasai Development.* Bloomington: Indiana University Press.

Howard, Mary, and Ann V. Millard. 1997. *Hunger and Shame: Child Malnutrition and Poverty on Mount Kilimanjaro.* New York and London: Routledge.

Hutchinson, Sharon. 1996. *Nuer Dilemmas: Coping with Money, War, and the State.* Berkeley: University of California Press.

Hyden, Goran. 1980. *Beyond Ujamaa in Tanzania: Underdevelopment and an Uncaptured Peasantry.* London: Heinemann.

Iliffe, John. 1979. *A Modern History of Tanzania.* Cambridge: Cambridge University Press.

Johnson, C. B. 1966. "Some Aspects of Iraqw Religion." *Tanzania Notes and Records* 65:53–56.

Kasfir, Nelson. 1986. "Are African Peasants Self-Sufficient?" *Development and Change* 17(4):677–506.

Kerner, Donna O. 1988. "Land Scarcity and Rights of Control in the Development of Commercial Farming in Northeast Tanzania." In *Land and Society in Contemporary Africa,* edited by R. E. Downs and S. P. Reyna. Hanover: University of New Hampshire.

Klima, George. 1970. *The Barabaig: East African Cattleherders.* New York: Holt, Rhinehart and Winston.

Kratz, Corinne A. 1994. *Affecting Performance: Meaning, Movement, and Experience in Okiek Women's Initiation.* Washington, D.C.: Smithsonian Institution Press.

Kwiatkowski, Lynn M. 1998. *Struggling with Development: The Politics of Hunger and Gender in the Philippines.* Boulder: Westview Press.

Lambek, Michael. 1993. *Knowledge and Practice in Mayotte: Local Discourses of Islam, Sorcery and Spirit Possession.* Toronto: University of Toronto Press.

Lawi, Yusufu Q. 2000. May the Spider Blind Witches and Wild Animals: Local Knowledge and the Political Ecology of Natural Resource Use in the Iraqwland, Tanzania, 1900–1985. Ph.D. Dissertation, Boston University.

Lees, E.C.L. 1936. "A Note on the Wambulu." *Tanzania Notes and Records* 2:106–107.

Little, Peter, and Michael Painter. 1995. "Discourse, Politics, and the Development Process: Reflections on Escobar's 'Anthropology and the Development Encounter.'" *American Ethnologist* 22(3):602–616.

Meek, C. I. 1953. "Stock Reduction in the Mbulu Highlands, Tanganyika." *Journal of African Administration* 5:158–167.

Middleton, John, and E. H. Winter. 1963. *Witchcraft and Sorcery in East Africa.* London: Routledge and Kegan Paul.

Middleton, John, and David Tait. 1958. *Tribes without Rulers: Studies in African Segmentary Systems.* London: Routledge and Kegan Paul.

Moore, Henrietta. 1986. *Space, Text and Gender: An Anthropological Study of the Marakwet of Kenya.* Cambridge: Cambridge University Press.

Moore, Sally Falk. 1986. *Social Facts and Fabrications.* Cambridge: Cambridge University Press.

Mous, Martin. 1988. *Iraqw-English Dictionary.* Unpublished manuscript.

Mous, Martin, Martha Qorro, and Roland Kiesling. 2002. *Iraqw-English Dictionary.* Koln: Rudiger Koppe Verlag.

Nyerere, Julius K. 1968. *Ujamaa: Essays on Socialism.* Dar es Salaam: Oxford University Press.

Ortner, Sherry B. 1989. *High Religion: A Cultural and Political History of Sherpa Buddhism.* Princeton: Princeton University Press.

Parker, Melissa. 1995. "Rethinking Female Circumcision." *Africa* 65(4):506–523.

Pigg, Stacy Leigh. 1992. "Inventing Social Categories Through Place: Social Representations and Development in Nepal." *Comparative Studies in Society and History* 34:491–513.

Piot, Charles. 1999. *Remotely Global: Village Modernity in West Africa.* Chicago: University of Chicago Press.

Prazak, Miroslava. 1999. "'We're on the Run': Ideas of Progress among Adolescents in Rural Kenya." *Journal of African Cultural Studies* 12 (1):93–110.

Pred, Allan, and Michael John Watts. 1992. *Reworking Modernity: Capitalisms and Symbolic Discontent.* New Brunswick, N.J.: Rutgers University Press.

Radcliffe-Brown, A. R., and Daryll Forde. 1950. *African Systems of Kinship and Marriage.* London: Oxford University Press.

Raikes, Philip. 1978. "Rural Differentiation and Class Formation in Tanzania." *Journal of Peasant Studies* 5(3):285–325.

_____. 1975a. The Development of Mechanized Commercial Wheat Production in North Iraqw, Tanzania. Ph.D. dissertation, Stanford University.

_____. 1975b. "Wheat Production and the Development of Capitalism in North Iraqw." In *Rural Cooperation in Tanzania,* edited by Lionel Cliffe et al. Dar es Salaam: Tanzania Publishing House.

Rekdal, Ole Bjørn. 1999. The Invention by Tradition: Creativity and Change among the Iraqw of Northern Tanzania. Doctoral thesis, University of Bergen.

_____. 1998. "When Hypothesis Becomes Myth: The Iraqi Origin of the Iraqw." *Ethnology* 37(1):17–38.

_____. 1996. "Money, Milk and Sorghum Beer: Change and Continuity among the Iraqw of Tanzania." *Africa* 66(3):367–386.

Rekdal, Ole Bjørn, and Astrid Blystad. 1999. "'We Are as Sheep and Goats': Iraqw and Datooga Discourses on Fortune, Failure and the Future." In *"The Poor Are Not Us": Poverty and Pastoralism in Eastern Africa,* edited by David Anderson and Vigdis Broch-Due. London: James Currey.

Rigby, Peter. 1981. "Pastors and Pastoralists: The Differential Penetration of Christianity among East African Cattle Herders." *Comparative Studies in Society and History* 23(1):96–129.

_____. 1969. *Cattle and Kinship among the Gogo.* Ithaca and London: Cornell University Press.

Rubin, Deborah. 1984. *People of Good Heart.* Ph.D. dissertation, Johns Hopkins University.

Sanders, Todd. 1999. "Modernity, Wealth and Witchcraft in Tanzania." *Research in Economic Anthropology* 20:117–131.

Schein, Louisa. 1999. "Performing Modernity." *Cultural Anthropology* 14(3):361–395.

Scott, James C. 1998. *Seeing Like a State: How Certain Schemes to Improve the Human Condition Have Failed.* New Haven: Yale University Press.

Shaw, Rosalind. 1997. "The Production of Witchcraft/Witchcraft as Production: Memory, Modernity, and the Slave Trade in Sierra Leone." *American Ethnologist* 24(4):856–876.

Shipton, Parker. 1989. *Bitter Money: Cultural Economy and Some African Meanings of Forbidden Commodities.* Washington, D.C.: American Anthropological Association.

Simon, Vendelin. 2002. Local Culture: Risk or Resource in Times of AIDS? A Case Study from Mbulu in Northern Tanzania. Master's thesis, University of Bergen, Norway.

Snyder, Katherine A. 2002. "Modern Cows and Exotic Trees: Identity, Personhood, and Exchange among the Iraqw of Tanzania." *Ethnology* 41(2):155–173.

_____. 2001. "Being of One Heart: Power and Politics among the Iraqw of Tanzania." *AFRICA* 71(1):128–148.

_____. 1999. "Gender Ideology, and the Domestic and Public Domains among the Iraqw." In *Those Who Play with Fire: Gender, Fertility and Transformation in East and Southern Africa,* edited by Henrietta L. Moore, Todd Sanders, and Bwire Kaare. New Brunswick, N.J.: Athlone Press.

_____. 1997. "Elders' Authority and Women's Protest: The Masay Ritual and Social Change among the Iraqw of Tanzania." *Journal of the Royal Anthropological Society* (N.S.) 3:561–576.

_____. 1996. "Agrarian Change and Land-Use Strategies among the Iraqw Farmers of Northern Tanzania." *Human Ecology* 24(3):315–340.

_____. 1993. "Like Water and Honey": Moral Ideology and the Construction of Community among the Iraqw of Northern Tanzania. Ph.D. Dissertation, Yale University.

Songstad, Nils Gunnar. 2002. Coexistence and Conflict: Political Domains in a Local Community in Tanzania. Master's Thesis, University of Bergen, Norway.

Spencer, Paul. 1988. *The Maasai of Matapato.* Bloomington and Indianapolis: Indiana University Press.

Stambach, Amy. 1996. "'Seeded' in the Market Economy: Schooling and Social Transformations on Mount Kilimanjaro." *Anthropology and Education Quarterly* 27(4):545–567.

Sturdy, D. 1936. "Agricultural Notes." *Tanganyika Notes and Records* 1:52–56.

Tanzania National Archives (TNA). File A3/1.

Thomas, Garry L. 1977. *Baseline Information and Situation Overview Requisite to the Design of Integrated Rural Development Projects in Mbulu District, Tanzania.* A report prepared for USAID/Tanzania.

Thornton, Robert J. 1982. "Modelling Spatial Relations in a Boundary-Making Ritual of the Iraqw of Tanzania." *Man* 17(3):528–545.

_____. 1980. *Space, Time, and Culture among the Iraqw of Tanzania.* New York: Academic Press.

Tripp, Aili Mari. 1997. *Changing the Rules: The Politics of Liberalization and the Urban Informal Economy in Tanzania.* Berkeley: University of California Press.

Wada, Shohei. 1984. "Female Initiation Rites of the Iraqw and the Gorowa." *Senri Ethnological Studies* 15:187–196.

_____. 1980. "Two Iraqw Marriage Rituals." *Senri Ethnological Studies* 6:79–91.

_____. 1978. "*Slufay*: Notes on an Iraqw Ritual Prayer." *Senri Ethnological Studies* 1:37–53.

_____. 1975. "Political History of Mbulu District—Power Struggles and Territorial Groupings of Medicine Men." *Kyoto University African Studies* 9:45–68.

_____. 1971. "Marriage Ceremonies and Customs among the Iraqw of Tanzania." *Kyoto University African Studies* 6:31–52.

_____. 1969a. "Local Group of the Iraqw—Their Structure and Functions." *Kyoto University African Studies* 3:109–131.

_____. 1969b. "Territorial Expansion of the Iraqw." *Kyoto University African Studies* 4:115–132.

Walley, Christine. 2003. "Our Ancestors Used to Buy their 'Development' in the Ground: Modernity and the Meanings of Development within a Tanzanian Marine Park." *Anthropological Quarterly* 76(1):33–54.

Watts, Michael J. 1992. "Capitalisms, Crises, and Cultures I: Notes Toward a Totality of Fragments." Chapter 1 of *Reworking Modernity: Capitalisms and Symbolic Discontent*, by Allan Pred and Michael John Watts. New Brunswick, N.J.: Rutgers University Press.

Weiss, Brad. 2002. "Thug Realism: Inhabiting Fantasy in Urban Tanzania." *Cultural Anthropology* 17(1):93–125.

_____. 2001. "Mal-Adjustments: Ritual and Reproduction in Neo-Liberal Africa." *Journal of Religion in Africa* 31(4):367–372.

Whiteley, W. H. 1958. *A Short Description of Item Categories in Iraqw*. London: School of Oriental and African Studies.

Williams, Raymond. 1977. *Marxism and Literature*. Oxford: Oxford University Press.

Winter, E. H. 1978. "Cattle-Raiding in East Africa: The Case of the Iraqw." *Anthropology* 2(1):53–59.

_____. 1968. "Some Aspects of Political Organization and Land Tenure among the Iraqw." *Kyoto University African Studies* 2:1–29.

_____. 1966. "Territorial Grouping and Religion among the Iraqw." In *Anthropological Approaches to the Study of Religion*, edited by M. Banton. London: Tavistock.

_____. 1964. "The Slaughter of a Bull: A Study of Cosmology and Ritual." In *Process and Pattern in Culture*, edited by R. A. Manners. Chicago: Aldine.

_____. 1962. "Livestock Markets among the Iraqw of Northern Tanganyika." In *Markets in Africa*, edited by P. Bohannon and G. Dalton. Evanston, Ill.: Northwestern University Press.

Winter, E. H., and L. Molyneaux. 1963. "Population Patterns and Problems among the Iraqw." *Ethnology* 11(4):490–505.

Yoneyama, Toshinao. 1973. "The Formation of National Cultures in Africa: A Comparative Study." *Kyoto University African Studies* 8:1–15.

_____. 1970. "Some Basic Notions among the Iraqw of Northern Tanzania." *Kyoto University African Studies* 5:81–100.

_____. 1969. "The Life and Society of the Iraqw." *Kyoto University African Studies* 4:79–114.

Index